How to Make Money in Stocks

A Winning System in Good Times or Bad

WILLIAM J. O'NEIL

THIRD EDITION

McGraw-Hill

New York   Chicago   San Francisco   Lisbon   London   Madrid
Mexico City   Milan   New Delhi   San Juan   Seoul
Singapore   Sydney   Toronto

Library of Congress Cataloging-in-Publication Data
O'Neil, William J.
  How to make money in stocks: a winning system in good times or bad /
by William J. O'Neil.—3rd ed.
     p. cm.
Includes index.
  ISBN 0-07-137361-6
  1. Investments. 2. Stocks. I. Title.
  HG4521 .O515 2002
  332.63'22—dc21

                                            2002004916

McGraw-Hill
A Division of The McGraw-Hill Companies

This text contains the following, which are trademarks, service marks, or registered trademarks of *Investor's Business Daily* Incorporated, William O'Neil + Co., Incorporated, or their affiliated entities, in the United States and/or other countries: CAN SLIM™, New Stock Market Ideas®, Daily Graphs Online®, SMR Rating™, Stock Checkup℠, O'Neil Database®.

    5 6 7 8 9 0   DOC / DOC   0 9 8 7 6 5 4 3 (Softcover Edition)
3 4 5 6 7 8 9 0   DOC / DOC   0 9 8 7 6 5 4 3 (Special Author Edition)

ISBN: 0-07-137361-6 (Softcover Edition)
ISBN: 0-07-140668-9 (Special Author Edition)

McGraw-Hill books are available at special quality discounts to use as premiums and sales promotions, or for use in corporate training programs. For more information, please write to the Director of Special Sales, McGraw-Hill, Professional Publishing, Two Penn Plaza, New York, NY 10121-2298. Or contact your local bookstore.

This book is printed on recycled, acid-free paper containing a minimum of 50% recycled, de-inked fiber.

Success in a free country is simple.
Get a job, get an education, and
learn to save and invest wisely.
Anyone can do it.
You can do it.

Some of the dedicated individuals who helped make this latest edition possible are to be thanked for their contributions: Wes Mann and Chris Gessel, as well as Deirdre Abbott, Leila Marsden Barth, Heather Davis, Yinghua Gao, Charles Harris, Hilary Kircher, Gil Morales, Justin Nielsen, Michelle Playford, Wendy Reidt, Lisa Rubin, Kathy Sherman, Gary Slemaker, and Mike Webster. I also want to thank Philip Ruppel and the outstanding staff at McGraw-Hill.

• CONTENTS •

How to Make Money in Stocks **gives you a proven, simple, fact-based system** called CAN SLIM™.° The system consists of buying and selling rules derived from an extensive analysis of all of the greatest winning stocks each year for the last half-century.

All known fundamental and technical (price and volume) variables and facts were studied in exacting detail to determine what common characteristics occurred just before these super stocks had huge price increases and how these variables changed when the stocks topped and began substantial declines.

The buying and selling rules in this book represent only the time-tested facts of how the stock market actually works, not my personal opinions and certainly not the current personal views and beliefs of most Wall Street analysts or strategists on TV.

In this third edition, as in earlier ones, we will site many references to Investor's Business Daily's more relevant stock tables, charts, data, and company news. We designed and published IBD to give business people and investors of all experience levels daily ongoing access via a newspaper and Web site, to the valuable research information described in *How to Make Money in Stocks.*

How have these rules worked in the battlefield of the real day-to-day marketplace? We now have on file more than 500 case histories of savvy *How to Make Money in Stocks* readers and Investor's Business Daily® subscribers who made and kept substantial gains of several hundred percent or more using the rules and principles in both publications.

Who are some of these savvy subscribers? R. and D. Tank, individual investors, said, "We both have been using IBD for about nine years, and

°CAN SLIM is the trademark for investment modeling associated with William J. O'Neil, Investor's Business Daily, and their affiliated entities. All rights reserved.

along with using CAN SLIM and reading your book, we have been able to rack up over a 5000% gain just since the beginning of 1998. The paper was critical for us in 2000. . . . It allowed us to spot the climax top in March 2000 in the Nasdaq and clearly illustrated the value of IBD. After all, in order to make money in the markets, you need to also learn how to keep what you make. We would never have had this chance without your efforts put forth in *How to Make Money in Stocks.* Thank you again for sharing your knowledge. Your teachings have proved to be invaluable to us and many people that are dear to us!"

P. Kaiser mentioned she had "tried other theories that didn't work. Finally I read William O'Neil's books. I never again followed anyone else. In the last two years, I have retired, bought a house and an apartment building from just using IBD and Daily Graphs! Thank you!"

Barbara James never bought a stock in her life; she was afraid of the market so she kept her savings in the local S&L. After attending one of our southern California free seminars in 1996, she traded on paper for a year before she had the confidence to apply the rules and buy her first stock, an odd lot of EMC Corp. It advanced 1300%. She sold it in September 2000. Her second stock increased 286%.

Allen Cecil, who you may have seen in IBD TV commercials talking about "If you teach a man to fish, you feed him for life," made over 1200% during the 1990s and was able to realize his dream of a nice five-bedroom home in Colorado by carefully following the system. Allen said, "Investor's Business Daily is scientifically based because of its database and the history that's behind it, and I don't find anything out there that comes close."

Jim Sugano attended a seminar in the mid 1980s when we discussed Home Depot. He checked it out according to the rules and bought many shares. Every time it made a new high, he bought more shares. He held it for more than 16 years while it split nine times.

One of Morgan Stanley's top brokers in New York City attended three of our all-day Saturday paid workshops and increased his own account from $250,000 to $6 million. A middle-aged attorney from the South also attended our sessions and ran $300,000 to $18 million in stocks like Yahoo!, AOL, and Qualcomm and then retired early from his practice.

K. Phillips said, "A few years back, my husband suggested I learn to handle some of our investments. I now love Investor's Business Daily and CAN SLIM. [There is] so much information and Mr. O'Neil gives the best lessons in *How to Make Money in Stocks.* Since I started using CAN SLIM and IBD, and now investors.com, I was able to make 359% on my original investment! IBD has so many features that help me find the great stocks. I'm grateful for all the work you do to help investors."

E. Boboch, individual investor, told us, "I started trading stocks in 1995 and subscribed to IBD, reread *How to Make Money in Stocks* four times, and analyzed my bad trades once a year to learn what not to do. I've now earned enough money in the market to buy a brand new car with cash, and I'm getting ready to pay off my house mortgage. Next goal is to work towards complete financial independence."

Mark Zeitchick and Vincent Mangone of Ladenburg Thalmann Financial Services, money managers and active IBD readers, cite the importance of "The Big Picture" in their daily decision-making processes: "It was 'The Big Picture' that ultimately led us out of the market during the spring of 2000, saving millions of dollars in investor capital. Every investor from novice to the professional should read 'The Big Picture' and 'Investor's Corner' on a daily basis. IBD is more than a newspaper; it's a necessary investment tool."

A clergyman, Dr. John Edmund Haggai, founder of the Haggai Institute, has done so well following the system he annually donates significant sums to certain charities. Then, of course, there are all of the people like Lee Freestone, David Ryan, Ced Moses, Dan Running, and Jay Plisco who either won or were among the top finishers in many different real money trading contests during the 1980s and 1990s following the CAN SLIM™ rules in *How to Make Money in Stocks.*

Based on surveys, we estimate up to 50,000 of IBD's experienced readers have made and nailed down significant gains during the 1990s. They did this by following the individual stock selling rules in Chapters 9 and 10 and the general market sell rules in Chapter 7 of *How to Make Money in Stocks* plus paying close attention to IBD's "The Big Picture" daily market column written by Chris Gessel. It tracked these same selling rules and was one of the rare sources that clearly told readers it was time to sell and raise cash in March and April 2000 and again in September 2000.

A difficult and serious problem for all investors today is that there is entirely too much free information, hype, promotion, personal opinion, and advice about the stock market. You get it from friends, relatives, people at work, the Internet, brokers, stock analysts, advisers, entertaining cable TV market programs, and other media. It can be very risky and potentially dangerous. Realistically, there are not too many people you can listen to if you want to avoid confusing, contradictory, and faulty personal market opinions.

You need to confine yourself to just a very few sources of relevant facts and data and a sound system that has proven to be accurate and profitable over time. Facts are always better than most people's opinions.

The American Association of Individual Investors compared the CAN SLIM™ system in *How to Make Money in Stocks* to other well-known methods of selecting stocks such as that of Peter Lynch, Warren Buffet, and many others for the bull market years of 1998 and 1999, as well as the bear market of 2000. Their independent study published in 2001 found that CAN SLIM™ had the best and most consistent performance record each year. The results were as follows: 1998, +28.2%; 1999, +36.6%; 2000, +30.2%.

Perhaps the longest real-time record of stock selection using the rules contained in *How to Make Money in Stocks* is from William O'Neil + Co.'s institutional advisory service called New Stock Market Ideas®. Its comprehensive record of over 8400 buy recommendations made weekly for over 24 years (1977 to 2001) is shown on the accompanying charts. It dramatically outperformed Value Line's number 1 ranked stocks over the last 10 and 20 years. Few firms publish the results of all of their many recommendations; however, we believe the record for New Stock Market Ideas® to be among the very best on Wall Street.

Following the rules in *How to Make Money in Stocks*, I had my second-best performance period ever in 1998 and 1999, up 401% and 322%, respectively. The biggest winners were America Online, Charles Schwab, Qualcomm, and Sun Microsystems.

Possibly more important, we had 10 different in-house money managers running money out of a separate holding company, Data Analysis, Inc. They together averaged 221% in 1998, 363% in 1999, and as of this writing, averaged 5% for 2000 and most of 2001 by primarily being out of the market and in money market funds for most of the period. The compounded result was a 1530% increase. All 10 operated independently, following and using the disciplined buy-and-sell rules in *How to Make Money in Stocks.*

Realistically, not everyone will make money buying stocks. In fact, many people will lose a lot of money because they do not follow sound time-tested buy-and-sell rules. Therefore, they simply do not learn how to protect their capital. For example, *How to Make Money in Stocks* was sent to most IBD subscribers, but less than half actually read it. Some that did failed to adopt and apply its essential loss-cutting rules. Furthermore, millions of investors have never studied or been exposed to Investor's Business Daily or *How to Make Money in Stocks.* My observation is many of them lost 50% to 75% in 2000 and 2001 following widely accepted, faulty buy-and-hold methods. These methods did not even take into consideration individual stock selling rules for when to take and nail down a profit, loss-cutting rules, and general market selling rules.

However, anyone who will take the time to read, carefully study, and understand this third edition of *How to Make Money in Stocks* can, with discipline and determination, dramatically improve his or her investment performance in both good and bad markets.

New Stock Market Ideas® Institutional List Performance Since Inception

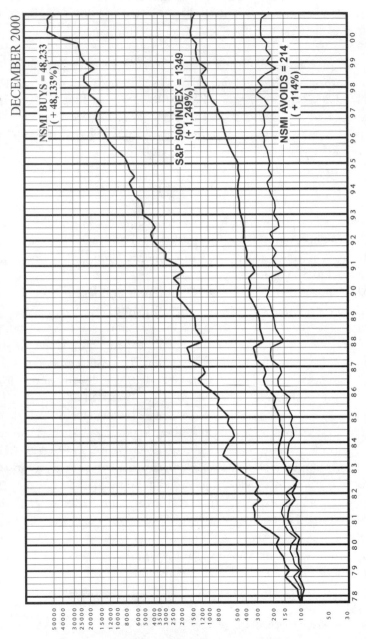

DECEMBER 2000

NSMI BUYS = 48,233
(+ 48,133%)

S&P 500 INDEX = 1349
(+ 1,249%)

NSMI AVOIDS = 214
(+ 114%)

PERFORMANCE COMPUTATIONS REFLECT A COMPOUNDING OF RATES OF RETURN WEEKLY BASED ON THE PUBLICATION DATE OF THE *NEW STOCK MARKET IDEAS*® LIST. DIVIDENDS AND COMMISSIONS WERE NOT CONSIDERED IN ANY COMPUTATIONS. THE ABOVE DOES NOT IMPLY COMPARABLE FUTURE PERFORMANCE. IT SHOULD BE RECOGNIZED THERE IS SUBSTANTIAL SPECULATIVE RISK IN MOST COMMON STOCKS.

X

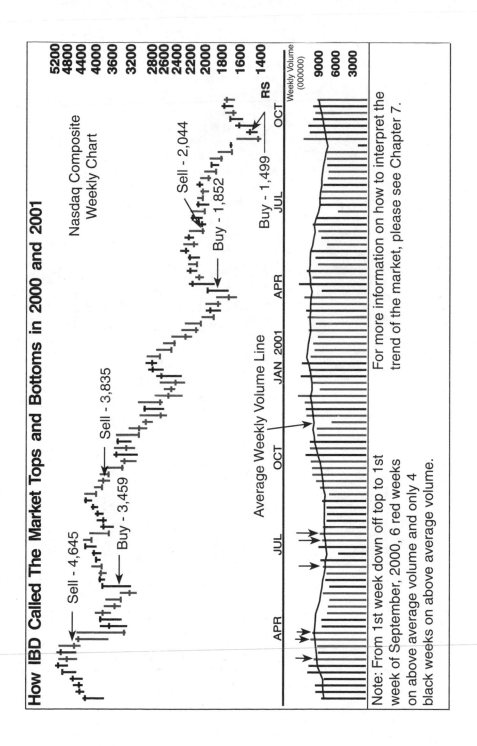

How IBD Called The Market Tops and Bottoms in 2000 and 2001

Nasdaq Composite
Weekly Chart

Sell - 4,645

Sell - 3,835

Buy - 3,459

Sell - 3,835

Sell - 2,044

Buy - 1,852

Buy - 1,499

RS

5200
4800
4400
4000
3600
3200
2800
2600
2400
2200
2000
1800
1600
1400

Average Weekly Volume Line

APR   JUL   OCT   JAN 2001   APR   JUL   OCT

Weekly Volume
(000000)

9000
6000
3000

Note: From 1st week down off top to 1st week of September, 2000, 6 red weeks on above average volume and only 4 black weeks on above average volume.

For more information on how to interpret the trend of the market, please see Chapter 7.

xi

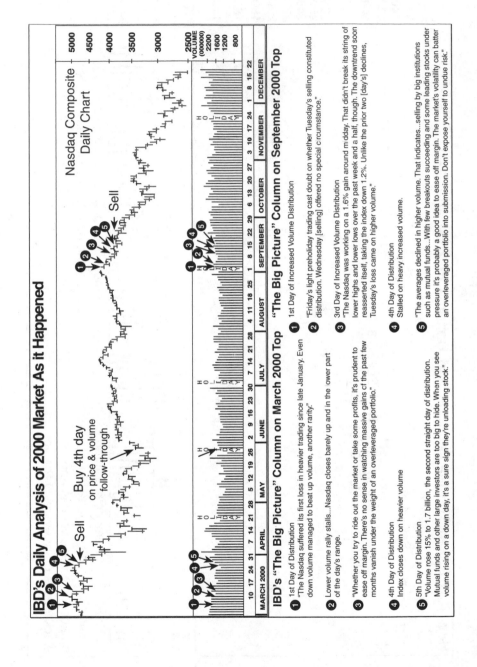

IBD's Daily Analysis of 2000 Market As it Happened

Nasdaq Composite
Daily Chart

Sell

Buy 4th day
on price & volume
follow-through

Sell

IBD's "The Big Picture" Column on March 2000 Top

1 1st Day of Distribution
"The Nasdaq suffered its first loss in heavier trading since late January. Even down volume managed to beat up volume, another rarity."

2 Lower volume rally stalls...Nasdaq closes barely up and in the ower part of the day's range.

3 "Whether you try to ride out the market or take some profits, it's prudent to ease off margin. There's no sense in watching massive gains cf the past few months vanish under the weight of an overleveraged portfolio."

4 4th Day of Distribution
Index closes down on heavier volume

5 5th Day of Distribution
"Volume rose 15% to 1.7 billion, the second straight day of distribution. Mutual funds and other large investors are too big to hide. When you see volume rising on a down day, it's a sure sign they're unloading stock."

"The Big Picture" Column on September 2000 Top

1 1st Day of Increased Volume Distribution

2 "Friday's light preholiday trading cast doubt on whether Tuesday's selling constituted distribution. Wednesday [selling] offered no special crcumstance."

3 3rd Day of Increased Volume Distribution
"The Nasdaq was working on a 1.6% gain around midday. That didn't break its string of lower highs and lower lows over the past week and a half, though. The downtrend soon reasserted itself, taking the index down 1.2%. Unlike the prior two [day's] declines, Tuesday's loss came on higher volume."

4 4th Day of Distribution
Stalled on heavy increased volume.

5 "The averages declined in higher volume. That indicates...selling by big institutions such as mutual funds....With few breakouts succeeding and some leading stocks under pressure it's probably a good idea to ease off margin. The market's volatility can batter an overleveraged portfolio into submission. Don't expose yourself to undue risk."

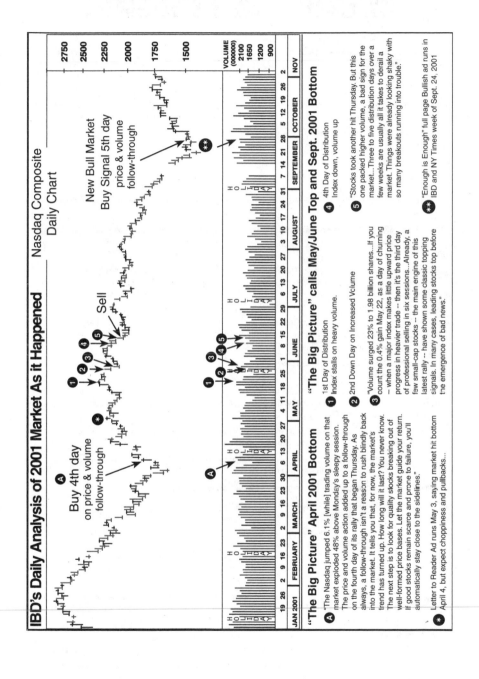

IBD's Daily Analysis of 2001 Market As it Happened

Nasdaq Composite Daily Chart

Buy 4th day on price & volume follow-through

Sell

New Bull Market Buy Signal 5th day price & volume follow-through

"The Big Picture" April 2001 Bottom

Ⓐ "The Nasdaq jumped 6.1% [while] trading volume on that market exploded 48% above Monday's sleepy session. The price and volume action added up to a follow-through on the fourth day of its rally that began Thursday. As always, a follow-through isn't a reason to rush blindly back into the market. It tells you that, for now, the market's trend has turned up. How long will it last? You never know. The next step is to look for quality stocks breaking out of well-formed price bases. Let the market guide your return. If good stocks remain scarce and prone to failure, you'll automatically stay close to the sidelines."

✱ Letter to Reader Ad runs May 3, saying market hit bottom April 4, but expect choppiness and pullbacks...

"The Big Picture" calls May/June Top and Sept. 2001 Bottom

❶ 1st Day of Distribution
Index stalls on heavy volume.

❷ 2nd Down Day on Increased Volume

❸ "Volume surged 23% to 1.98 billion shares...If you count the 0.4% gain May 22, as a day of churning -- when a major index makes little upward price progress in heavier trade -- then it's the third day of professional selling in six sessions...Already, a few small-cap stocks -- the main engine of this latest rally -- have shown some classic topping signals. In many cases, leading stocks top before the emergence of bad news."

❹ 4th Day of Distribution
Index down, volume up

❺ "Stocks took another hit Thursday. But this one packed higher volume, a bad sign for the market...Three to five distribution days over a few weeks are usually all it takes to derail a market. Things were already looking shaky with so many breakouts running into trouble."

✱✱ "Enough is Enough" full page Bullish ad runs in IBD and NY Times week of Sept. 24, 2001

A LETTER TO OUR READERS FROM WILLIAM J. O'NEIL

Enough is Enough!

A great American president, Franklin Delano Roosevelt, in another trying time said, "We have nothing to fear but fear itself." It's now time for Americans to stop fearing and become positive. Positive about the American stock market and investing in our many future opportunities. Positive about flying and traveling. Positive about buying or refinancing a home at historically low interest rates or buying a new car under new no-interest offers. Or just positive about normal day-to-day shopping.

America is the strongest nation in the world. We lead in new technology, computer software, innovative new entrepreneurial companies, military power, medical advancements and in freedom and opportunity for all.

Our Congress is now united and ready to act to assure future recovery and economic growth.

Investor's Business Daily suggests the following actions by our government:

1. Reduce the long-term capital gains rate to 15% and consider changing the required time period to 6 months as it was under the Kennedy administration. From 1979 to 1982, the cap gains rate was cut from 35% to 20%. In the five years before 1979, initial public offerings averaged fewer than 30 a year. The first year after the lower 20% incentive in 1982, IPOs soared to 681. New start-up companies spawned new jobs, new products, new markets, new industries and new ways of doing business.

Who were a few of these new 1980s companies? Home Depot, Franklin Resources, Amgen, Compaq, United Healthcare, Microsoft, Oracle, EMC, Sun Microsystems, Adobe Systems, Dell Computer, Cisco Systems, Qualcomm, PeopleSoft and America Online. They created millions of new jobs (and taxpayers) and drove most of the last 20 years of unparalleled growth.

Capital gains rates are not just for the rich. They are for all Americans, 50% of whom are now investors. Other Americans would love to start a business. This is the best way to create more long-term investors and form thousands of new companies that in turn produce jobs and new taxpayers.

We should not fear that lower rates will cause more public selling in the market, because most investors have losses in the last 18 months. Also, the public rarely determines important market price movements. Giant mutual funds all across the nation dominate price action, and they do not pay taxes on fund portfolio gains. (The government's income will also increase from a lower capital gains rate.)

2. Lower corporate income taxes and enact accelerated depreciation allowances for companies to speed recovery and re-employment of workers.

3. Lower interest rates by another 1/2 point in October to assist recovery. The technology market and our economy are in the aftermath of a euphoric market boom and bust in 1998, 1999 and early 2000. It will take more incentives and time than typical to recover from those excesses.

4. Open up the deep interior of Alaska and other oil-bearing areas where few people live to oil drilling, so the U.S. will become more energy self-sufficient and less dependent on unpredictable foreign oil supply and prices.

5. Begin funding a missile defense system so we can't be threatened or damaged by the first terrorist nation to acquire an intercontinental missile capable of hitting our East Coast cities.

This nation has enormous resources and reserves. This is the time to use them…that's what they're for.

Long-term mutual fund investors should consider increasing their monthly buying of diversified domestic equity funds now and over the next 3 months – not selling at this late stage.

If individual investors didn't choose to follow Investor's Business Daily's rules for selling and cutting losses at 8%, or the specific "sell and raise cash" advice suggested in "The Big Picture" column in March, April and September of 2000, it's probably too late to be selling a broad list of stocks now. We see similarities today to the market lows of June 1962 when that bear market shakeout low undercut the prior market index low for five days. Put-call ratios reached highs recently — another positive psychological sign.

Investor's Business Daily is in the process of expanding with new contract printing facilities in Seattle, Pittsburgh, Des Moines and possibly Denver. In early October, Investor's Business Daily will introduce a whole new redesign of IBD that will utilize more color, easier-to-read type and other key features. Our improved investors.com Web site will also be introducing important new services for subscribers.

We would like to take this opportunity to thank all of our advertisers and subscribers for their continued support.

In times like this, it is important to remember, Rule #1 in Investor's Business Daily's "10 Secrets to Success"…"How You Think is Everything. Always be positive. Think success…not fear."

INVESTOR'S BUSINESS DAILY

CHOOSE SUCCESS.™

Ad appeared in *The New York Times* and *IBD* the week of Sept. 24, 2001.

PART
I

A Winning System: CAN SLIM™

Learning From the Greatest Winners

In the following chapters, I will show you exactly how to pick big winners in the stock market and nail down the profits in them, as well as how to substantially reduce your losses and mistakes.

Many people who dabble in stocks either have mediocre results or lose money because of their lack of knowledge, but no one has to lose money. You can definitely learn to invest wisely. This book will provide you with the investment understanding, skills, and methods you need to become a more successful investor.

I believe that most people in this country and many others throughout the free world, young and old, regardless of profession, education, background, or economic position, positively should own common stock. This book isn't written for the elite but for the millions of guys and gals everywhere who want a chance to be better off financially. You are never too old or too young to start investing.

● **YOU CAN START SMALL—If you are a typical working person or a beginning investor, it doesn't take a lot of money to start. You can begin with as little as $500 to $1000 and add to it as you earn and save more money. I began with the purchase of just five shares of Procter & Gamble when I was only 21 and fresh out of school.**

You live in a fantastic time of unlimited opportunity, an era of outstanding new ideas, emerging industries, and new frontiers. However, you have to read the rest of this book to learn how to recognize and take advantage of these amazing new situations.

The opportunities are out there for everyone. You are now in a continually changing New America. We lead the world in high technology, the Internet, medical advancements, computer software, military capability, and innovative new entrepreneurial companies. The communist/socialist system and concept of a "command economy" is now relegated to the ash heap of history. Our system of freedom and opportunity serves as a model of success for most countries in the world.

It is not enough today for you to just work and earn a salary. To do the things you want to do, to go the places you want to go, to have the things you want to have in your life, you absolutely must save and invest intelligently. The second income from your investments and the net profits you can make will let you reach your goals and provide real security. This book will just change your whole life.

● **SECRET TIP—The first step in learning to pick big stock market winners is for you to examine leading big winners of the past to learn all the characteristics of the most successful stocks. You will learn from this observation what type of price patterns these stocks developed just before their spectacular price advances.**

Other key factors you will discover include what the quarterly earnings of these companies were at the time, what the annual earnings histories of these organizations had been in the prior three years, what amount of trading volume was present, what degree of relative price strength occurred in the price of the stocks before their enormous success, and how many shares of common stock were outstanding in the capitalization of each company. You'll also learn that many of the greatest winners had significant new products or new management and that many were tied to strong industry group moves caused by important changes occurring in an entire industry.

It's easy to conduct this type of practical, commonsense analysis of all past successful leaders. I have already completed such a comprehensive study. In our historical analysis, we selected the greatest winning stocks in the stock market each year (in terms of percentage increase for the year), spanning the past half-century.

We call the study *The Model Book of Greatest Stock Market Winners*. It covers the period from the 1950s through 2000 and analyzes in detail over 600 of the biggest winning companies in recent stock market history: super stocks such as Texas Instruments, whose price soared from $25 to $250 from January 1958 through May 1960; Xerox, which escalated from $160 to the equivalent of $1340 from March 1963 to June 1966; Syntex, which leaped from $100 to $570 in only six months during the last half of 1963; Dome Petroleum and Prime Computer, which respectively advanced 1000% and 1595% in the 1978–1980 stock market; Limited Stores, which wildly excited lucky shareowners with a 3500% increase between 1982 and 1987; and Cisco Systems, which advanced from a split-adjusted $0.10 to $82 between October 1990 and March 2000. Home Depot and Microsoft both increased more than 20 times during the 1980s and early 1990s. Home Depot was one of the all-time great performers, jumping 20-fold in less than two years from its initial public offering in September 1981 and then climbing another 10 times from 1988 to 1992. All of these companies offered exciting new products and concepts.

Would you like to know the common characteristics and rules of success we discovered from this intensive study of all past stock market leaders?

It's all covered in the next few chapters and in a simple, easy-to-remember formula we have named CAN SLIM™. Each letter in the words CAN SLIM stands for one of the seven chief characteristics of these greatest winning stocks at their early developing stages, just before they made huge profits for their shareholders. Write the formula down, and repeat it several times so you won't forget it. The reason CAN SLIM continues to work cycle after cycle is because it is based solely on the reality of how the stock market actually works rather than our personal opinion or anyone else's, including Wall Street's. Further, human nature at work in the market simply doesn't change. So CAN SLIM does not get outmoded as fads, fashions, and economic cycles come and go. It will beat big egos and personal opinions every time.

You can definitely learn how to pick big winners in the stock market, and you can become part owner in the best companies in the world. So, let's get started right now. Here's a sneak preview of CAN SLIM:

C Current Quarterly Earnings per Share: *The Higher, the Better*

A Annual Earnings Increases: *Look for Significant Growth*

N New Products, New Management, New Highs: *Buying at the Right Time*

S Supply and Demand: *Shares Outstanding Plus Big Volume Demand*

L Leader or Laggard: *Which Is Your Stock?*

I Institutional Sponsorship: *Follow the Leaders*

M Market Direction: *How to Determine It*

Please begin immediately with Chapter 1. Go for it. You can do it.

C = Current Quarterly Earnings per Share: The Higher, the Better

Dell Computer, America Online, Cisco Systems—why, among the thousands of stocks that trade each day, did these three perform so well during the 1990s? And what traits, among the hundreds that can move stocks up and down, did they all have in common? (We'll discuss when to sell and take your profit in Chapter 10.)

These are not idle questions. The answers unlock the secret to true success in the stock market.

Our study of all the stock market superstars from the past half-century found they did indeed share common characteristics. However, none stood out as boldly as the profits each big winner reported in the latest quarter or two before its major price advance. For example:

- Cisco Systems posted earnings-per-share gains of 150% and 155% in the two quarters ending October 1990, prior to its 1467% price run-up over the next three years.

- America Online's quarterly earnings were up 900% and 283% before its price jumped 557% in only six months from October 1998.

- Dell Computer's earnings soared 74% and 108% in the two quarters prior to its 27-month price increase of 1780% from November 1996.

- Ascend Communications saw earnings up 1500% in August 1994 just prior to its 1380% price move over the next 15 months.

- Accustaff showed a 300% profit increase just before its price gain of 1486% in the 16 months from January 1995.

In fact, if you look down a list of the market's biggest winners, you'll instantly see the relationship between booming profits and booming stocks. And you'll see why our studies have concluded that:

The stocks you select should show a major percentage increase in current quarterly earnings per share (the most recently reported quarter) when compared to the prior year's same quarter.

Seek Stocks Showing Huge Current Earnings Increases

In our models of the 600 best-performing stocks from 1952 to 2001, three out of four showed earnings increases averaging more than 70% in the latest publicly reported quarter *before* they began their major advances. The remaining 25% that *did not show* solid current quarterly earnings increases did so *the very next quarter* and had an average earnings increase of 90%!

If the best stocks had profit increases of this magnitude before they advanced rapidly in price, why should you settle for anything less? You may find that only 2% of all stocks listed on the Nasdaq or the New York Stock Exchange will show earnings gains of this size. But remember: You're looking for stocks that are exceptional, not lackluster. Don't worry; they're out there. However, as with any search, there can be traps and pitfalls along the way, and you need to know how to avoid them.

The earnings-per-share (EPS) number you want to focus on is calculated by dividing a company's total after-tax profits by the number of common shares outstanding. This percentage change in EPS is the single most important element in stock selection today. The greater the percentage increase, the better.

And yet, during the Internet boom of the late 1990s, some people bought stocks based on big stories of profits and riches to come while most Internet and dot-com companies had only shown deficits to date. Given that companies like AOL and Yahoo! were actually showing earnings, risking your hard-earned money in other unproven stocks was simply not necessary. AOL and Yahoo! were the real leaders at that time. When the inevitable market correction (downturn) hit, lower grade, more speculative companies with no earnings rapidly suffered the largest declines. You don't need that added risk.

I am continually amazed at how some professional money managers, let alone individual investors, buy common stocks with the current reported quarter's earnings flat (no change) or down. There is absolutely no good reason for a stock to go anywhere in a big, sustainable way if current earnings are poor.

Even profit gains of 5% to 10% are insufficient to fuel a major price movement in a stock. It's also more likely for a company showing a mere increase of 8% or 10% to suddenly report lower earnings the next quarter.

Unlike some institutional investors who may be restricted by the size of their funds, individual investors have the luxury of investing in only the very best stocks in each bull cycle. While some of these stocks with no earnings (like Amazon.com and Priceline.com) had big moves in 1998–1999, most investors were better off buying stocks like America Online and Charles Schwab that had strong earnings. Following the CAN SLIM™ strategy's emphasis on earnings ensures an investor will always be led to the strongest stocks in any market cycle, regardless of any temporary, highly speculative "bubbles" or euphoria. But remember, don't buy on earnings growth alone. We'll cover the other key factors in the chapters that follow.

Watch Out for Misleading Earnings Reports

Have you ever read a corporation's quarterly earnings report that stated:

We had a terrible first three months. Prospects for our company are turning down due to inefficiencies at the home office. Our competition just came out with a better product, which will adversely affect our sales. Furthermore, we are losing our shirt on the new Midwestern operation, which was a real blunder on management's part.

No way! Here's what you see:

Greatshakes Corporation reports record sales of $7.2 million versus $6 million (+20%) for the quarter ended March 31.

If you're a stockholder, this may be wonderful news. You certainly aren't going to be disappointed. After all, this is a fine company (otherwise you wouldn't have invested in it in the first place), and the report confirms your thinking.

But is this "record-breaking" sales announcement a good report? Let's suppose the company also had record earnings of $2.10 per share, up 5% from the $2.00 per share reported for the same quarter a year ago. Is it even better now? The questions you have to ask are why were sales up 20% but earnings only ahead 5%? What does this say about the company's profit margins?

Most investors are impressed with what they read, and companies love to put their best foot forward in press releases and TV appearances. Even though this company's sales grew 20% to an all-time high, it didn't mean much for the company's profits. The key question for the winning investor must always be:

**How much are the current quarter's earnings per share up
(in percentage terms) from the same quarter the year before?**

Let's say your company discloses that sales climbed 10% and net income advanced 12%. Sounds good, right? Not necessarily. You shouldn't be concerned with the company's total net income. You don't own the whole organization; you own shares in it. The company might have issued additional shares or "diluted" the common stock in other ways. So while net income may be up 12%, earnings per share—your main focus as an investor—may have inched up only 5% or 6%.

You must be able to see through slanted presentations. Don't let their use of words like "sales" and "net income" divert your attention from the truly vital facts like current quarterly earnings. To further clarify this point:

> **You should always compare a company's earnings per share to
> the same quarter a year earlier, not to the prior quarter, to avoid any
> distortion due to seasonality. In other words, you don't compare the
> December quarter's earnings to the prior September quarter's earnings
> per share. Rather, compare the December quarter of this year to the
> December quarter of last year for a more accurate evaluation.**

Omit a Company's One-Time Extraordinary Gains

The winning investor should avoid the trap of being influenced by nonrecurring profits.

If a computer maker reports earnings for the last quarter that include nonrecurring profits from activities such as the sale of real estate, this portion of earnings should be subtracted from the report. Such earnings represent a one-time, nonrecurring event and not the true, ongoing profitability of corporate operations. Ignore the earnings that result from these types of events.

Set a Minimum Level for Current Earnings Increases

Whether you're a new or experienced investor, I would advise against buying any stock that doesn't show earnings per share up at least 18% or 20% in the most recent quarter versus the same quarter the year before. In our study of the greatest winning companies, we found that they all had this in common *prior* to their big price moves. Many successful investors use 25% or 30% as their minimum earnings parameter. To be even safer, insist that both of the last two quarters show significant earnings gains.

During bull markets (major market uptrends), I prefer to concentrate on stocks that show powerful earnings gains—from 40% to 500% or more. You have thousands of stocks to choose from. Why not buy the very best merchandise available?

To further sharpen your stock selection process, look ahead to the next quarter or two and check the earnings that were reported for those same quarters the previous year. See if the company will be coming up against unusually large or small earnings achieved a year ago.

When the unusual year-earlier results are not due to seasonal factors, this step may help you anticipate a strong or poor earnings report in the coming months. Also, be sure to check consensus earnings estimates (projections that combine the earnings estimates of a large group of analysts) for the next several quarters—as well as the next year or two—to make sure the company is projected to be on a positive track. Some earnings estimate services even show an estimated annual earnings growth rate for the next five years for many companies.

Many individuals and even some institutional investors (mutual funds, banks, and insurance companies) buy stocks with earnings down in the most recently reported quarter just because they like a company and think its stock price is cheap. Usually they accept the story that earnings will rebound strongly in the near future. In some cases this may be true, but in many cases it isn't. The point is you have the choice of investing in thousands of companies, many of which are actually showing strong operating results. You don't have to accept promises of earnings that may never occur.

The Debate on Overemphasis of Current Earnings

It has been suggested in past years that Japanese firms concentrate more on long-term profits than current earnings per share. They spend money on projects that will strengthen the company's future, such as research and development.

Their concept is sound and one that better-managed organizations in the United States (a minority of companies) also follow. It's how leading companies create colossal earnings increases: they spend years on the research and development of superior new products.

But don't be confused. As an individual investor, you can afford to wait until the company proves its efforts have been successful by showing real earnings improvement. Requiring that current quarterly earnings be up a hefty amount is just another smart way the intelligent investor can reduce the risk of mistakes in stock selection.

Many older American corporations have mediocre management that continually produces second-rate earnings results. I call them the "entrenched maintainers" or "caretaker management." These are the companies you want to avoid until someone has the courage to change top management. Not coincidentally, they are generally the companies that strain to pump up their current earnings a dull 8% or 10%. True growth companies with outstanding new products or improved management do not have to maximize current results.

Look for Accelerating Quarterly Earnings Growth

Our analysis of the most successful stocks also showed that, in almost every case, earnings growth *accelerated* sometime in the 10 quarters before a towering price move began.

In other words, it's not just increased earnings that cause a big move. It's also the *size* of the increase plus the *improvement* from the company's prior percentage rate of earnings growth. Wall Street now calls many of these "earnings surprises."

If a company's earnings are up 15% a year and suddenly begin spurting 40% to 50% or more, it usually creates the conditions for important stock price improvement.

Look for Sales as Well as Earnings Growth

Strong, improved quarterly earnings should always be supported by sales growth of at least 25% for the latest quarter or at least an acceleration in the rate of sales percentage improvement over the last three quarters. Many newer issues (initial public offerings) may show the last 8, 10, or 12 quarters of huge sales increases sometimes averaging 100% or more.

Some professional investors bought Waste Management at $50 in early 1998 because earnings had jumped three quarters in a row from 24% to 75% and 268%. However, sales were up only 5%. Several months later the stock collapsed to $15 a share. What this demonstrates is that earnings can be inflated for a few quarters by cost reduction or reducing R&D, depreciation, reserves, advertising, or other constructive activities. However, to be sustainable, earnings growth must be supported by sales increases. Such was not the case with Waste Management.

It also helps improve your batting average if your stock selections show the latest quarter's after-tax profit margins are either at or near a new high.

Two Quarters of Major Earnings Deceleration Can Mean Trouble

Just as it's important to recognize when quarterly earnings growth is accelerating, it's also important to know when earnings begin to *decelerate,* and significantly slow down. By this I mean if a company growing at a 50% rate suddenly reports earnings gains of only 15%, that usually spells trouble and you probably want to avoid it.

When this happens, the stock frequently has either topped out permanently—regardless of what Wall Street analysts say—or its rate of upward progress will flatten into a lengthy and unrewarding period of price consolidation (sideways price movement without further price progress up).

However, before turning negative on a company's earnings I prefer to see two quarters of *material* slowdown, usually a two-third decline from the prior several quarters' rate of growth. Even the best organizations can have one slow quarter every once in a while.

Consult Log-Scale Weekly Graphs

Understanding the principle of earnings acceleration or deceleration is essential. Securities analysts who recommend stocks because of an absolute level of earnings expected for the following year could be looking at the wrong set of facts. A stock that earned $5 per share and expects to report $6 the next year (a "favorable" 20% increase) could mislead you unless you know the previous trend in the percentage rate of earnings change. What if previously it was up 60%? This partially explains why so few investors make significant money following the buy and sell recommendations of securities analysts.

Logarithmic-scale graphs are of great value in analyzing stocks because acceleration or deceleration in the percentage rate of quarterly earnings increases can be seen very clearly. Log graphs show percentage changes accurately, since 1 inch anywhere on the price or earnings scale represents the same percentage change. This is not true of arithmetically scaled charts. For example, on an arithmetically scaled chart, a 100% price increase from $10 to $20 a share would show the same space change as a 50% increase from $20 to $30 a share. In contrast, a logarithmic graph would show the 100% increase as twice as large as the 50% increase.

You, as a do-it-yourself investor, can take the latest quarterly earnings per share (EPS), along with the prior three quarters' EPS, and plot them on a logarithmic-scale graph to get a clear picture of earnings acceleration or deceleration. The plotting of the most recent 12-month earnings each quarter should, in the best companies, put the earnings per share point close to or already at new highs.

Check Other Stocks in the Group

For additional validation, check the earnings of other companies in your stock's industry group. If you can't find one or two other impressive stocks in the group displaying strong earnings, chances are you may have selected the wrong investment.

Where to Find Current Quarterly Earnings Reports

Quarterly corporate earnings statements are published every day in the business sections of most local newspapers and financial publications. *Investor's Business Daily* goes one step further and separates all new earnings reports into companies with "up" earnings from those reporting "down" results, so you can easily see who produced excellent gains and who didn't.

Chart services, like Daily Graphs®, Daily Graphs Online®, and others, also show earnings reported during the week as well as the most recent earnings figures for every stock they chart. Once you locate the percentage change in earnings per share when compared to the same year-ago quarter, also compare the percentage change in EPS on a quarter-by-quarter basis. Looking at the March quarter and then at the June, September, and December quarters will tell you if a company's earnings growth is accelerating or decelerating.

185 Ups
Median Change +19%

CACI INTL INC		CACI 52.67
Computer-Services		Eps 94 Rel 98
Qtr. Sep 30:	v2001	(OTC) 2000
Sales +16%↓	146,621,000	126,295,000
Net Income	6,575,000	4,352,000
Avg shares	11,472,000	11,354,000
Earn/shr +50%↑	0.57	0.38
Share earns (diluted):		
Net earn per shr	0.56	0.38
v-Results reflect adoption of SFAS No. 141 and No. 142.		

Investor's Business Daily®
October 19, 2001

Sample earnings report

You now have the first critical rule for improving your stock selection:

Current quarterly earnings per share should be up a major percentage–at least 25% to 50% or more–over the same quarter the previous year. The best companies might show earnings up 100% to 500% or more!

A mediocre 10% or 12% isn't enough. When picking winning stocks, it's the bottom line that counts.

A = Annual Earnings Increases: Look for Significant Growth

Any company can report a good earnings quarter every once in a while, and as we've seen, strong current quarterly earnings are critical to picking most of the market's biggest winners. But it's not enough.

To ensure that the latest results aren't just a flash in the pan, and that the company you are looking at is a quality one, you must insist on more proof. The way to do that is by reviewing the company's annual earnings growth rate.

Look for annual earnings per share that have increased every year for the last three years. You normally don't want the second year's earnings down, even if the following year rebounds and is in new high ground. It is the combination of strong earnings in the last few quarters plus a record of solid growth in recent years that creates a superb stock, or at least one with a higher probability for success.

Select Stocks With 25% to 50% or More Annual Growth Rates

The annual rate of earnings growth in the companies you pick should be 25%, 50%, even 100% or more. Between 1980 and 2000, the median annual growth rate of all outstanding stocks in our study at their early emerging stage was 36%. Three out of four of the biggest winners showed at least some positive annual growth rate over the five years preceding the stock's big run-up.

A typical earnings-per-share progression for the five years preceding the stock's move might be something like $0.70, $1.15, $1.85, $2.65, and $4.00.

In a few cases you might accept one down year in the last five as long as the following year's earnings quickly recover and move back to new high ground.

It's possible that a company could earn $4.00 a share one year, $5.00 the next, $6.00 the next, and then $2.00 a share. If the next annual earnings statement was, say, $2.50 per share versus the prior year's $2.00, it would still not be a good report despite the 25% increase. The only reason it seems attractive is that the previous ($2.00 a share) year was so depressed that any improvement would look good. The point is profits are recovering slowly and are still well below the company's annual peak earnings of $6.00 a share.

The consensus earnings estimate for the next year should also be up: the greater the increase, the better. Remember, however, that estimates are opinions, and opinions may be wrong. Actual reported earnings are facts.

Also, you should not ignore a company's annual return on equity (ROE). Our studies show that the greatest winning stocks of the past 50 years had ROEs of at least 17%. Return on equity helps separate the well-managed companies from the poorly managed ones. Additionally, look for growth stocks showing annual cash flow per share greater than actual earnings per share by at least 20%.

Check the Stability of a Company's Three-Year Earnings Record

Through our research, we've developed an additional factor that has proved to be important in selecting growth stocks: the stability and consistency of annual earnings growth over the past three years. Our stability measurement, which is expressed on a scale from 1 to 99, is calculated differently than most statistics. The lower the figure, the more stable the past earnings record. The figures are calculated by plotting quarterly earnings for the past five years and fitting a trend line around the plot points to determine the degree of deviation from the basic trend.

Growth stocks with steady earnings tend to show a stability figure below 20 or 25. Companies with stability ratings over 30 are more cyclical and a little less dependable in terms of their growth. All other things being equal, you may want to look for stocks showing a greater degree of sustainability, consistency, and stability in past earnings growth. When the quarterly earnings are plotted on a log chart for several years, the earnings line should be on a nearly straight line, consistently moving up.

Earnings stability numbers are usually shown immediately after a company's annual growth rate, although most analysts and investment services do not bother to make the calculation. We show them in many of our insti-

Unitedhealth Group Inc.	
Annual Growth Rate	20%
Earnings Stability	7
EPS Rating	96
Sales, Margins + ROE Rating	B

Daily Graphs Online®
October 16, 2001
Sample earnings stability

tutional products as well as in Daily Graphs® and Daily Graphs Online®, designed for individual investors.

If you restrict your stock selections to ventures with proven growth records, you avoid the hundreds of investments with erratic histories or cyclical recoveries in profits. Such stocks may "top out" as they approach the peaks of their prior earnings cycle.

What Is a Normal Stock Market Cycle?

History demonstrates that most bull (up) market cycles last two to four years and are followed by a recession or bear (down) market; then another bull market starts.

In the beginning phase of a new bull market, growth stocks are usually the first to lead and make new price highs. Basic industry groups such as steel, chemical, paper, rubber, machinery, and other so-called cyclical stocks usually lag.

Young growth stocks will usually dominate for at least two bull cycles. Then the emphasis may change for a short period to turnarounds, cyclicals, or other newly improved sectors.

While three out of four big market winners in the past were growth stocks, one in four was a turnaround situation. In 1982, Chrysler and Ford were two such spirited turnaround plays. Cyclical and turnaround opportunities led in the market waves of 1953–1955, 1963–1965, and 1974–1975. Cyclicals like paper, aluminum, autos, chemicals, and plastics returned to the fore in 1987. Home-building stocks (also cyclical) have led in other cycles. IBM was a great example of a turnaround situation in 1994.

Yet even in these periods there were some pretty dramatic young growth stocks available. Basic-industry stocks in the United States often represent older, more inefficient industries, some of which are no longer internationally competitive and growing. They do not represent America's future.

Rallies in cyclical stocks tend to be short-lived and prone to falter at the first hint of an earnings slowdown. Should you decide to buy strong turn-around stocks, the annual earnings growth rate could be 5% to 10%. Requiring a turnaround company to show two consecutive quarters of sharp earnings recovery should put the earnings for the latest 12 months into or very near new high ground. Look at the 12 months earnings line on a stock chart; the sharper the upswing the better. If the profit upswing is so dramatic that it reaches a new high, sometimes one quarter of earnings turnaround will suffice.

How to Weed Out the Losers in a Group

Using three-year annual earnings per share growth criteria will help you weed out 80% of stocks in any industry group. Growth rates for most stocks in most groups are lackluster, or worse, nonexistent, unlike the following stocks, all of which showed signs of their future major advances:

- When Xerox's stock soared 700% from March 1963 to June 1966, its earnings growth rate averaged 32% a year.
- Wal-Mart Stores, which rocketed 11,200% from 1977 to 1990, sported an annual growth rate of 43% prior to its big move.
- Cisco Systems' growth rate in October 1990 was an enormous 257% per year and Microsoft's was 99% in October 1986, prior to their long advances.

Keep in mind that an annual growth record doesn't necessarily mean a company is a growth stock. In fact, many so-called growth stocks report substantially slower growth than they did in earlier market periods.

A company with an outstanding three-year growth record of 30% but whose earnings in the last several quarters have slowed significantly to 10% and 15% acts like a fully mature growth stock. Older and larger organizations often show slowed growth and in most cases should be avoided. From 1998 to 2000, McDonald's Corp had a three-year growth rate of only 10%, which is substandard in today's growth-stock markets.

Insist on Both Annual and Current Quarterly Earnings Being Excellent

A standout stock needs a sound growth record during recent years, but also a strong current earnings record in the last few quarters. It is the powerful combination of these two critical factors, rather than one or the other, which creates a super stock, or at least one that has a higher chance for true success.

The fastest way to find a company with strong and accelerating current earnings and solid three-year growth is by checking the Earnings Per Share (EPS) Rating provided for every stock listed in *Investor's Business Daily*. The EPS Rating is defined as:

A proprietary rating that measures a company's two most recent quarters' earnings growth rate compared to the same quarters one year prior. Then, the company's three-year annual growth rate is examined. The results are compared to all other publicly traded companies and rated on a scale from 1 to 99, with 99 being best. An EPS Rating of 99 means that a company has outperformed 99% of all other companies in terms of both annual and recent quarterly earnings performance.

If an initial public offering doesn't show a three-year earnings record, look for the last five or six quarterly earnings reports to be up a huge amount and even more quarters of enormous sales increases. One or two quarters of profitability is frequently not enough and represents a less proven stock that might fall apart somewhere down the line.

Are Price-Earnings Ratios Really Important?

If you're like most investors, you've probably learned that the most important thing you need to know about a stock is its price-to-earnings (P/E) ratio. Well, prepare yourself for a bubble-bursting surprise.

While P/E ratios have been used for years by analysts as their basic measurement tool in deciding if a stock is undervalued (has a low P/E) and should be bought, or is overvalued (has a high P/E) and should be sold, our ongoing analysis of the most successful stocks from 1952 to present shows that P/E ratios were not a relevant factor in price movement and have very little to do with whether a stock should be bought or sold. P/Es are an end effect, not a cause. Much more crucial, we found, was the percentage increase in earnings per share. To say a security is "undervalued" because it's selling at a low P/E or because it's in the low range of its historical P/E is nonsense. **Primary consideration should be given to whether the rate of change in earnings is substantially increasing or decreasing.**

From 1953 through 1985, the average P/E ratio for the best-performing stocks at their early emerging stage was 20. (The P/E of the Dow Jones Industrial Average at the time averaged 15.) While advancing, the biggest winners expanded their P/Es by 125% to about 45. During the 1990–95 period, the real leaders began with an average P/E of 36 and expanded into the 80s. Since these are averages, the beginning P/E range for most big winners was 25 to 50 and the P/E expansions varied from 60 to 115. The late

1990s market euphoria saw these valuations increase to even greater levels. Value buyers missed all of these tremendous investments.

Why You Missed Some Fabulous Stocks!

While the above-mentioned numbers are just averages, they do strongly suggest that if you were not willing to pay an average of 25 to 50 times earnings or even much more for growth stocks, you automatically eliminated most of the best investments available! Thus, you would have missed out on Microsoft, Cisco Systems, Home Depot, and America Online during their periods of greatest market performance.

High P/Es were found to occur because of bull markets. Low P/Es, with the exception of cyclical stocks, generally occurred because of bear markets. In a roaring bull market, don't overlook a stock just because its P/E seems too high. It could be the next great stock market winner.

Never buy a stock solely because the P/E ratio makes it look like a bargain. There are usually good reasons why P/Es are low, and there's no golden rule in the stock market that protects a stock that sells at 8 or 10 times earnings from going even lower and selling at 4 or 5 times earnings.

Many years ago, when I first began to study the market, I bought Northrop at 4 times earnings and watched in disbelief as the stock declined to a P/E ratio of 2.

How Price-Earnings Ratios Are Misused

Many Wall Street analysts put a stock on their "buy" list because it's selling in the low end of its historical P/E range. They'll also recommend a stock when the price starts to drop, thereby lowering the P/E and making it seem like an even bigger bargain. In 1998, Gillette and Coca-Cola looked like great buys because they sold off several points and their P/Es looked more attractive. In actuality, the earnings growth in both companies showed material deceleration, which justified a lower P/E valuation. Much of this questionable method of P/E analysis is based on personal opinions and theories handed down through the years by analysts, academicians, and others who often have questionable track records when it comes to making money in the market. Reliance on P/E ratios often ignores more basic trends. For example, the general market may have topped out, in which case all stocks are headed lower. It's ridiculous and somewhat naïve to say a company is undervalued because at one time it was 22 times earnings and it can now be bought for 15 times earnings.

One way I use P/E ratios is to estimate the potential price objective for a growth stock over the next 6 to 18 months based on its estimated future earnings. I take the earnings estimate for the next two years and multiply it by the stock's P/E ratio at the initial chart base buy point multiplied by 130%. This 130% is the degree of P/E expansion expected on average if a growth stock has a major price move. This tells what a growth stock could potentially sell for during bull market conditions. For example, if Charles Schwab's stock breaks out of its first base at $43.75 per share and its P/E ratio at the beginning buy point is 40, multiply 40 by 130% to see that the P/E ratio could possibly expand to 92 if the stock has a huge price move. Now multiply the potential P/E ratio of 92 by the consensus earnings estimate two years out of $1.45 per share. This tells you what a possible price objective for your growth stock might be.

The Wrong Way to Analyze Companies in an Industry

Another faulty use of price-earnings ratios, by amateurs and professionals alike, is to evaluate stocks in an industry and conclude that the one selling at the cheapest P/E is always undervalued and therefore the most attractive purchase. The reality is that the lowest P/E usually belongs to the company with the most ghastly earnings record, and that's precisely why it sells at the lowest P/E.

The simple truth is that stocks at any one time usually sell near their current value. The stock that sells at 20 times earnings is there for one set of market-determined reasons, and the stock that trades for 15 times earnings is there for another set of reasons. A stock selling at, say, 7 times earnings does so because its overall record is more deficient than a stock with a higher P/E ratio. Also, keep in mind that cyclical stocks normally have lower P/Es; in good periods they do not show the P/E expansion that happens in growth stocks. You can't buy a Mercedes for the price of a Chevrolet.

Everything sells for about what it is worth at the time. If a company's price and P/E ratio change in the near future, it's because conditions, events, psychology, and earnings continue to improve or suddenly start to deteriorate as the weeks and months pass.

Eventually, a stock's P/E will reach a peak, but this normally occurs when the general market averages are topping out and starting a significant decline. It could also be a signal that the stock is about to lose its earnings momentum.

It is true that high P/E stocks will be more volatile, particularly if they are in the volatile high-tech area. The price of a high P/E stock can also get temporarily ahead of itself, but the same can also be said for lower P/E stocks.

Examples of High P/Es That Were Great Bargains

In situations where small but captivating growth companies have revolutionary new products, what seems like a high P/E ratio can actually be low. For instance:

- Xerox sold for 100 times earnings in 1960—before it advanced 3300% in price (from a split-adjusted $5 to $170).
- Syntex sold for 45 times earnings in July 1963—before it advanced 400%.
- Genentech was priced at 200 times earnings in November 1985, and it bolted 300% in five months.
- America Online sold for over 100 times earnings in November 1994 before increasing 14,900% from 1994 to its top in December 1999.

These companies had fantastic new products: the first dry copier, the oral contraceptive pill, the use of genetic information to develop new wonder drugs, and access to the revolutionary new world of the Internet. If you had a bias against P/Es you considered too high, you would have missed out on the tremendous price advances these stocks had. Therefore, it usually pays to avoid having a P/E bias during bull markets.

Don't Sell High P/E Stocks Short

In June 1962, when the stock market was at rock bottom, a big Beverly Hills investor barged into the office of a broker friend of mine and shouted that, at 50 times earnings, Xerox was drastically overpriced. He sold 2000 shares short at $88. (He borrowed stock from his broker to sell in the hope that the stock would decline and he could later buy it back cheaper, making money on the difference in price.)

The stock took off immediately and ultimately reached a price equal to $1300 (before adjusting for splits). So much for opinions about P/Es being too high! Investors' personal opinions are generally wrong; the market is almost always right.

In summary, **concentrate on stocks with proven records of significant earnings growth in each of the last three years plus strong recent quarterly improvements.** Don't accept anything less.

· CHAPTER ·

N = New Products, New Management, New Highs: Buying at the Right Time

It takes something new to produce a startling advance in the price of a stock. It can be an important new product or service that sells rapidly and causes earnings to accelerate above previous rates of increase. Or it can be a change of management that brings new vigor, new ideas, or at least a new broom to sweep everything clean. New industry conditions—shortages, price increases, or revolutionary technologies, for example—can affect most stocks in an industry group in a positive way.

In our study of the greatest stock market winners from 1952 through 2001, we discovered that more than 95% of stunning successes in American industry met at least one of the above criteria.

New Products That Created Super Successes

One of the ways a company can achieve enormous success, thereby enjoying large gains in its stock price, is by introducing new products into the marketplace. We're not talking about a new formula for dish soap. These products and companies have to revolutionize the way we live. Here are some examples from the past:

1. Rexall's new Tupperware division in 1958 helped push the company's stock to $50 a share from $16.

2. Thiokol in 1957–1959 came out with new rocket fuels for missiles, propelling its shares from $48 to the equivalent of $355.

3. Syntex in 1963 marketed the oral contraceptive pill. In six months, the stock soared from $100 to $550.

4. McDonald's, with low-priced fast-food franchising, snowballed from 1967 to 1971 into a 1100% profit for stockholders.

5. Levitz Furniture's stock soared 660% in 1970–1971 on the popularity of the company's giant warehouse discount-furniture centers.

6. Houston Oil & Gas, with a major new oil field, ran up 968% in 61 weeks in 1972–1973 and picked up another 367% in 1976.

7. Computervision's stock advanced 1235% in 1978–1980 with the introduction of new Cad-Cam factory-automation equipment.

8. Wang Labs' Class B shares grew 1350% in 1978–1980 on the development of its new word processing office machines.

9. Price Company's stock shot up more than 15 times in 1982–1986 with the opening of a southern California chain of innovative wholesale warehouse membership stores.

10. Amgen developed two successful new biotech drugs, Epogen and Neupogen, and the stock raced ahead from $60 in 1990 to the equivalent of $460 in early 1992.

11. Cisco Systems, another California company, created routers and networking equipment that enabled companies to link up geographically dispersed local area computer networks. The stock rocketed to nearly 2000% in 3½ years from November 1990 to March 1994. In 10 years, from 1990 to 2000, Cisco increased an unbelievable 75,000%.

12. International Game Technology surged 1600% in 1991–1993 with new microprocessor-based gaming products.

13. Microsoft carried its stock up almost 1800% from March 1993 to the end of 1999 as its innovative Windows software products dominated the personal computer market.

14. Peoplesoft, the number one maker of personnel software, exploded for a 20-fold increase in the 3½ years from August 1994.

15. Dell Computer, the leader and innovator in build-to-order, direct PC sales advanced 1780% from November 1996 to January 1999.

16. EMC, with superior computer memory devices, capitalizing on the ever-increasing need for network storage, raced up 478% from January 1998 in 15 months.

17. AOL and Yahoo!, the two top Internet leaders providing consumers with the new "portals" they needed to access the wealth of services and information available on the Internet, both produced 500% gains beginning in the fall of 1998 to their peaks in 1999.

18. Oracle's database and e-business applications software drove its stock in September 1999 from $20 to $90 in only 29 weeks.

19. Charles Schwab, the number one online discount broker during a period that showed a shift to online trading, racked up a 414% move in just six months from late 1998.

20. Sun Microsystems emerged with new leading network products and bolted more than 700% from October 1998 to March 2000.

Don't ever let yourself get discouraged and give up on the opportunity that is the U.S. stock market. There will be hundreds of future leaders just like the ones we've mentioned above. Study and prepare yourself so you will be able to recognize the next big round of new winners.

The Stock Market's "Great Paradox"

There is another fascinating phenomenon we found in the early stage of all winning stocks. We call it the "great paradox." Before I tell you what this is, I want you to look at the accompanying graphs of three typical stocks. Which one looks like the best buy to you, A, B, or C? Which would you avoid? We'll give you the answer at the end of this chapter.

The staggering majority of individual investors, whether new or experienced, take delightful comfort in buying stocks that are down substantially

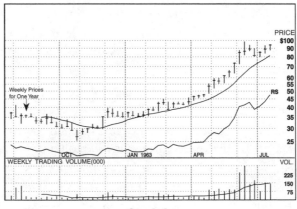

Stock A

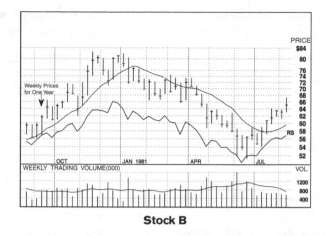

Stock B

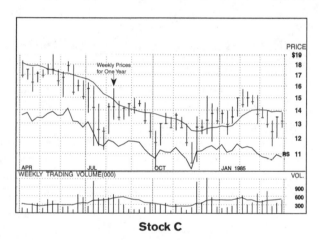

Stock C

from their peaks, thinking they're getting a bargain. Among the hundreds of thousands of individual investors attending my investment lectures in the 1970s, 1980s, and 1990s, 98% said they do not buy stocks that are making new highs in price.

This phenomenon is not limited to individual investors. I have provided extensive research for more than 600 major institutional investors and have found that many of them are also "bottom buyers." They, too, feel it's safer to buy stocks that look like bargains because they're either down a lot in price or actually selling near their lows.

Our study of the greatest stock market winners proved (surprisingly) that the old adage "buy low, sell high" was completely wrong. In fact, our study proved the exact opposite. The hard-to-believe Great Paradox in the stock market is:

What seems too high in price and risky to the majority usually goes higher, and what seems low and cheap usually goes lower.

Are you finding this "high-altitude paradox" a little difficult to act upon? Let me cite another study we conducted. In this one, we analyzed two groups of stocks over many market periods: those that made new highs and those that made new lows.

The results were conclusive: Stocks on the new-high list tended to go higher in price, while those on the new-low list tended to go lower in price.

Based on our research, a stock on IBD's "New Price Low" list tends to be a pretty poor prospect and should be avoided. In fact, decisive investors should sell such stocks long before they get on the "New Price Low" list. A stock making the new-high list—especially for the first time while trading on big volume during a bull market—might be a prospect with big potential.

How Does a Stock Go from $50 to $100?

Ask yourself: What does a stock that has traded between $40 and $50 a share over many months, and is now selling at $50, have to do to double in price? Doesn't it first have to go through $51, then $52, and $53, $54, $55, and so on—all new price highs—before it can reach $100?

As a smart investor, your job is to buy when a stock looks too high to the majority of conventional investors and sell after it moves substantially higher and finally begins to look attractive to some of those same investors. If you bought Cisco at the highest price it ever sold for in 1990 when it just made a new high and looked scary, you would have enjoyed a nearly 75,000% increase from that point forward.

When to Correctly Begin Buying a Stock

Just because a stock is making a new price high does not necessarily mean it's the right time to buy. Using stock charts is an important piece of the stock selection process. A stock's historical price movement should be reviewed carefully, and you should look for stocks making new price highs as they break out of price consolidation areas (or "bases"). (See Chapter 12 for more detail on chart reading and identifying chart patterns.) Why? Because this is the point where most really big price advances begin, and it is the time where the probability of a significant price move is the greatest. A sound consolidation, or base-building, period could last from seven or eight weeks up to 15 months. So some bases are short and some are longer timewise.

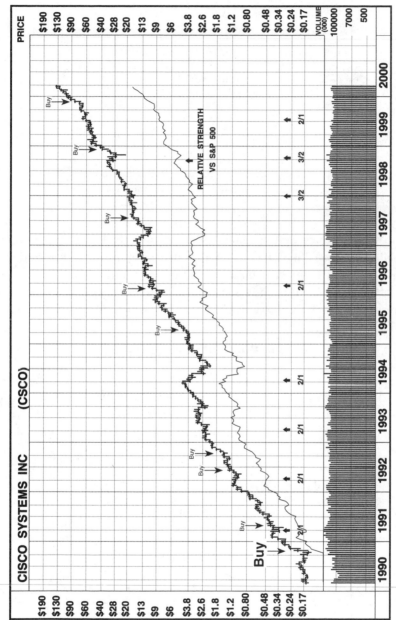

Up nearly 75,000% in 10 years

480% increase in just under 6 months

The perfect time is during a bull market just as a stock is starting to break out of its price base. (See America Online chart.) This is what is referred to as the "pivot" or buy point. You should avoid buying once the stock is more than 5% or 10% above the exact buy point off the base; otherwise, your chance of getting shaken out in the next correction or pullback in price greatly increases.

Answers to the Market's Great Paradox

Now that you know the great paradox, would you still pick the same stock you did earlier in the chapter? The right one to buy was Stock A, Syntex Corp., which is shown below. The arrow pointing to July 1963's weekly price movements is the buy point. This arrow coincides with the price and volume

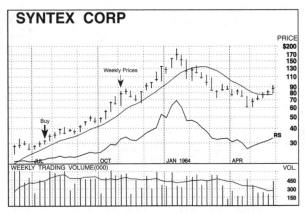

Stock A: 482% increase in 6 months from buy arrow

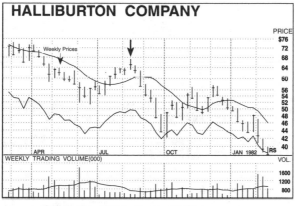

Stock B: –42% in 6 months from arrow

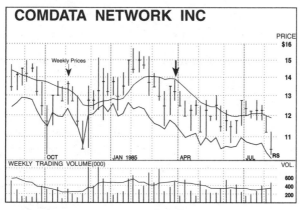

Stock C: –21% in 5 months from arrow

activity at the end of the Stock A chart, adjusted for a 3 to 1 split. Syntex enjoyed a major price advance from its July 1963 buy point. In contrast, Stocks B (Halliburton) and C (Comdata Network) both declined, as you can see from their charts. (The arrows indicate where the corresponding charts shown earlier left off.)

In conclusion, **search for companies that have developed important new products or services, or benefited from new management or new industry conditions. Then buy their stocks when they are emerging from price consolidation patterns and are close to, or actually making, new price highs.**

S = Supply and Demand: Shares Outstanding Plus Big Volume Demand

The law of supply and demand determines the price of almost everything in your daily life. At the grocery store, for instance, what you pay for your lettuce, tomatoes, eggs, and beef depends on how much of each item there is and how many people want these items. It impacted the price of food and consumer goods even in former Communist countries. There, state-owned items were always in short supply and often available only to the privileged class or on the black market to those who could pay the exorbitant prices.

This basic principle of supply and demand also applies to the stock market, where it is more important than all the analyst opinions on Wall Street.

Big or Small Supply of Stock

The price of a common stock with 5 billion shares outstanding is harder to budge because there's such a large supply. It takes a large volume of buying, or demand, to create a rousing price increase.

On the other hand, if a company has only 50 million shares outstanding— a relatively small supply—just a reasonable amount of buying, or demand, can push the price up more rapidly.

If you are choosing between two stocks to buy, one with 5 billion shares outstanding and the other with 50 million, the smaller one will usually be the better performer, if other factors are equal. However, since smaller-capitalization stocks are less liquid, they can come down as fast as they go up, sometimes even faster. In other words, with greater opportunity comes significant additional risk. But there are definite ways of minimizing your risk, which will be discussed in Chapter 9.

The total number of shares outstanding in a company's capital structure represents the potential amount of stock available. But market professionals also look at the "floating supply," the shares left for possible purchase after subtracting stock that is closely held. Companies in which top management owns a large percentage of the stock (at least 2% to 3% in a large company, and more in small companies) generally are your better prospects because they have a vested interest in the stock.

There's another fundamental reason, besides supply and demand, why companies with a large number of shares frequently produce slower results: The companies themselves may be much older, growing at a slower rate, and simply too big and sluggish.

During the 1990s, a phenomenon occurred where for several years big-cap stocks outperformed small-cap stocks. This was in part related to the size problem experienced by the mutual fund community that suddenly found itself awash in huge amounts of new cash as more and more people bought mutual funds. As a result, the industry was forced to buy bigger-cap stocks. It appeared that funds favored bigger-cap stocks because of the need to put more money to work. This was contrary to the normally favorable supply/demand effect found in smaller-cap stocks with fewer shares around to meet increases in investor demand. Big-cap stocks do have some advantages: greater liquidity, less downside volatility, better-quality, and usually less risk. The immense buying power of large funds can make a top-notch, big stock advance nearly as fast as shares of a smaller company.

Pick Entrepreneurial Management Rather Than Caretakers

Great size may create seeming power and influence, but size in corporations can also produce a lack of imagination. Big companies are often run by older and more conservative "caretaker management" less willing to innovate, take risks, and keep up with the times. In most cases, top managers of large companies don't own a lot of their company's stock. This is a serious defect that should be corrected since it implies to the savvy investor that the company's management and employees don't have any personal interest in seeing the company succeed.

Also, in some cases, multiple layers of management separate the senior executives from what's really going on at the customer level. And in a capitalist economy, the ultimate boss in a company is the customer.

Times are changing at an ever-faster rate. A company with a hot new product today will find sales slipping within two or three years if it doesn't continue to bring relevant new products to market. Most new products, services, and inventions come from young, hungry, innovative, small- and medium-sized companies with entrepreneurial management. Not coincidentally, these organizations grow much faster and create most of the new jobs. Many are in the service or technology industries. This is where the great future growth of America lies. Microsoft, Cisco Systems, and Oracle are just a few examples of dynamic small-cap innovators of the 1980s and 1990s that continually grew and became big-cap stocks.

In contrast, if a mammoth older company creates an important new product, it may not materially help its stock because the product will probably account for only a small percentage of the company's total sales and earnings. The product is simply a small drop in a bucket that's just too big.

Excessive Stock Splits May Hurt

From time to time, companies make the mistake of excessively splitting their stocks. This is sometimes done on advice from Wall Street investment bankers.

In my opinion, it's usually better for a company to split its shares 2 for 1 or 3 for 2 than 3 for 1 or 5 for 1. (When a stock splits 2 for 1, you get two shares for each share previously held, but the new shares sell for half the price.)

Oversized splits create a substantially larger supply and may put a company in the more lethargic, big-cap status sooner.

It may be unwise for a company whose stock has gone up in price for a year or two to declare an extravagant split near the end of a bull market or in the early stage of a bear market. Yet, this is exactly what many corporations do.

Generally speaking, these companies feel the lower-priced stock will attract more buyers. This may be the case with some smaller buyers, but it also may produce the opposite result—more sellers—especially if it's the second split in the last year or two. Knowledgeable pros and a few shrewd individual traders will probably use the excitement generated by the oversized split as an opportunity to sell and take their profits.

A stock will often top in price around the second or third time it splits. Our study of the biggest winners found only 18% of them had splits in the year preceding their great price advances.

Large holders who are thinking of selling might figure it's easier to unload their 100,000 shares *before* a 3-for-1 split than sell 300,000 shares afterward.

And smart short sellers pick on stocks that are heavily owned by institutions and starting to falter after huge price run-ups.

Look for Companies Buying Their Own Stock in the Open Market

In most but not all cases it's usually a good sign when a company, and especially a small- to medium-sized growth company that meets the CAN SLIM™ criteria, buys its own stock in the open marketplace over a consistent period of time. (A 10% buyback would be considered big.) This reduces the number of shares in the marketplace and usually implies the company expects improved sales and earnings in the future.

As a result of the buyback, the company's net income will be divided by a smaller number of shares, thereby increasing earnings per share. As we've discussed, the percentage increase in earnings per share is one of the principal driving forces behind outstanding stocks.

From the mid-1970s to the early 1980s, Tandy, Teledyne, and Metromedia successfully repurchased their own stock. All three produced notable results in their earnings-per-share growth and in the price advance of their stock. Tandy's (split-adjusted) stock increased from $2.75 to $60 between 1973 and 1983. Teledyne stock zoomed from $8 to $190 from 1971 to 1984, and Metromedia soared from $30 to $560 from 1971 to 1977. Teledyne shrank its capitalization from 88 million shares to 15 million and increased its earnings from $0.61 a share to nearly $20 per share with eight separate buybacks.

In 1989 and 1990, International Game Technology announced they were buying back 20% of their stock. By September 1993, IGT had advanced more than 20 times. NVR Inc. had big buybacks in 2001.

A Low Corporate Debt-to-Equity Ratio Is Generally Better

After you've found a stock with a reasonable number of shares, check the percentage of the company's total capitalization represented by long-term debt or bonds. Usually, the lower the debt ratio, the safer and better the company.

Earnings per share of companies with high debt-to-equity ratios could be clobbered in difficult periods of high interest rates. These highly leveraged companies are generally of lower quality and higher risk.

A corporation that's been reducing its debt as a percent of equity over the last two or three years is worth considering. If nothing else, interest costs will be sharply reduced, helping generate higher earnings per share.

Additionally, the presence of convertible bonds in the capital structure could dilute earnings if and when the bonds are converted into shares of common stock.

Evaluating Supply and Demand

The best way to measure a stock's supply and demand is by watching its daily trading volume. When a stock pulls back in price, you want to see volume dry up indicating no significant selling pressure. When it rallies up in price, you want to see volume rise, which usually represents institutional buying. When a stock breaks out of a price consolidation area (see Chapter 12 on chart reading and identifying price patterns of winning stocks), trading volume should be at least 50% above normal. In many cases, it will increase 100% or more for the day, indicating solid buying of the stock and the possibility for further increases in price. Using daily and weekly charts helps you analyze and interpret a stock's price and volume action.

Remember, **any size capitalization stock can be bought under the CAN SLIM™ method, but small-cap stocks will be substantially more volatile, both on the upside and the downside. From time to time, the market will shift its emphasis from small to large caps and vice versa. Companies buying back their stock in the open market and companies showing stock ownership by management are preferred.**

L = Leader or Laggard: Which Is Your Stock?

People tend to buy stocks they like, stocks they feel good about, or stocks they feel comfortable with, but in an otherwise exciting stock market, these sentimental securities often lag the market rather than lead it.

Suppose you want to buy a stock in the computer industry. If you buy the leader in the group, and if your timing is right, you have a crack at real price appreciation. But if you buy a stock that hasn't yet moved, or is down the most in price (because you feel safer with it and think you're getting a real bargain), you might have bought a stock with little upward price potential. Why else would it be at the bottom of the pile?

Don't just dabble in stocks. Dig in, do some detective work, and find out what really works.

Buy Among the Best Two or Three Stocks in a Group

The top two or three stocks in a strong industry group can have unbelievable growth, while others in the pack may hardly stir.

In 1979 and 1980, Wang Labs, Prime Computer, Datapoint, Rolm Corp., Tandy Corporation, and other small computer companies had five-, six-, and seven-fold advances before topping and retreating. Grand old IBM, on the other hand, just sat there, and giants Burroughs, NCR, and Sperry Rand turned in lifeless performances. However, in the next bull market cycle IBM sprang to life and produced excellent results.

Home Depot advanced 10 times from 1988 to 1992, while Waban and Hechinger, the group's laggards, dramatically underperformed.

37

You should buy the really great companies—the ones that lead their industries and are number 1 in their particular field. All of my best big winners, Syntex in 1963, Pic-N-Save from 1976 to 1983, Price Company from 1982 to 1985, Franklin Resources from 1985 to 1986, Genentech from 1986 to 1987, Amgen from 1990 to 1991, America Online from 1998 to 1999, Charles Schwab from 1998 to 1999, Sun Microsystems from 1998 to 1999, and Qualcomm in 1999, were the number one companies in their industries at the time they were purchased. The number one market leader is not the largest company or the one with the most recognized brand name; it's the one with the best quarterly and annual earnings growth, return on equity, profit margins, sales growth, and price action. It will also have a superior product or service and be gaining market share from its older, less innovative competitors.

Avoid Sympathy Stock Moves

As our studies show, very little in the stock market is really new; history just keeps repeating itself. In the summer of 1963, I bought stock in Syntex, the developer of the birth-control pill, which then shot up 400%. Most people wouldn't buy it because it had just made a new price high at $100 and its P/E ratio, at 45, seemed too high.

Instead, several investment firms recommended G.D. Searle as a "sympathy play." It looked much cheaper in price and had a product similar to Syntex's, but it failed to produce the same market results. Syntex was the leader; Searle, the laggard.

A sympathy play is a stock in the same group as a leading company, and it's bought in the hope that the leader's luster will rub off onto it, but the profit and price records of sympathy plays usually pale in comparison. Eventually they'll try to move up "in sympathy" with the real leader, but they never do as well.

In 1970, Levitz Furniture, the leader in the then-new warehouse business, became an electrifying market winner. Wickes Corp. copied Levitz, and many people bought its shares because they were cheaper in price, but Wickes never performed and ultimately got into financial trouble. Levitz, meanwhile, appreciated 900% before it finally topped.

As steel industry pioneer Andrew Carnegie said in his autobiography: "The first man gets the oyster; the second, the shell."

How to Separate the Leaders From the Laggards: Using Relative Price Strength

If you own a portfolio of stocks, you must learn to sell the worst performers first and keep the best ones a little longer. In other words, always sell your losers and mistakes, and watch your better selections to see if they progress into your big winners.

There's a fast and easy way to tell if your stock is a leader or a laggard: check IBD's Relative Price Strength (RS) Rating. The RS Rating is defined as:

A proprietary rating that measures the price performance of a given stock against the rest of the market for the past 52 weeks. Each stock is assigned a performance rating from 1 to 99, with 99 being best. An RS Rating of 99 means the stock has outperformed 99% of all other companies in terms of price performance.

If your stock's RS Rating is below 70, it's lagging the better-performing stocks in the overall market. That doesn't mean it can't go up in price—it just means that if by some chance it does go up, it'll probably go up less.

The average RS Rating of the best-performing stocks each year from the early 1950s through 2000 was 87 *before* their major run-ups. So the determined winner's rule: Avoid laggard stocks and sympathy moves. Look for the genuine leaders!

The Relative Price Strength Rating is shown each day for all NYSE, Nasdaq, and Amex stocks listed in *Investor's Business Daily's* stock tables. You can't find this information in any other newspaper. Updated RS Ratings are also shown on the Daily Graphs Online® charting service.

In addition to IBD's proprietary RS Rating, you'll also want to look on a chart for the relative strength line. If it has been sinking for seven months or more, or if the line has an abnormally sharp decline for four months or more, the stock's price behavior is highly questionable.

Pick 80s and 90s That Are in a Chart Base Pattern

Want to upgrade your stock selection and concentrate on the best leaders? Restrict your purchases to companies showing a Relative Price Strength Rating of 80 or higher. There's no point to buying a stock that's straggling behind many others in the market, yet that's exactly what many investors do. Most do it without ever looking at a relative strength line or RS Rating, including some of America's largest investment firms.

I don't like to buy stocks with Relative Price Strength Ratings less than 80. In fact, the really big money-making selections generally have RS Ratings of 90 or higher just before breaking out of their first or second base structure. The RS Rating of a potential winning stock should be in the same league as a pitcher's fastball. The average big league fastball is clocked about 86 miles per hour, and the best pitchers throw "heat" in the 90s.

When you buy, make absolutely sure the stock is coming out of a sound base (price consolidation area) and that you buy it at its exact pivot buy point. (For more on bases and pivot points, please read Chapter 12.) Also, be sure it's not extended more than 5% or 10% above the precise buy point of this base. This will keep you from chasing stocks that have raced up in price too rapidly above their bases. Buying stocks that are extended percentagewise too far from a correct buy point will result in more sharp sell-offs in price that will shake you out of a stock.

The unwillingness of investors to set and follow minimum standards for stock selection reminds me of doctors years ago who were ignorant of the need to sterilize their instruments before each operation. They kept killing off patients until surgeons finally and begrudgingly accepted studies by researchers Louis Pasteur and Joseph Lister.

Ignorance rarely pays off in any walk of life, and it's no different in the stock market.

Finding New Leaders in Market Corrections

Corrections, or price declines, in the general market can help you recognize new leaders—if you know what to look for. The more desirable growth stocks normally correct 1½ to 2½ times the general market averages. In a bull market correction, growth stocks declining the least (percentagewise) are usually your best selections. The stocks that drop the most are normally your weakest.

Say the general market average suffers an intermediate-term correction of 10%, and three of your successful growth stocks come off 15%, 20%, and 30%. The two off only 15% or 20% are likely to be your best investments after they recover. A stock sliding 35% to 40% in a general-market decline of 10% could be flashing a warning signal. In most cases, you should heed it.

Once a general-market decline is definitely over, the first stocks that bounce back to new price highs are almost always your authentic leaders. These breakouts continue week by week for about three months.

Pros Make Mistakes Too

Many professional investment managers make the serious mistake of buying stocks that have just suffered unusually large price drops. As our studies indicate, this is a surefire way to get yourself in trouble.

In June 1972, a normally capable institutional investor in Maryland bought Levitz Furniture after its first abnormal price break—a one-week drop from

$60 to around $40. The stock rallied for a few weeks, rolled over and broke to $18.

In October 1978, several institutional investors bought Memorex when it had its first unusual price break. It later plunged.

In September 1981, certain money managers in New York bought Dome Petroleum on a break from $16 to $12. To them, it seemed cheap, and there was a favorable story about the stock going around Wall Street. Months later, Dome sold for $1.

Institutional buyers snapped up Lucent Technologies at the start of 2000 when it broke from $78 to $50. Later in the year it collapsed to $5.

None of these pros recognized the difference between normal price declines and highly abnormal big-volume corrections that signal potential disaster.

The real problem, of course, was these experts all relied solely on fundamental analysis (and stories) and their personal opinion of value (lower P/E ratios). They didn't pay attention to the market action that could have told them what was really going on. Those who ignore what the market says usually pay a heavy price. Those who listen and who learn the difference between normal and abnormal action are said to have a "good feel for the market."

Look for Abnormal Strength in a Weak Market

In the spring of 1967, I remember walking through a broker's office in New York on a day when the Dow Jones Industrial Average was down over 12 points (12 points was a lot in those days!). When I looked up at the electronic ticker tape, showing prices moving across the wall, I saw that Control Data was trading at $62, up 3½ points on heavy volume. I bought the stock at once. I knew Control Data well, and this was abnormal strength in the face of a weak overall market. The stock later ran up to $150.

In April 1981, just as the 1981 bear market was getting underway, MCI Communications, a Washington, D.C.-based telecommunications stock trading in the over-the-counter market, broke out of a price base at $15. It advanced to the equivalent of $90 in 21 months.

This was another great example of abnormal strength during a weak market. Lorillard did the same thing in the 1957 bear market. Software Toolworks soared in the down market of early 1990. In 1999, Qualcomm made big progress even during its difficult mid-year market, and Taro Pharmaceutical soared in the last part of 2000.

So don't forget: **It seldom pays to invest in laggard stocks, even if they look tantalizingly cheap. Look for, and confine your purchases to, market leaders.**

I = Institutional Sponsorship: Follow the Leaders

It takes big demand to move prices up, and by far the largest source of big demand for stocks is institutional investors (mutual funds, pension funds, banks, etc.) who account for the lion's share of each day's market activity.

What Is Institutional Sponsorship?

Institutional sponsorship refers to the shares of a stock owned by institutions, such as mutual funds, corporate pension funds, insurance companies, large investment counselors, hedge funds, bank trust departments, and state, charitable, and educational institutions. (For measurement purposes, I do not consider brokerage research reports or analyst recommendations as institutional sponsorship, although a few may exert strictly short-term influence on some securities. Investment advisory services and market newsletters also aren't considered to be institutional or professional sponsorship by this definition because they lack the concentrated or sustained buying or selling power of institutional investors.)

A winning stock doesn't need a huge number of institutional owners, but it should have at least several. Ten might be a minimum reasonable number of institutional sponsors, although most stocks have a good many more. If a stock has no professional sponsorship, chances are that its performance will be more run-of-the-mill. Odds are that at least several of the more than a thousand institutional investors have looked at the stock and passed it over. Even if they're wrong, it still takes large buying volume to stimulate an important price increase.

42

Look for Both Quantity and Quality

Diligent investors go yet another level deeper. They want to know not only how *many* institutional sponsors a stock has and if that number has increased in recent quarters, but they also want to know *who* those sponsors are. They look for stocks held by at least one or two of the more savvy portfolio managers who have the best performance records. This is referred to as analyzing the *quality* of sponsorship.

When analyzing the quality of a stock's sponsorship, the latest 12 months plus the last three-year period of performance of an institutional sponsor are usually the most relevant. One quick and easy way to do this is by checking a fund's 36-Month Performance Rating in *Investor's Business Daily*. An "A+" rating indicates a fund in the top 5% of all funds in terms of performance. Funds with ratings of A− or higher are considered your better performers.

However, results may change significantly as key portfolio managers leave one money-management firm and go to another. The institutional leaders continually rotate and change. For example, until 1981, the trust investment division of California-based Security Pacific Bank (since merged into Bank of America) enjoyed only modest success, but with the addition of new management and the introduction of more realistic investing concepts, it polished up its act to the point it ranked at the very top in performance in 1982. In 1984, Security Pacific's top manager left and formed his own company, Nicholas-Applegate of San Diego, CA, which from its start has been one of William O'Neil + Co.'s (our institutional services firm) major clients.

Financial services such as Vickers and Wiesenberger Thomson Financial publish fund holdings and investment performance records of various institutions. In the past, mutual funds tended to be more aggressive in the market, but banks also manage large amounts of money. More recently, many new "entrepreneurial-type" investment-counseling firms have cropped up to manage institutional moneys.

Buy Companies That Show Increasing Sponsorship

As mentioned previously, it's less crucial to know *how many* institutions own a stock than *which* of the better-performing institutions own or have bought a stock recently. It's also key to know if the total number of sponsors is increasing or decreasing. The main thing to look for is the recent quarterly trend. It's always best to buy stocks showing an increasing number of institutional owners over several recent quarters. You can also get an overall picture of a stock's sponsorship using *Investor's Business Daily*'s proprietary

Sponsorship Rating found in the stock tables. It ranges from A (best) to E (worst). Stocks with an A rating indicate increased buying by the better money managers in the market.

Note New Stock Positions Bought in the Last Quarter

A significant, new institutional investment position taken in the most recently reported period is generally more relevant than existing positions held for some time. This is because when a fund establishes a new position, chances are that it will continue to add to that position and may be less likely to sell it in the near future. Reports on such activities, which are available about six weeks after the end of a fund's quarter or six-month period, are very helpful to those who can identify the wiser picks and who understand correct timing and the proper analysis of daily and weekly charts. Many investors feel disclosure of a fund's new commitments are published too long after the fact to be of any real value. This is really not true.

Institutional trades also tend to show up on the ticker tape in transactions from 1000 to 100,000 shares or more. Institutional buying and selling account for more than 70% of the activity in most leading companies. This is the sustained force behind most important price moves. It's important to note that about half the institutional buying that shows up on the New York Stock Exchange ticker tape may be in humdrum stocks; much of it may also be wrong, but out of the other half you may have some truly phenomenal selections.

Your task, then, is to separate intelligent, highly informed institutional buying from poor, faulty buying. Though difficult, this will become easier as you learn to apply and follow the proven rules, guidelines, and principles presented in this book.

To gain a better sense for what works in the market, it's important to study the investment strategies of well-managed mutual funds. When reviewing *Investor's Business Daily's* mutual fund tables, look for funds with A ratings, and then call to obtain a prospectus. In doing so, you'll learn the investment philosophy and techniques used by certain funds. For example:

- Jim Stower's American Century Ultra and Growth Investors funds use computer screening to find volatile, aggressive stocks that show accelerating percentage increases in recent sales and earnings.
- The Fidelity, Contra, and New Millennium funds scour the country to get in early on every new concept or story in a stock.
- Keystone S-4 usually remains fully invested in the most aggressive growth stocks it can find.

- Other managements with growth funds worth tracking might include AIM Management, Nicholas-Applegate, Berger, Columbia Funds, Strong Funds, Phoenix Engemann, Sun America, and CGM. Some funds buy on new highs; others buy around lows and may sell on new highs.

Is Your Stock "Overowned" by Institutions?

It is possible for a stock to have too much sponsorship. "Overowned" is a term we coined in 1969 to describe stocks whose institutional ownership had become excessive. The danger is that excessive sponsorship might translate into large potential selling if something goes wrong at the company or a bear market begins. Janus Funds alone owned more than 250 million shares of Nokia and 100 million shares of America Online that contributed to an adverse supply/demand imbalance in 2000 and 2001. WorldCom (in 1999) and JDSU, Nokia, and Cisco Systems (in 2000 and 2001) were examples of overowned stocks.

Thus, the "favorite 50" and other widely owned institutional stocks can be rather poor, potentially risky prospects. By the time a company's attractive performance is so obvious that almost all institutions own the stock, it's probably too late to climb aboard. The heart is already out of the watermelon. For instance, stocks such as America Online in the summer of 2001 and Cisco Systems in the summer of 2000 are examples of those that were overowned by more than a thousand institutions. This potential heavy supply can adversely affect a stock during bear market periods.

An Unassailable Institutional Growth Stock Tops

While it may seem like some stocks are invincible, the old saying is true: What goes up, must eventually come down. No company is immune forever from management problems, economic slowdowns, and changes in market direction. The savvy investor knows that in the stock market there are few "sacred cows."

For instance, in June 1974, no one could believe it when William O'Neil + Co. put Xerox on its institutional sell list at $115. Xerox was then one of the most widely held institutional stocks and had been amazingly successful up to that point, but our research indicated it had topped and was headed down. It was also overowned. However, institutional investors went on to make Xerox their most widely purchased stock for that year. When the stock tumbled in price, it showed the true condition of the company at that time.

The episode did bring widespread attention to our institutional services firm and our first global insurance company account, American International Group (AIG) in New York City. The company had been buying Xerox on the way down in the $80s until we persuaded them they should be selling instead of buying.

We also received a lot of argument in 1998 when we put Gillette, another sacred cow, on our avoid list near $60 before it tanked. Enron was removed from our buy list on November 29, 2000, at $72.91 due to its poor action. Here is just a partial list of the technology stocks removed from our New Stock Market Ideas® (NSMI) institutional service buy list in 2000 at a time when most securities analysts were incorrectly saying they were buys. The lesson here: Don't be swayed by a stock's broad-based popularity.

Leading Stocks Removed From NSMI Buys in 2000

Symbol	Name	Date Removed	Price Removed	Low Price as of 10/30/01	Percent Decline as of 10/30/01*
AMAT	Applied Materials	5/11/2000	$80.56	$26.59	67%
CSCO	Cisco Systems	8/1/2000	$63.50	$11.04	83%
CNXT	Conexant Systems	3/3/2000	$84.75	$6.57	92%
DELL	Dell Computer Corp	5/9/2000	$46.31	$16.01	65%
EMC	E M C Corp	12/15/2000	$74.63	$10.01	87%
EXDS	Exodus Communications	3/30/2000	$69.25	$0.14	100%
INTC	Intel Corp	9/15/2000	$58.00	$18.96	67%
JDSU	J D S Uniphase	10/10/2000	$90.50	$5.12	94%
MOT	Motorola	3/30/2000	$51.67	$10.50	80%
NXTL	Nextel Communications	4/12/2000	$55.41	$6.87	88%
NT	Nortel Networks	10/2/2000	$59.56	$4.76	92%
PMCS	P M C Sierra Inc	8/1/2000	$186.25	$9.37	95%
QLGC	Qlogic Corp	3/14/2000	$167.88	$17.21	90%
SEBL	Siebel Systems Inc	12/15/2000	$76.88	$12.24	84%
SUNW	Sun Microsystems	11/9/2000	$49.32	$7.52	85%
VIGN	Vignette Corp	3/15/2000	$88.33	$3.08	97%
YHOO	Yahoo!	3/30/2000	$175.25	$8.02	95%

*Percentages have been rounded to the nearest whole number.

Institutional Sponsorship Means Market Liquidity

Another benefit to you as an individual investor is that institutional sponsorship provides buying support when you want to get out of your investment. If there's no sponsorship, and you try to sell your stock in a poor market, you may have problems finding someone to buy it. Daily marketability is one of the tremendous advantages of owning stock in the United States. (Real estate is far less liquid, and commissions and fees are much higher.) Institutional sponsorship provides continuous liquidity.

In summary, **only buy stocks that have at least a few institutional sponsors with better-than-average recent performance records, and invest in stocks showing an increasing total number of institutional owners in recent quarters.** Utilize institutional sponsorship and always make it an extremely important tool as you research a stock for purchase.

M = Market Direction: How to Determine It

You can be right on every one of the factors in the first six chapters, but if you're wrong about the direction of the general market, three out of four of your stocks will plummet with the market averages and you will certainly lose money big time as many people did in 2000. Therefore, in your analytical tool kit you absolutely must have a reliable method to determine if you're in a bull (up) market or a bear (down) market.

But that's not enough. If you're in a bull market, are you in the early stage or the latter stage? And more importantly, what is the market doing right now? Is it weak and acting badly, or is it merely going through a normal decline (typically 8% to 12%)? Is the market doing just what it should be, based on current conditions in the country, or is it acting abnormally strong or weak?

In order to answer these and other vital questions, you'll want to learn to analyze the overall market correctly, and you must start at the most logical point. The best way to determine the direction of the market is to follow, interpret, and understand what the general market averages are doing every day. It might sound overwhelming at first, but with patience and practice, you'll soon be analyzing the market like a pro. This is the most important lesson you can learn.

Remember, don't let anyone tell you that you can't time the market. We've heard from thousands of readers of this chapter and IBD's "The Big Picture" column who have done just that. As a result, they had the foresight to sell stocks and raise cash in March 2000, protecting much of their gains made during 1998 and 1999. The erroneous belief that no one can time the market evolved more than 30 years ago when most mutual funds that tried it weren't successful at it. This is because they had to both sell exactly right and then get back in the market at exactly the right time, but due to their asset size problems, it took weeks to raise cash and weeks to reenter the market. Funds lost relative performance during the fast turnarounds that frequently happen at market bottoms (called the "bounce back effect"). Therefore, the top management at these mutual funds imposed rules on their money managers that required them to remain fully invested (95% to 100% of assets). This fits well with the sound concept that mutual funds are truly long-term investments. Also, because funds are typically widely diversified (owning a hundred or more stocks spread among many industries), in time they will recover as the market recovers.

What Is the General Market?

The "general market" is a term that usually refers to the most commonly used market indices. These indices tell you the approximate strength or weakness in each day's overall trading activity and can be one of your earliest indications of emerging trends. These indices include:

- *The Standard & Poor's (S&P) 500:* Consisting of 500 companies, this index is a broader, more modern representation of market action than the Dow. New York Stock Exchange-traded stocks are featured prominently in this index, as opposed to stocks traded on the American Stock Exchange and the Nasdaq, which are featured less prominently.

- *The Dow Jones Industrial Average (DJIA):* This index consists of 30 widely traded stocks, and while it used to focus primarily on large, cyclical, industrial issues, it has broadened a little in recent years to include companies like Coca-Cola and Home Depot. It's a simple but rather out-of-date average to study because it's dominated by established, old-line companies that grow more slowly than today's more modern, entrepreneurial companies. Also, its 30 stocks can be more easily manipulated over short time periods.

- *The Nasdaq Composite:* The more relevant and volatile index in recent years, the Nasdaq is home to the market's younger, more innovative and fast-growing companies. It includes over 4000 companies that trade via the Nasdaq network of market makers, and it is more heavily weighted toward the technology sector.

Why Is Skilled, Careful Market Observation So Important?

A Harvard professor once asked his students to do a special report on fish. His scholars went to the library, read books about fish, and then wrote their expositions. The students were shocked when, after turning in their papers, the professor tore them up and threw them in the wastebasket.

When they asked what was wrong with the reports, the professor said, "If you want to learn anything about fish, sit in front of a fish bowl and look at fish." He then made his students sit and watch fish for hours. Then they rewrote their assignment solely on their observations of the objects themselves.

Being a student of the market is like being a student in this professor's class: If you want to learn about the market, you must observe and study the major indices carefully. In doing so, you'll come to recognize meaningful changes in the daily market averages' behavior at key turning points like market tops and bottoms and learn to capitalize upon them. Recognizing when the market has hit a top or has bottomed out is frequently 50% of the whole complicated ballgame. It's also the key investing skill virtually all amateur and professional investors alike seem to lack. In fact, Wall Street analysts completely missed calling the market top in 2000, particularly the top in every one of the high-technology leaders.

The Stages of a Stock Market Cycle

The winning investor should understand how a normal business cycle unfolds and over what period of time. Particular attention should be paid to recent cycles. There's no guarantee that just because cycles lasted three or four years in the past, they'll last that long in the future.

Bull and bear markets don't end easily. It usually takes two or three pullbacks to fake out or shake out the few remaining speculators. After everyone who can be run in or run out has thrown in the towel, there isn't anyone left to take action in the same direction. Then the market will finally turn and begin a whole new trend.

Bear markets usually end while business is still in a downtrend. The reason is that stocks are anticipating, or "discounting," economic events months in advance. Similarly, bull markets usually top out and turn down before a recession sets in. For this reason, use of economic indicators to tell you when to buy or sell stocks is not recommended. Yet, some investment firms do this very thing.

The predictions of many economists also leave a lot to be desired. A few of our nation's presidents have had to learn this lesson the hard way. In early

1983, just as the economy was in its first few months of recovery, the head of President Reagan's Council of Economic Advisers was a little concerned. The capital goods sector was not very strong, he fretted. This was the first hint that this adviser might not be as sound as he should be. Had he understood historical trends, he would have seen that capital goods demand had never been strong in the early stage of recovery, especially in the first quarter of 1983 when U.S. plants were operating at a low percentage of capacity.

You should check earlier cycles to learn the sequence of industry group moves at various stages of the market. For example, railroad equipment, machinery, and other capital goods industries are late movers in a business or stock market cycle. This knowledge can help you get a fix on where you are now. When these groups start running up, you know you're near the end. In early 2000, it was computer companies supplying Internet capital goods and infrastructure that were the last-stage movers along with telecommunications equipment suppliers.

Dedicated market students who want to learn more about cycles and the longer-term history of U.S. economic growth may want to write to Securities Research Company, 101 Prescott Street, Wellesley Hills, MA 02481, and purchase one of their long-term wall charts.

Some charts of market averages include major news events over the last 12 months. These can be very valuable, especially if you keep and review back copies. You then have a history of both the market averages and events that have influenced their direction. It helps to know, for example, how the market has reacted to new faces in the White House, rumors of war, controls on wages and prices, changes in discount rates, or just to "panics" in general. The accompanying chart of the S&P 500 Index on page 52 shows several past cycles with the bear markets shaded.

Study the General Market Every Day

In bear markets, stocks usually open strong and close weak. In bull markets, they tend to open weak and close strong. The general market averages need to be studied closely every day since reverses in trends can begin on any given day. Relying on these primary indices is a much more practical and effective method for analyzing the market's behavior and determining its direction. Don't rely on other, subsidiary indicators because they haven't been proven as effective. Listening to the many market newsletter writers, technical analysts, or strategists who pour over 30 different technical or economic indicators and then tell you what they think the market should be doing is generally a waste of time. Investment newsletters can create doubt, uncertainty, and confusion in an investor's mind. Interestingly enough, his-

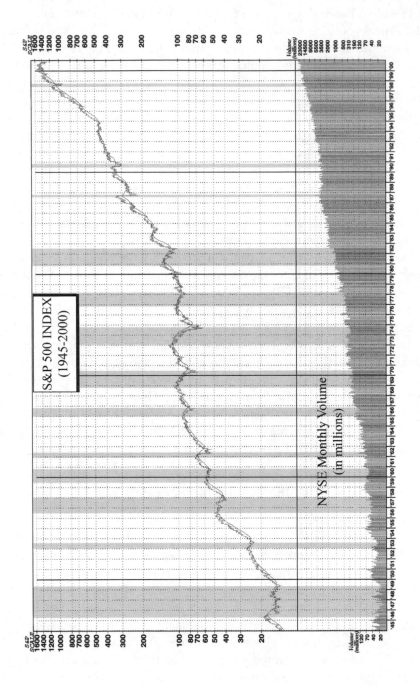

S&P 500 INDEX
(1945-2000)

NYSE Monthly Volume
(in millions)

tory shows that the market tends to go up just when these experts are most skeptical and uncertain.

You must sell when the general market tops to raise at least some cash as well as get off margin (using borrowed money) in order to protect your account. As an individual investor, you can easily raise cash and get out in one or two days and can likewise reenter later when the market is right. If you don't sell and raise cash when the general market tops, your diversified list of former market leaders can decline sharply and several may never recover to former levels.

Your best bet is to learn to interpret daily price and volume charts of the key general market averages. If you do, you can't get too far offtrack, and you won't need much else. It doesn't pay to argue with the market. Experience teaches that fighting the market can be a very expensive lesson.

1973–1974: The Worst Market Plunge Since 1929

The Watergate scandal and hearings, plus the 1974 oil embargo by OPEC, combined to make 1973–1974 the worst stock market catastrophe at the time since the 1929–1933 depression. The Dow corrected 50%, but the average stock plummeted more than 70%.

This was a catastrophe for stockholders and was almost as severe as the 90% correction the average stock showed from 1929 to 1933. (However, in 1933, industrial production was only 56% of the 1929 level, and more than 13 million Americans were unemployed.)

The markets were so demoralized in 1973–1974 that most members on the floor of the New York Stock Exchange were afraid the exchange might not survive as a viable institution. This is why it's absolutely critical to study the market averages and protect yourself against catastrophic losses, for the sake of your health as well as your portfolio.

A 33% Drop Requires a 50% Rise to Break Even

The importance of knowing the direction of the general market cannot be overemphasized. A 33% loss in a portfolio of stocks requires a 50% gain just to get to your break-even point. For example, if a $10,000 portfolio is allowed to decline to $6666 (a 33% decline), the portfolio has to rise $3333 (or 50%) just to get you back where you started.

You positively must always act to preserve as much as possible of the profit that you've built up during the bull market rather than ride your investments back down through difficult bear market periods. To do this, you have to learn historically proven selling rules. (See Chapters 9 and 10 for more on selling rules.)

The Myth Surrounding "Long-Term Investing"

Many investors like to think of, or at least describe, themselves as "long-term investors." Their strategy is to stay fully invested through thick and thin. Some institutions do the same thing, but this inflexible approach can bring tragic results, particularly for individual investors. Individuals and institutions alike may get away with standing pat through relatively mild (20% or less) bear markets, but many bear markets are not mild. Some are downright devastating.

The problem always comes at the beginning, when you start to sense an impending bear market. You cannot, in every case, project how bad economic conditions might become or how long they could linger. For example, the war in Vietnam, inflation, and a tight money supply helped turn the 1969–1970 correction into a two-year decline of 36.9%. Before that, bear markets averaged only nine months and took the averages down 26%.

Most stocks fall during a bear market, but not all of them recover. If you hold on during even a modest bear correction, you can get stuck with damaged merchandise that may never see its former highs. You must learn to sell when the overall environment changes and your stocks are not working.

Buy-and-hold investors fell in love with Coca-Cola during the 1980s and 1990s. The soft drink maker chugged higher year after year, rising and falling with the market, but it stopped working in 1998 along with Gillette. When the market slipped into its mild bear correction that summer, Coke followed along. Two years later—after some of the market's most exciting gains in decades—Coke was still stuck in a downtrend. In some instances, these kinds of stocks may come back, but this much is certain: Coke investors missed huge advances in names such as America Online and Qualcomm. The buy-and-hold strategy was also disastrous to anyone who held technology stocks in 2000. Many highfliers lost 75% to 90% of their value, and some will never return to their prior highs.

Protecting Yourself From Market Downturns

Napoleon once wrote that never hesitating in battle gave him an advantage over his opponents, and for many years he was undefeated. In the battlefield that is the stock market, there are the quick and there are the dead!

After you see the first several definite indications of a market top, don't wait around. Sell quickly before real weakness develops. When market indices peak and begin major downside reversals, you should act immediately by raising 25% or more cash, selling your stocks at market prices. Use of limit orders (buying or selling at a specific price, as opposed to a market order, which is bought or sold at market prices) is not recommended. The thing to focus on is your ability to get in or out of a stock when you need to. By quibbling over an eighth- or quarter-point (or their decimal equivalents), you could miss your opportunity to buy or sell a stock.

Lightning-fast action is even more critical if your stock account is on margin. If your portfolio is fully margined, with half of the money in your stocks borrowed from your broker, a 20% decline in the price of your stocks will cause you to lose 40% of your money. A 50% decline in your stocks could wipe you out!

In the final analysis, there are only two things you can really do when a new bear market begins: sell and get out or go short. When you get out, you should stay out until the bear market is over. This usually means five or six months, but in the prolonged, problem-ridden 1969–1970 and 1973–1974 periods, it meant two years. In addition, the bear market that began in March 2000 during the last year of the Clinton administration lasted longer and was more severe than normal. Nine out of 10 investors lost a lot of money, particularly in high-tech stocks. It was the end of a period of many excesses during the late 1990s. It was a decade where America got careless and let its guard down.

Selling short can be profitable, but it's a very difficult and highly specialized skill that should only be attempted during bear markets. But be forewarned: Few people make money shorting. Chapter 11 discusses short selling in more detail.

Using Stop-Loss Orders

If stop-loss orders are used or mentally recorded and acted upon, a market that is starting to top out will mechanically force you, robotlike, out of many of your stocks. A stop-loss order instructs the specialist in the stock on the exchange floor that once the stock drops to your specified price, it then becomes a market order and will be sold out on the next transaction.

It's usually better not to enter stop-loss orders. In doing so, you and other similarly minded investors are showing your hand to market makers. At times, they might drop the stock to shakeout stop-loss orders. Instead, watch your stocks closely and know ahead of time the exact price at which you will immediately sell to cut a loss. However, some people travel a lot and aren't able to watch their stocks closely. Others have a hard time making sell decisions and getting out when they are losing. In such cases, stop-loss orders help protect against distance and indecisiveness.

If you use them, remember to cancel the stop-loss order if you change your mind and sell a stock before the stop-loss order is executed. Otherwise, you could later accidentally sell a stock you no longer own. Such errors can be costly.

How to Identify Stock Market Tops

To detect a market top, keep a close eye on the daily S&P 500, Dow 30, and Nasdaq Composite as they work their way higher. On one of the days in the uptrend, volume for the market as a whole will increase from the day before, but the average itself will show stalling action (significantly less price increase for the day compared to the prior day's price increase). I call this "heavy volume without further price progress up." The average doesn't have to close down for the day, but in most instances it will, making it much easier to see the distribution (selling) as professional investors liquidate stock. The spread from the average's daily high to its daily low may be a little wider than on previous days.

Normal liquidation near the market peak will usually occur on three to five days over one, two, or three weeks. In other words, the market comes under distribution while it is advancing! This is one reason so few people know how to recognize distribution. After four or five days of definite distribution, the general market will almost always turn down.

Four days of distribution, if correctly spotted over a two- or three-week period, are often enough to turn a previously advancing market into a decline. Sometimes distribution can be spread over six or seven weeks if the market attempts to rally back to new highs. If you miss the topping signals given off by the S&P 500, Nasdaq, or Dow (which is easy to do, since they sometimes occur on only a few days), you could be wrong about the market direction and therefore wrong on almost everything you do.

One of the biggest problems is the time it takes to reverse investors' positive personal opinions and views. If you sell and always cut all losses 7% or 8% below your buy points, you will automatically be forced into selling at least some stocks as a correction in the general market starts to develop. This should get you into a questioning, defensive frame of mind sooner. Following this one simple but powerful rule of ours saved a lot of people big money in 2000's devastating decline in technology leaders.

The Initial Market Decline Can Be on Lower Volume

Right after the first selling near the top, a vacuum exists where volume may subside and the market averages will sell off for four days or so. The second and probably last early chance to recognize a top reversal is when the market attempts its first rally. This usually comes several days down from the peak.

Most stock market technicians are fooled by the initial market decline off the top if they see volume contracting. They don't understand that this is a normal occurrence after heavy volume distribution has occurred on the way up around the top.

Volume begins to pick up on the downside days or weeks later, when the weakness becomes obvious to more investors. As in anything else, if you wait until the writing's on the wall, it's going to cost you more. You'll be selling late.

After the Initial Decline off the Top, Track Each Rally Attempt on the Way Down

Following several days of increased volume distribution around the top and the first decline resulting from it, there will be either a poor rally in the market averages, followed by a rally failure, or a positive and powerful follow-through on price and volume. You should learn in detail exactly what signals to look for and remain unbiased about the market. Let the day-by-day market averages tell you what the market has been doing and is doing. (See "How You Can Spot Stock Market Bottoms" later in this chapter for further discussion of market rallies.)

Three Signs the First Rally Attempt May Fail

After the market does top out, it typically will rally feebly and then fail. For instance, after the first day's rebound, the second day will open strongly, but toward the end of the session the market will suddenly close down. The abrupt failure of the market to follow through on its first recovery attempt should probably be met by further selling on your part.

You'll know the initial bounce back is feeble if (1) the index advances in price on the third, fourth, or fifth rally day but on volume lower than the day before; (2) the average makes little net upward price progress compared with the progress the day before; or (3) the market average recovers less than half of the initial drop from its former absolute intraday high. Further selling is advisable when you see these weak rallies and failures.

How CAN SLIM™ and IBD Red-Flagged
the March 2000 Nasdaq Top

In October 1999, the market took off on a furious advance. Fears of a Y2K meltdown on January 1 had faded. Companies were announcing strong profits from the third quarter, which had just ended the month prior. Leading tech stocks as well as speculative Internet and biotechnology issues racked up huge gains in just five months, but cracks started to appear in early March 2000. Many leaders suffered from classic climax tops.

On March 7, the Nasdaq closed lower on higher volume, the first instance in more than six weeks. That's unusual action during a roaring bull market, but one day of distribution isn't always significant on its own. Still, it was a yellow flag worth carefully watching.

Three days later the Nasdaq bolted more than 85 points to a new high in the morning but reversed in the afternoon. It finished the day up only 2 points as volume remained heavy. That churning action (a lot of trading action but no real progress—a clear sign of distribution) was all the more important because leading stocks started showing their own symptoms of hitting a climax top, action that will be discussed in Chapters 9 and 10.

Over the next week, many leaders broke down as the Nasdaq corrected 13%. The index managed to put together a suspect rally from March 16 to 24, but it soon ran out of steam and rolled over in heavier volume, a final, definite confirmation of the March 10 top.

During the next two weeks, the Nasdaq, as well as the S&P 500 and Dow, suffered repeated bouts of distribution as the indices sold off in heavier volume than the prior day. Astute CAN SLIM investors had all long since taken their profits.

Study the examples of this and other market tops in the next section. History repeats itself when it comes to the stock market; you'll see this type of action happen again in the future.

Historical Tops for Further Study

Historically, intermediate term distribution tops (usually tops that then decline 8% to 12%) in the general market averages occur as they did the first week of August 1954, where there was increased New York Stock Exchange volume without further upward price progress on the Dow Jones Industrials, followed the next day by heavy volume without further price progress up and a wide price spread from high to low on the Dow. One also occurred in the first week of July 1955, which was characterized by a price climax with a wide price spread from the day's low to its high, followed the next day by increased volume, with the Dow Jones Industrial Average closing down in price, and three days later, increased New York Stock Exchange volume again with the Dow Jones closing down.

Other market tops for study include:

September 1955	October 1973
November 1955	July 1975
April 1956	September 1976
August 1956	September 1978
January 1957	September 1979
July 1957	February 1980
November 1958	November 1980
January 1959	April 1981
May 1959	June 1981
June 1959	December 1981
July 1959	May 1982
January 1960	January 1984
June 1960	July 1986
April 1961	September 1986
May 1961	April 1987
September 1961	August 1987
November 1961	October 1987
December 1961	October 1989
March 1962	January 1990
June 1963	July 1990
October 1963	June 1992
May 1965	February 1994
February 1966	September 1994
April 1966	May 1996
June 1966	March 1997
May 1967	October 1997
September 1967	July 1998
December 1967	August 1999
December 1968	January 2000
May 1969	April 2000
April 1971	September 2000
September 1971	February 2001
January 1973	May 2001

If you study the seven following daily market average graphs of several tops closely and understand how they came about, you'll come to recognize these same patterns as you observe future market environments. Each numbered day on these charts is a distribution day.

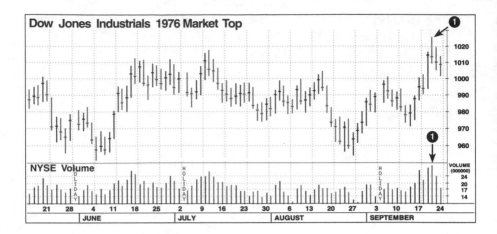

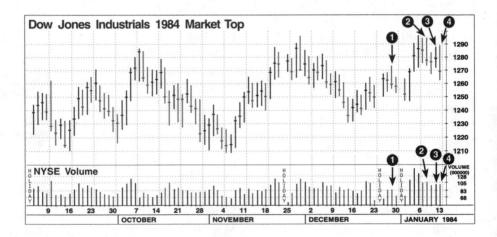

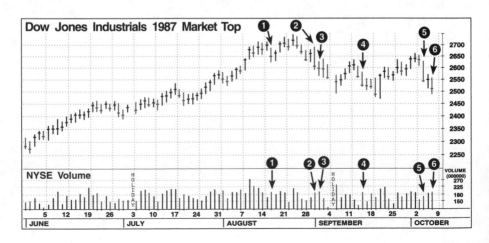

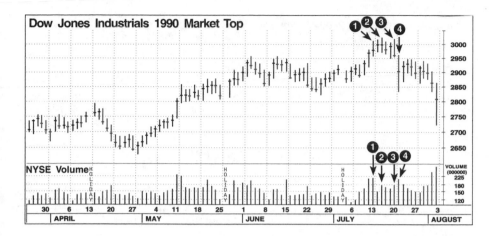

Dow Jones Industrials 1990 Market Top

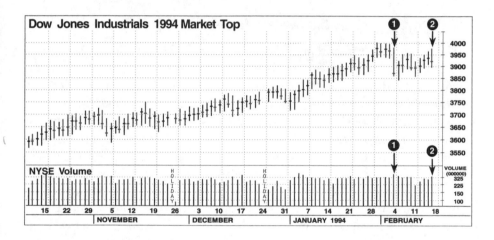

Dow Jones Industrials 1994 Market Top

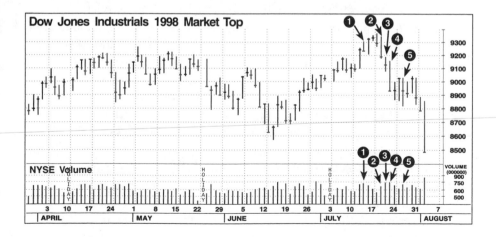

Dow Jones Industrials 1998 Market Top

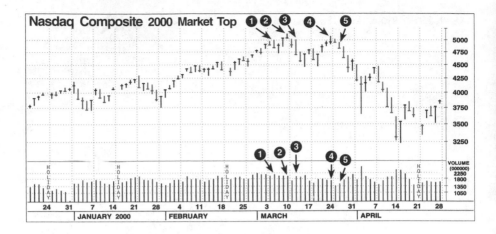

Follow the Leaders for Market Top Clues

The second most important indicator of primary changes in market direction after the daily averages is the way leading stocks act. After the market has advanced for a couple of years, you can be fairly sure it's headed for trouble if most of the individual stock leaders start acting abnormally.

One example of abnormal activity can be seen when leading stocks break out of third- or fourth-stage chart base formations on the way up. Most of these base structures will be faulty, with price fluctuations appearing much wider and looser. A faulty base (wide, loose, and erratic) can best be recognized and analyzed by studying charts of a stock's daily or weekly price and volume history. Another sign of abnormal activity is the "climax" top. Here, a leading stock will run up more rapidly for two or three weeks in a row after having advanced for many months. (See Chapter 10 on selling.)

A few leaders will have their first abnormal price break off the top on heavy volume and then be unable to rally more than a small amount from the lows of their correction. Still others will show a serious loss of upward momentum in their most recent quarterly earnings reports.

Shifts in market direction can also be detected by reviewing the last four or five stock purchases in your own portfolio. If you haven't made a dime on any of them, you could be picking up signs of a new downtrend.

Investors who use charts and understand market action know that there are very few leading stocks that will be attractive around market tops. There simply aren't any stocks coming out of sound chart bases that can be bought. Most bases are wide, loose, and erratic, a giant sign of real danger you must learn to understand and obey. Also, the tendency is for laggard stocks to show strength at this stage. The sight of sluggish or low-priced, lower-quality laggards strengthening is a signal to the wise market operator that the upward market move may be near its end. Even turkeys can try to fly in a windstorm.

During bear markets, certain leading stocks will seem to be bucking the trend by holding up in price, creating the impression of strength, but what you're seeing is just a postponement of the inevitable. When they raid the house, they usually get everyone, and eventually all the leaders will succumb to the selling. This is exactly what happened in the 2000 bear market. Cisco and other high-tech leaders all eventually collapsed in spite of how many analysts incorrectly said they should be bought.

Market tops, whether intermediate (usually 8% to 12% declines) or primary bull market peaks, sometimes occur five, six, or seven months after the last major buy point in leading stocks and in the averages. Thus, top reversals are usually late signals—the last straw before a cave-in. In most cases, distribution, or selling, has been going on for days or even weeks in individual market leaders. Use of individual stock selling rules, which we'll discuss in Chapters 9 and 10, should have already led you to sell one or two of your holdings on the way up, just before the market peak.

Other Bear Market Warnings

When the original market leaders begin to falter, you may see lower-priced, lower-quality, more speculative stocks begin to move up. Watch out! When the old dogs begin to bark, the market is on its last feeble leg.

Among the telltale signs are the poor-quality stocks that start to dominate the most active list on market "up" days. It's simply a matter of weak leadership trying to command the market. If the best ones can't lead, the worst certainly aren't going to for very long.

Many top reversals (when the market closes at the bottom of its trading range after making a new high that day) have occurred from the third to the ninth day of a rally after the averages moved into new high ground off small chart bases (meaning the time span from the start to the end of the pattern is short). It's important to note the conditions under which the tops occurred were all about the same.

At other times, a topping market will recover for a couple of months and get back near or even above its old high before breaking down in earnest. This occurred in December 1976, January 1981, and January 1984. There's an important psychological reason for this: The majority of people in the market can't be exactly right at exactly the right time. In 1994, the Nasdaq didn't top until weeks after the Dow did. A similar thing happened in early 2000.

The majority in the stock market will be fooled first. This includes both professional and individual investors. If you were smart enough to sell or sell short in January 1981, the powerful rebound in February and March probably forced you to cover your short sales at a loss or buy some stocks back during the strong rally. It was an example of how treacherous the market really is.

Don't Jump Back in Too Early

I didn't have much problem recognizing and acting upon the early signs of the many bear markets from 1962 through 2000, but a couple of times I made the mistake of buying back too early. When you make a mistake in the stock market, the only sound thing to do is correct it. Pride and ego never pay off; neither does vacillation when losses start to show up.

The typical bear market (and some aren't typical) usually has three separate phases, or legs, of decline interrupted by a couple of rallies that last just long enough to convince investors to begin buying. In 1969 and 1974, a few of these phony, drawn-out rallies lasted up to 15 weeks. Most don't last that long.

Many institutional investors love to "bottom fish." They'll start buying stocks off a supposed bottom and help make the rally convincing enough to draw you in. You're better off staying on the sidelines in cash until a real new bull market starts.

How You Can Spot Stock Market Bottoms

Once you've recognized a bear market and have scaled back your stock holdings, the big question is how long you should remain on the sidelines. If you plunge back in the market too soon, the apparent rally may fade and you'll lose money, but if you hesitate at the brink of the eventual roaring recovery, opportunities will pass you by. Again, the daily general market averages provide the best answer by far.

At some point in every correction—whether mild or severe—the stock market will always attempt to rally. Don't jump back in right away. Wait for the market itself to confirm the new uptrend.

A rally attempt begins when a major market average closes higher after a decline, either from earlier in the day or the previous session. For example, the Dow plummets 3% in the morning but then recovers later in the day and closes higher. Or the Dow closes down 2% and then rebounds the next day. The session in which the Dow closes higher is the first day of the attempted rally. Sit tight and be patient. The first few days of improvement can't tell you if the rally will succeed.

Starting on the fourth day of the attempted rally, look for one of the major averages to "follow through," meaning it shows a booming 2% or more gain on heavier volume than the day before. This tells you the rally is much more likely to be real. The most powerful follow-throughs usually occur on the fourth to seventh days of the rally. Follow-throughs after the tenth day may indicate a positive but somewhat weaker new uptrend.

A follow-through day should give the feeling of an explosive rally that is strong, decisive, and conclusive, not begrudging and on the fence, barely up 1%. The market's volume for the day should be above its average daily volume in addition to always being higher than the prior day's trading.

Occasionally, a follow-through occurs as early as the third day of the rally. In such a case, the first, second, and third days must all be very powerful, with a major average up 1% to 2% or more each session in heavy volume.

I used to use 1% as the required percentage increase for a valid follow-through day. However, in recent years as institutional investors learned of our system, we've moved up the requirement to 2% to minimize professionals manipulating a few stocks in the Dow averages to create false or faulty follow-through days.

There will be a few cases in which confirmed rallies fail. A few large institutional investors, armed with their immense buying power, can run up the averages on a particular day and create the impression of a follow-through. Unless the smart buyers are back on board, the rally will implode—usually crashing in heavy volume within the next day or two.

However, just because the market corrects the day after a follow-through, it doesn't mean the follow-through was false. When a bear market bottoms, it frequently pulls back and settles above or near the lows made during the previous few weeks. It is more constructive when these pullbacks or "tests" hold up at least a little above the absolute intraday lows made recently in the market averages.

A follow-through signal doesn't mean you should rush out and buy with abandon. It gives the go-ahead to begin buying quality stocks as they break out of sound price bases, and it is a vital second confirmation that the attempted rally is succeeding.

Remember, no new bull market has ever started without a strong price and volume follow-through confirmation. It pays to wait and listen to the market. The seven following graphs are examples of several bottoms in the stock market between 1974 and 2001.

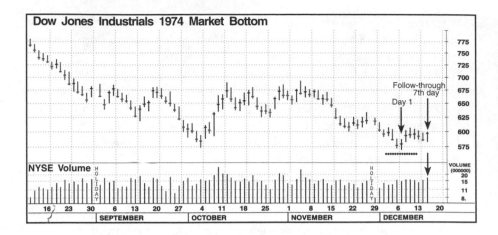

Dow Jones Industrials 1974 Market Bottom

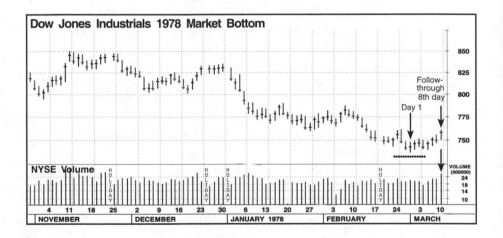

Dow Jones Industrials 1978 Market Bottom

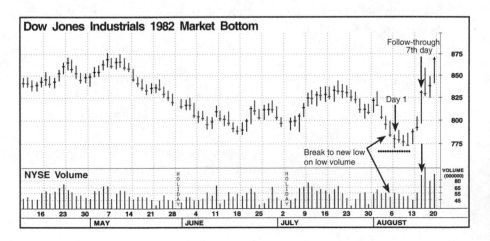

Dow Jones Industrials 1982 Market Bottom

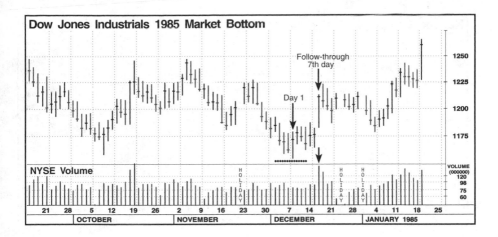

Dow Jones Industrials 1985 Market Bottom

Follow-through
7th day

Day 1

NYSE Volume

VOLUME
(000000)
120
98
75
60

21 28 5 12 19 26 2 9 16 23 30 7 14 21 28 4 11 18 25

OCTOBER   NOVEMBER   DECEMBER   JANUARY 1985

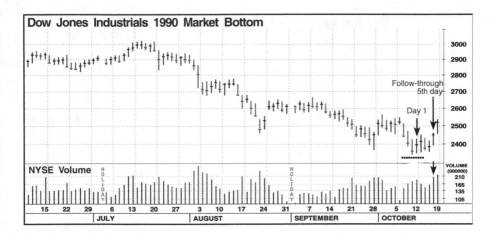

Dow Jones Industrials 1990 Market Bottom

Follow-through
5th day

Day 1

NYSE Volume

VOLUME
(000000)
210
165
135
105

15 22 29 6 13 20 27 3 10 17 24 31 7 14 21 28 5 12 19

JULY   AUGUST   SEPTEMBER   OCTOBER

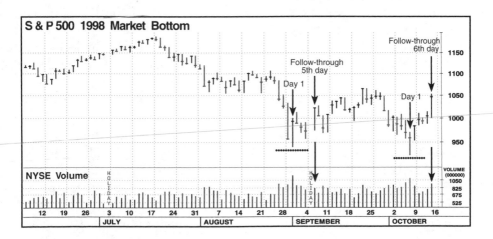

S & P 500 1998 Market Bottom

Follow-through
6th day

Follow-through
5th day

Day 1

Day 1

NYSE Volume

VOLUME
(000000)
1050
825
675
525

12 19 26 3 10 17 24 31 7 14 21 28 4 11 18 25 2 9 16

JULY   AUGUST   SEPTEMBER   OCTOBER

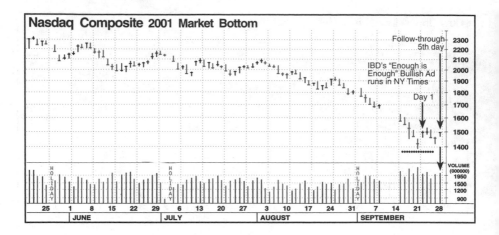

Nasdaq Composite 2001 Market Bottom

The Big Money Is Made in the First Two Years

The really big money is usually made in the first one or two years of a normal bull market cycle. It is at this point you must recognize, and fully capitalize upon, the golden opportunities presented.

The rest of the "up" cycle usually consists of back and forth movement in the market averages, followed by a bear market. The year 1965 was one of the few exceptions, but that strong market in the third year of a new cycle was caused by the beginning of the Vietnam War.

In the first or second year of a new bull market, you should have a few intermediate-term declines in the market averages. These usually last a couple of months, with the market indices dropping 8% to an occasional 15%. After several sharp downward adjustments of this nature, and once two years of a bull market have passed, heavy volume without further upside progress in the daily market averages could indicate the beginning of the next bear market.

Since the market is governed by supply and demand, you can decipher a chart of the general market averages about the same way as you read the chart of an individual stock. The Dow Jones Industrial Average and S&P 500 are displayed prominently in the better publications. (*Investor's Business Daily* displays the Nasdaq Composite, Dow, and S&P 500 stacked on one page for easier comparison.) These charts should show the high, low, and close of the market averages day by day for 6 to 12 months, together with the daily NYSE and Nasdaq volume in millions of shares traded.

Normal bear markets show three legs of price movement down, but there's no rule saying you can't have four or even five down-legs. You have to objectively evaluate overall conditions and events in the country and let the market averages tell their own story. And you have to understand what that story is.

Additional Ways to Identify Key Market Turning Points

Look for Divergence of Key Averages

Several averages should be checked at market turning points to see if there are significant divergences, meaning they are moving in different directions (one up and one down) or one is advancing/declining at a much greater rate from another. For example, if the Dow is up 100 and the S&P 500 is up only the equivalent of 20 on the Dow for the day (the S&P 500 being a broader index), it would indicate the rally is not as broad and strong as it appears. To compare the S&P 500 change to the Dow, divide the S&P 500 into the Dow average and then multiply by the change in the S&P 500. For example, if the Dow closed at 10,000 and the S&P 500 finished at 2500, the 10,000 Dow would be four times the S&P 500 index. Therefore, if the Dow, on a particular day, is up 100 points and the S&P 500 is up 10, you can multiply the 10 by 4 and find that the S&P 500 was only up the equivalent of 40 points on the Dow.

The Dow's new high in January 1984 was accompanied by a divergence in the indices: the broader-based, more significant S&P 500 did not hit a new high. This is the reason most professionals plot the key indices together—to make it easier to spot nonconfirmations at key turning points. Institutional investors periodically run up the 30-stock Dow while the broader Nasdaq is under liquidation.

Certain Psychological Market Indicators Can Help

Now that speculation in *put* and *call* options is the get-rich-quick scheme for many investors, you can plot and analyze the ratio of calls to puts for another valuable insight into crowd temperament. Options traders buy calls, which are options to buy common stock, or puts, which are options to sell common stock. A call buyer hopes prices will rise; a buyer of put options wishes prices to fall. If the volume of call options in a given period of time is greater than the volume of put options, one may logically assume that option speculators as a group are expecting higher prices and are bullish on the market. If the volume of put options is greater than that of calls, speculators hold a bearish attitude. When option players buy more puts than calls, the put to call ratio index increases above 1.0, which coincided with general market bottoms in 1990, 1996, 1998, and April and September 2001.

The *percentage of investment advisers who are bearish* is an interesting measure of investor sentiments. When bear markets are near the bottom, the great majority of advisory letters will usually be bearish. Near market tops, most will be bullish. The majority is usually wrong when it's most important to be right. However, you cannot blindly assume that because 65% of investment advisers were bearish the last time the general market hit bottom, a major market decline will be over the next time the investment advisers' index reaches the same point.

The *short-interest ratio* is the amount of short selling on the New York Stock Exchange, expressed as a percentage of total NYSE volume. This ratio can reflect the degree of bearishness shown by speculators in the market. Along bear market bottoms, you will usually see two or three major peaks showing sharply increased short selling. There's no rule governing how high the index should go, but studying past market bottoms can give you an idea of what the ratio looked like at key market junctures.

An index sometimes used to measure the degree of speculative activity is the *Nasdaq volume as a percentage of NYSE volume.* This measure provided a helpful tip-off of impending trouble during the summer of 1983, when Nasdaq volume significantly increased relative to the Big Board's (NYSE). When a trend persists and accelerates, indicating wild, rampant speculation, you're close to a general market correction.

Interpret the Overrated Advance-Decline Line

Some technical analysts religiously follow advance-decline (A-D) data. Technicians take the number of stocks advancing each day versus the number declining, and then plot that ratio on a graph. Advance-decline lines are far from precise because they frequently prematurely veer down sharply long before a bull market finally tops. In other words, the market keeps advancing toward higher ground but is being led by fewer but better stocks. The advance-decline line is simply not as accurate as the key general market indexes because analyzing the market's direction is not a total numbers game. All stocks are not created equal; it's better to know where the real leadership is and how it's acting than it is to know how many more mediocre stocks are advancing and declining.

The NYSE A-D line peaked in April 1998. It trended lower during the new bull market that broke out six months later in October. The A-D line continued to fall from October 1999 to March 2000, missing one of the market's most powerful rallies.

An advance-decline line can sometimes be helpful when a clear-cut bear market attempts a short-term rally. If the A-D line lags the market averages and can't rally, it's giving an internal indication that, despite the rally strength in the Dow or S&P, the broader market remains frail. In such instances, the rally usually fizzles. In other words, it takes more than just a few leaders to make a new bull market.

At best, the advance-decline line is a secondary indicator of limited value. If you hear commentators or TV market strategists extolling its virtues bullishly or bearishly, they probably haven't done their homework.

Watch Federal Reserve Board Rate Changes

Among fundamental general market indicators, changes in the Federal Reserve Board's discount rate (the interest rate the FRB charges member banks for loans), the Fed Funds rate (the interest rate that banks with fund reserves charge for loans to banks without fund reserves), and occasionally stock margin levels, are valuable indicators to watch.

As a rule, interest rates provide the best confirmation of basic economic conditions, and changes in the discount rate and Fed Funds rate are by far the most reliable. Three successive significant hikes in the discount rate have generally marked the beginning of bear markets and impending recessions. Bear markets have usually but not always ended when the rate was finally lowered. On the downside, the discount rate increase to 6% in September 1987, just after Alan Greenspan became chairman, led to the severe market break that October.

Money market indicators mirror general economic activity. At times I follow selected government and Federal Reserve Board measurements, including 10 indicators of the supply and demand for money and indicators of interest rate levels.

History proves that the direction of the general market, as well as of several industry groups, is often affected by changes in interest rates because the level of interest rates is usually tied to tight or easy Fed monetary policy.

For the investor, the simplest and most relevant monetary indicators to follow and understand are the changes in the Federal Reserve Board discount rate and the Fed Funds rate. With the advent of program trading and various hedging devices, some funds hedge portions of their portfolio in an attempt to provide some downside protection during risky markets. The degree to which these are successful again depends greatly on skill and timing, but one possible effect for some managers may be to lessen the pressure to dump portfolio securities on the market.

Most funds operate under a plan of wide diversification and a fully or near fully invested policy at all times. This is because most fund managers, with today's great size (billions of dollars), have difficulty in getting out and into cash at the right time and, most importantly, then getting back in fast enough to participate in the initial powerful rebound off the ultimate bottom. So in times of monetary tightening and a topping market, many funds aren't allowed to raise large amounts of cash. They will try to shift their emphasis to big-cap, semidefensive groups.

Changes in T-bill rates and the erratic, tricky Fed Funds rate sometimes help predict impending discount rate changes. The monetary base and the velocity of money are other measures sometimes used by professionals. The Fed also watches economic data such as unemployment figures, inflation data, gross domestic product (GDP), and many others.

The Fed Crushes the 1981 Economy.   The bear market and the costly protracted recession that began in 1981, for example, were created solely because the Fed increased the discount rate in rapid succession on September 26, November 17, and December 5 of 1980. Its fourth increase, on May 8, 1981, thrust the discount rate to an all-time high of 14%. That finished off the U.S. economy, our basic industries, and the stock market.

Such actions and their result starkly demonstrate how much our federal government, not Wall Street or business, may at times influence our economic future. However, Fed rate changes should not be your primary market indicator because the stock market itself is always your best barometer. Our analysis of market cycles turned up three key market turns that the discount rate did not help predict.

Washington Causes the 1962 Stock Market Break.   The most notable stock market break was in 1962. That spring, nothing was wrong with the economy, but the market got skittish after the Securities and Exchange Commission (SEC) announced a major investigation of the stock market. President Kennedy jumped on the steel companies for raising prices against his wishes. IBM dropped 50%. That fall, after the Cuban missile showdown with the Russians, a new bull market sprang to life. All of this happened with no change in the discount rate.

There have also been situations in which the discount rate was lowered six months after the market bottom was reached. In such cases, you would be late in the game if you waited for the discount rate to drop. A few times Fed rate cuts occurred and the markets continued to whipsaw sideways or continued lower for several months. This dramatically occurred again in 2000 and 2001.

The Hourly Market Index and Volume Changes

At key turning points, an active market operator can watch market indices and volume changes hour by hour and compare them to volume in the same hour of the day before.

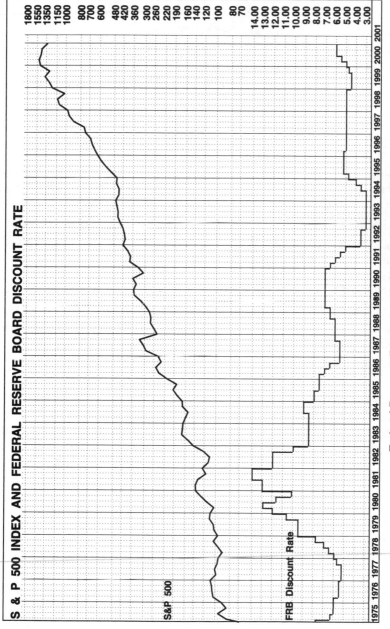

Federal Reserve discount rate changes for 25 years

73

A good time to watch hourly volume figures is during the first attempted rally following the initial decline off the market peak. You should be able to see if volume is dull or dries up on the rally. You can also see if the rally starts to fade late in the day, with volume picking up as it does, a sign that the rally is weak and will probably fail.

Hourly volume data also come in handy when the market averages reach an important prior low point and start breaking that "support" area. (A support area is a previous price level below which investors hope an index will no longer continue to fall.) What you want to know is whether selling picks up dramatically or by just a small amount as the market collapses into new low ground. If selling picks up dramatically, this will represent significant downward pressure on the market.

After the market has undercut previous lows for a few days, but on only slightly higher volume, look for one or two days of increased volume without the general market index going lower. If you see this, you may be in a "shakeout" area (when the market pressures many traders to sell, often at a loss), ready for an upturn after scaring out weak holders. This occurred on April 23 and 24, 1990.

Overbought/Oversold: Two Risky Words

The short-term overbought/oversold indicator has an avid following among some individual technicians and investors. It's a 10-day moving average of advances and declines in the market. But be careful: at the start of a new bull market the overbought/oversold index can become substantially "overbought." This should not be taken as a sign to sell stocks.

A big problem with indices that move counter to the trend is that you always have the question of how bad it can get before everything finally turns. Many amateurs follow and believe almost religiously in overbought/oversold indicators.

Something similar can happen in the early stage or first leg of a major bear market, when the index becomes unusually oversold. This is really telling you that a bear market may be imminent. The market was "oversold" all the way down during the brutal market implosion of 2000.

I once hired a well-respected professional who relied on such technical indicators. During the 1969 market break, at the very point when everything told me the market was getting into serious trouble, and I was aggressively trying to get several portfolio managers to liquidate stocks and raise large amounts of cash, he was telling them that it was too late to sell because his overbought/oversold indicator said the market was already very oversold. You guessed it: The market then split wide open.

Needless to say, I rarely pay attention to overbought/oversold indicators. What you learn from years of experience is usually more important than the opinions and theories of experts using their many different favorite indicators.

Other General Market Indicators

Upside/downside volume is a short-term index that relates trading volume in stocks that close up in price for the day to volume in stocks that close down. This index, plotted on a 10-day moving average, may show divergence at some intermediate turning points in the market. For example, after a 10% to 12% dip, the general market averages may continue to penetrate into new low ground for a week or two. Yet the upside/downside volume may suddenly shift and show steadily increasing upside volume with downside volume easing. This switch usually signals an intermediate-term upturn in the market. Of course, you'll pick up the same signals if you watch the changes in the daily Dow, Nasdaq, or S&P 500, and market volume.

Some services measure the *percentage of new money flowing into corporate pension funds* that is invested in common stocks and the amount invested in cash equivalents or bonds. This opens another window to institutional investor psychology. However, majority—or crowd—thinking is seldom right, even when it's done by professionals. Every year or two, Wall Street seems to be of one mind, with everyone following each other like a herd of cattle. They either all pile in or pile out.

An *index of "defensive" stocks*—more stable and supposedly safer issues such as utilities, tobaccos, foods, and soaps—may often show strength after a couple of years of bull market conditions. This may indicate "smart money" slipping into defensive positions and a weaker general market ahead.

Also helpful in evaluating the stage of a market cycle is determining the *percentage of stocks making new price highs in the defensive or laggard categories.* In pre-1983 cycles, some technicians rationalized their lack of concern with market weakness by citing the number of stocks still making new highs, but analysis of new high lists shows that a large percentage of preferred or defensive stocks signal bear market conditions. Superficial knowledge can hurt you in the stock market.

To summarize this complex but vitally important chapter: Learn to interpret the daily price and volume changes of the general market indices and the action of individual market leaders. Once you know how to do this correctly, you can stop listening to all the costly, and uninformed, personal market opinions of amateurs and professionals alike. As you can see, **the key to staying on top of the stock market is not predicting or knowing what the market**

is going to do, but knowing what the market has actually done recently and what it is currently doing. We don't want to give personal opinions and predictions; we carefully observe daily market supply and demand as it changes.

One of the great values to this system of interpreting the market averages' price and volume changes is not just the ability to recognize major market tops and bottoms, but also the ability to track each rally attempt when the market is on its way down. By waiting for powerful follow-through days you can normally prevent yourself from being drawn into the market prematurely when rally attempts ultimately end in failure. In other words, you have rules that will continue to keep you out of a declining market so that you don't get sucked into phony rallies. This is how we were able to stay out of the market and in money market funds for most of 2000 and 2001, and preserve gains made in 1998 and 1999. There is a fortune for you in this paragraph.

Part I Review: How to Remember and Use What You've Read So Far

It isn't enough just to read. You need to remember and apply *all* of what you read. To help you remember what you've read so far, we've come up with the simple two-word acronym: CAN SLIM™. Each letter in CAN SLIM stands for one of the seven basic fundamentals of selecting outstanding stocks. Most successful stocks have these seven common characteristics at emerging growth stages, so they are worth committing to memory. Repeat this formula until you can recall and use it easily:

C = Current Quarterly Earnings per Share: They must be up at least 18% or 20%. The higher, the better. Also, quarterly sales should be accelerating or up 25%.

A = Annual Earnings Increases: Require significant growth for each of the last three years and a return on equity of 17% or more.

N = New Products, New Management, New Highs: Look for new products or services, new management, or significant new changes in industry conditions. And most important, buy stocks as they emerge from sound chart bases and begin to make new highs in price.

S = Supply and Demand—Shares Outstanding Plus Big Volume Demand: Any size capitalization is acceptable in today's new economy as long as a company fits all other CAN SLIM rules. Look for big volume increases when a stock begins to move out of its basing area.

L = Leader or Laggard: Buy market leaders and avoid laggards. Buy the number one company in its field. Most leaders' Relative Price Strength Rating will be 80 to 90 or higher.

I = Institutional Sponsorship: Buy stocks with increasing sponsorship and at least a few institutional sponsors with top-notch recent performance records. Also look for companies with management ownership.

M = Market Direction: Learn to determine overall market direction by accurately interpreting the daily market indices' price and volume movements and the action of individual market leaders. This can determine whether you win big or lose.

Is CAN SLIM Momentum Investing?

I'm not even sure what "momentum investing" is. Some analysts and reporters who don't understand how we invest have given that name to what we recommend and do. They say it's "buying the stocks that have gone up the most in price" and that have the strongest relative price strength. No one in his or her right mind invests that way. What we do is identify companies with strong fundamentals—large sales and earnings increases resulting from unique new products or services—and then buy their stocks when they emerge from price consolidation periods and before they run up dramatically in price.

Experts, Education, and Egos

On Wall Street, wise men can be just as easily drawn into booby traps as fools. From what I've seen, in fact, the length and quality of one's education have very little to do with making big money investing in the market.

The more intelligent people are, the more they think they know what they're doing, and the more they may have to learn the hard way how little they really know about outsmarting the stock market. The few people I've known over the years who've been unquestionably successful making money in stocks were decisive individuals without huge egos. The market has a simple way of whittling all excessive pride and overblown egos down to size. After all, the whole idea is to be completely objective and recognize what the marketplace is telling you, rather than try to prove what you said or did yesterday or six weeks ago was right. The fastest way to take a bath in the stock market is to try to prove that you are right and the market is wrong. Humility and commonsense provide essential balance.

Sometimes, the more widely quoted and accepted the expert, the more trouble you can get yourself into. A well-known expert, in the spring and summer of 1982, insisted that government borrowing was going to crowd out the private sector and that interest rates and inflation would soar back to new highs. The exact opposite happened, inflation broke and interest rates came crashing down. Another expert's bear market call in the summer of 1996 backfired as it came only one day from the market bottom. In the 2000 bear market, one expert after another kept saying week after week on CNBC that it was time to buy high-tech stocks only to watch the techs continue to plummet further. Many high-profile analysts and strategists kept telling investors to capitalize on these once-in-a-lifetime "buying opportunities" on the way down! Buying on the way down can be a dangerous pastime.

Conventional wisdom or consensus thinking is seldom right in the market. I never pay any attention to the parade of experts voicing their personal opinions on the market. It just creates entirely too much confusion and can cost you a great deal of money. Some strategists in 2000 were telling people to buy the dips (short-term declines in price) because the cash position of mutual funds had increased greatly, such that there was all this money sitting on the sidelines. All anyone had to do to prove this wrong was to look at the General Markets & Sectors page in *Investor's Business Daily.* It showed that while mutual fund cash positions had indeed risen, the move was still significantly under historical highs and even under historical averages. The only thing that works is to let the market indices tell you the time to enter and exit. Never fight the market—it's bigger than you are.

PART II

Be Smart From the Start

CHAPTER

Nineteen Common Mistakes Most Investors Make

Knute Rockne, the famous winning Notre Dame football coach, used to say, "Build up your weaknesses until they become your strong points." The reason people either lose money or achieve mediocre results in the stock market is they simply make too many mistakes. It's the same in your business, life, or career. You are held back or have reverses, not because of your strengths, but because of your mistakes or weaknesses that you do not recognize and correct. Most people just blame somebody else. It is much easier to have excuses and alibis than it is to realistically examine your own behavior.

Since the early 1960s, I have known or dealt with countless individual risk-takers, from inexperienced beginners to smart professionals. What I've discovered is that it doesn't matter whether you're just getting started or have many years, even decades, of investing experience. In fact, experience is harmful if it continuously reinforces your bad habits. Success in the market is achieved by avoiding the classic mistakes made most often by the least successful investors. These are the mistakes you must avoid:

1. Stubbornly holding onto losses when they are very small and reasonable. Most could get out cheaply, but because people are human, emotions take over. You don't want to take a loss, so you wait and you hope, until your loss gets so large it costs you dearly. This is by far the number one mistake most investors make; they don't understand that all stocks are highly speculative and can involve huge risks. Without exception, you should cut every single loss short. My rule is to always cut all losses immediately when a stock falls 7% or 8% below my purchase price. Following this simple rule will ensure you will survive another day to invest and capitalize on future opportunities.

2. Buying on the way down in price, thus ensuring miserable results. A declining stock seems a real bargain because it's cheaper than it was a few months earlier. An acquaintance of mine bought International Harvester in March 1981 at $19 because it was down sharply. This was his first investment, and he made the classic tyro's mistake: He bought a stock near its low for the year. As it turned out, the company was in serious trouble and headed for possible bankruptcy. In late 1999, a young woman I know bought Xerox when it dropped abruptly to a new low at $34 and seemed really cheap. A year later it traded at $6. Why try to catch a falling dagger?

3. Averaging down in price rather than up when buying. If you buy a stock at $40 and then buy more at $30 and average out your cost at $35, you are following up your losers and putting good money after bad. This amateur strategy can produce serious losses and weigh your portfolio down with a few big losers.

4. Buying large amounts of low-priced stocks rather than smaller amounts of higher-priced stocks. Many think it's smarter to buy more shares in round lots of 100 or 1000 shares. This makes people feel like they're getting a lot more for their money. They'd be better off buying 30 or 50 shares of higher-priced, better-performing companies. Think in terms of *dollars* when you invest, not the number of shares you can buy. Buy the best merchandise available, not the cheapest. Many investors can't resist $2, $5, or $10 stocks, but most stocks selling for $10 or less are cheap for a reason. They've either been deficient in the past or have something wrong with them now. Stocks are like anything else: The best quality never comes at the cheapest price.

That's not all. Low-priced stocks usually cost more in commissions and markups. And since they can drop 15% to 20% faster than most higher-priced issues, they also carry greater risk. Most professionals and institutions won't normally invest in $5 and $10 stocks, so they do not have a top-notch following. Penny stocks are even worse. As we discussed earlier, institutional sponsorship is one of the ingredients needed to help propel a stock higher in price. Cheap stocks also have larger spreads in terms of the percentage difference between the bid and ask price. Compare a $5 stock that trades $5 bid, $5.25 ask versus a $50 stock that trades $50 bid, $50.25 ask. On your $5 stock that $0.25 difference is almost 5% of the bid price. On your $50 stock that $0.25 difference is a negligible 0.5%. The difference is a factor of 10. As a result, with low-priced stocks you tend to have much more ground to make up from your initial buy point just to break even and overcome the spread.

5. Wanting to make a quick and easy buck. Wanting too much, too fast—without doing the necessary preparation, learning the soundest methods, or acquiring the essential skills and discipline—can be your downfall. Chances are, you'll jump into a stock too fast and then be too slow to cut your losses when you are wrong.

6. Buying on tips, rumors, split announcements, and other news events, stories, advisory-service recommendations, or opinions you hear from supposed market experts on TV. In other words, many people are too willing to risk their hard-earned money on what someone else says, rather than taking the time to study, learn, and know for sure what they're doing. As a result, they risk losing a lot of money. Most rumors and tips you hear simply aren't true. Even if they are true, in most cases the stock concerned will ironically go down, not up.

7. Selecting second-rate stocks because of dividends or low price-earnings (P/E) ratios. Dividends and P/E ratios aren't as important as earnings per share growth. In many cases, the more a company pays in dividends, the weaker it may be. It may have to pay high interest rates to replenish funds paid out in the form of dividends. Better-performing companies will typically not issue dividends. Instead, they reinvest their capital into research and development (R&D) or other corporate improvements. Also, keep in mind that you can lose the amount of a dividend in one or two days' fluctuation in the price of the stock. As for P/E ratios, a low P/E is probably low because the company's past record is inferior. Most stocks sell for what they're worth at the time.

8. Never getting out of the starting gate properly due to poor selection criteria and not knowing exactly what to look for in a successful company. Many buy fourth-rate, "nothing-to-write-home-about" stocks that are not acting particularly well, have questionable earnings, sales growth, and return on equity, and are not the true market leaders. Others overly concentrate in highly speculative or lower-quality, risky technology securities.

9. Buying old names you're familiar with. Just because you used to work for General Motors doesn't necessarily make it a good stock to buy. Many of the best investments will be newer names that you won't know, but which, with a little research, you could discover and profit from before they become household names.

10. Not being able to recognize (and follow) good information and advice. Friends, relatives, certain stockbrokers, and advisory services might all be sources of *bad* advice. Only a small minority are successful enough themselves to merit your consideration. Outstanding stockbrokers or advisory services are no more plentiful than outstanding doctors, lawyers, or ball players. Only one out of nine baseball players who sign professional contracts ever make it to the big leagues. Most of the ball players that graduate college simply are not professional caliber.

11. Not using charts and being afraid to buy stocks that are going into new high ground in price. Over 98% of the masses will generally think that a stock making a new high price seems too high, but personal feelings and opinions are far less accurate than the market itself. The best time to buy a stock during a bull market is when the stock initially emerges from a price consolidation or sound "basing" area of at least seven or eight weeks.

12. Cashing in small, easy-to-take profits while holding the losers. In other words, doing exactly the opposite of what you should be doing: cutting losses short and giving your profits more time.

13. Worrying too much about taxes and commissions. The name of the game is to first make a net profit. Excessive worrying about taxes usually leads to unsound investment decisions in the hope of achieving a tax shelter. You can also fritter away a good profit by holding on too long, trying to get a long-term capital gain. Some investors convince themselves they can't sell because of taxes, but that's ego trumping judgment.

The commissions associated with buying and selling stocks, especially through an online broker, are minor compared with the money to be made by making the right decisions in the first place and taking action when needed. The fact that you pay relatively low commissions and can get out of your investment much faster are two of your biggest advantages of owning stock over real estate. With instant liquidity, you can protect yourself quickly at low cost and take advantage of highly profitable new trends as they continually evolve.

14. Concentrating your time on what to buy and once the buy decision is made, not understanding when or under what conditions the stock must be sold. Most investors have no rules or plan for selling stocks, doing only half of the homework necessary to succeed.

15. Failing to understand the importance of buying quality companies with good institutional sponsorship and the importance of learning how to use charts to significantly improve selection and timing.

16. Speculating too heavily in options or futures because they're thought to be a way to get rich quick. Some investors also focus mainly on shorter-term, lower-priced options that involve greater volatility and risk. The limited time period works against short-term option holders. Some also write "naked options" (selling options on stocks they do not even own), which amounts to taking great risk for a potentially small reward.

17. Rarely transacting "at the market" and preferring to put price limits on their buy and sell orders. By doing so, they're quibbling for eighths and quarters of a point (or their decimal equivalents), rather than focusing on the stock's larger and more important movement. With limit orders, you run the risk of missing the market completely and not getting out of stocks that should be sold to avoid substantial losses.

18. Not being able to make up your mind when a decision needs to be made. Many don't know if they should buy, sell, or hold, and the uncertainty shows that they have no guidelines. Most people don't follow a proven plan, a set of strict principles or buy and sell rules, to correctly guide them.

19. Not looking at stocks objectively. Many pick favorites and cross their fingers. Instead of relying on hope and their own opinions, successful investors pay attention to the market, which is usually right.

How many of these describe your own past investment beliefs and practices? Poor principles and methods yield poor results; sound principles and methods yield sound results.

After all of this, don't feel discouraged. Just remember what Rockne would say: "Build up your weaknesses until they become your strong points." It takes time and a little effort to get it right, but in the end, it's worth every minute.

When to Sell and Cut Your Losses

Now that you've learned how and when to buy nothing but the best stocks, it's time to learn how and when to sell them. You've probably heard the sports cliché: "The best offense is a strong defense." The funny thing about clichés is they are usually true; a team that's all offense and no defense seldom wins the game. In fact, a strong defense can often propel a team to great heights. During the glory days of President and General Manager Branch Rickey, the Brooklyn Dodgers typically had good pitching. In the game of baseball, the combination of pitching and fielding represent the defensive side of a team and probably 70% of the game. It's almost impossible to win without them.

The same holds true in the stock market. Unless you have a strong defense to protect yourself against large losses, you absolutely can't win big in the game of investing.

Bernard Baruch's Secret Market Method of Making Millions

Bernard Baruch, a famous market operator on Wall Street and trusted adviser to U.S. presidents, said it best: "If a speculator is correct half of the time, he is hitting a good average. Even being right 3 or 4 times out of 10 should yield a person a fortune if he has the sense to cut his losses quickly on the ventures where he has been wrong."

As you can see, even the most successful investors make mistakes. These poor decisions will lead to losses, some of which can become quite awful if you're not disciplined and careful. No matter how smart you are, how high your I.Q. or education, how good your information, or how sound your analysis, you're simply just not going to be right all the time. In fact, you'll probably be right less than half the time! You positively must understand and accept that rule number one for the highly successful individual investor is . . . always cut short and limit every loss. To do this takes discipline and courage.

Baruch's point was driven home to me with an account I managed back in 1962. The general market had taken a 29% nosedive, and we were right on only one of every three commitments we had made in this account. Yet the account was ahead at the end of the year. The reason was that the average profit on the 33% correct decisions was more than twice the average of the small losses we took when we were off-target.

The whole secret to winning big in the stock market is not to be right all the time but to lose the least amount possible when you're wrong. You've got to recognize when you may be wrong and sell without hesitation to cut short every one of your losses.

How can you tell when you may be wrong? That's easy: The price of the stock will drop below the price you paid for it! Each point your favorite brainchild falls below your cost increases both the chance you're wrong as well as the price you're going to pay for being wrong.

Are Successful People Lucky or Always Right?

People think that to be successful, you have to be lucky or right most of the time. Not so. Successful people make many mistakes, but their success is due to hard work, not luck. They just try harder and more often than the average person. There aren't many overnight successes; success takes time.

In search of a filament for his electric lamp, Thomas Edison carbonized and tested 6000 specimens of bamboo. Three of them worked. Before that, he tried thousands of other materials, from cotton thread to chicken feathers. Babe Ruth worked so hard for his home run record that he also held the lifetime record for strikeouts. Irving Berlin wrote more than 600 songs, but no more than 50 were hits. Before they made it big, every record company in England turned down the Beatles. Michael Jordan was once cut from his high school varsity basketball team, and Albert Einstein made an "F" in math.

It takes a lot of trial and error before you can own and nail down substantial gains in stocks like Brunswick and Great Western Financial when they doubled in 1961, Chrysler and Syntex in 1963, Fairchild Camera and Polaroid in 1965, Control Data in 1967, Levitz Furniture in 1970–1972, Prime Computer and Humana in 1977–1981, MCI Communications in

1981–1982, Price Company in 1982–1983, Microsoft in 1986–1992, Amgen in 1990–1991, International Game Technology in 1991–1993, Cisco Systems from 1995 to 2000, America Online and Charles Schwab in 1998–1999, and Qualcomm in 1999. These stocks dazzled the market with gains ranging from 100% to more than 1000%.

Over the years, I've found that only one or two out of ten stocks bought turned out to be truly outstanding and capable of making these kinds of substantial profits. In other words, to get the one or two stocks that make big money, you have to look for and buy ten. Which begs the question, what do you do with the other eight? Sit with them and hope, like most people do, or sell them and keep trying until you come up with even more big successes?

When Does a Loss Become a Loss?

When you say, "I can't sell my stock because I don't want to take a loss," you assume that what you want has some bearing on the situation. But the stock doesn't know who you are, and it couldn't care less what you hope or want. Besides, selling doesn't give you the loss; you already have the loss. If you think a loss isn't incurred until you sell the stock, you're kidding yourself. The larger the paper loss, the more real it will become. For example, if you paid $40 per share for 100 shares of Can't Miss Chemical, and it's now worth $28 per share, you have $2800 worth of stock that cost you $4000. You have a $1200 loss. Whether you convert the stock to cash or hold it, it's still worth only $2800.

Even though you didn't sell, you took your loss as the stock dropped in price. You'd be better off selling and going back to a cash position where you can think far more objectively. When you're holding on to a big loss, you are rarely able to think straight; you rationalize and say, "It can't go any lower." However, keep in mind that there are many other stocks to choose from where your chance of recouping your loss could be greater.

Here's another suggestion that may help you decide whether to sell: Pretend you don't own the stock and you have $2800 in the bank. Then ask yourself, "Do I really want to buy this stock now?" If your answer is "no," then why are you holding onto it?

Always, Without Exception, Limit Losses to 7% or 8% of Your Cost

Individual investors should definitely set firm rules limiting the loss on initial invested capital in each stock to an absolute maximum of 7% or 8%. Because of large position size problems, and broad diversification that lessens overall risk, most institutional investors do not have the flexibility to follow such a quick loss-cutting plan. It is very difficult for institutions to move quickly in and out of stocks, which is necessary in order for them to follow this loss-cutting rule. This is a terrific advantage you, the individual investor, have over the institutions. So use it.

When the late Gerald M. Loeb of E. F. Hutton was writing his last book on the stock market, I had the pleasure of discussing this idea with him. In his first work, *The Battle for Investment Survival,* Loeb advocated cutting all losses at 10%. I was curious and asked him if he always followed the 10% loss policy himself. "I would hope," he replied, "to be out long before they ever reach 10%." Loeb made millions in the market.

Bill Astrop, president of Astrop Advisory Corporation in Atlanta, Georgia, suggests a minor revision of the 10% loss-cutting plan. He thinks individual investors should sell half of their position in a stock if it is down 5% from their cost and the other half once it's down 10%. This is sound advice.

To preserve your hard-earned money, I think a 7% or 8% loss should be the limit. The average of all your losses should be less, perhaps 5% or 6%, if you're strictly disciplined and fast on your feet. If you can keep the average of all your mistakes and losses to 5% or 6%, you'll be like the football team that opponents can never move the ball on. If you don't give up many first downs, how can they ever beat you?

Now here's a giant secret: If you use charts to time your buys precisely at correct buy or "pivot" points coming off of *sound* chart bases (price consolidation areas), your stocks will rarely ever drop 8% from a correct buy point. (See Chapter 12 for further discussion.) This is a big key for your future success.

Also, there's no rule that says you have to wait until every single loss reaches 7% to 8% before you take it. On occasion, you will sense that the general market index is under distribution (selling) or that your stock isn't acting right and that you are starting off amiss. In such cases, you can cut your loss sooner, when a stock may be down only one or two points. Before the market broke wide open in October 1987, for example, there was ample time to sell and cut losses short. That correction actually began on August 26. If you are foolish enough to try bucking the market by buying stocks during a bear market, I would move up your absolute loss-cutting point to 3% or 4%.

After years of experience, your average losses should become less as your stock selection and timing improve and you learn to make small "follow-up buys" in your best stocks. It takes a lot of time to learn to safely make follow-up buys when a stock is up, but this method of money management forces you to move your money from slower-performing stocks into your stronger ones. (See Chapter 10 for more information.) You'll end up selling stocks that are not yet down 7% or 8% because you are raising money to add to your best winners during clearly strong bull markets.

Remember, 7% to 8% is your absolute loss limit. You must sell without hesitation—no waiting a few days to see what might happen or hoping the stock rallies back; no need to wait for the day's market close. Nothing but the fact you're down 7% or 8% should have a bearing on the situation at this point.

Once you're ahead and have a good profit, you can afford to give the stock a good bit more than 7% or 8% room for normal fluctuations in price. Do *not* sell a stock just because it's off 7% to 8% from its peak price. It's important that you understand the difference. In one case you are probably starting off wrong. The stock is not acting the way you expected, and you are beginning to lose your own hard earned money and may be about to lose a lot more. In the other case you have begun right. The stock has acted better, and you have a gain. You're working on a profit so you can afford to give the stock more room to fluctuate and avoid getting shaken out on a normal 10% to 15% correction. The key is timing your stock purchases exactly at breakout points to minimize the chance that a stock will drop 8%. (See Chapter 12 for more on using charts to select stocks.)

All Common Stocks Are Speculative and Risky

There is considerable risk in all common stocks, regardless of their name, quality, purported blue-chip status, previous performance record, or current good earnings. Keep in mind that most growth stocks top when their earnings are excellent and analysts' estimates are still rosy.

Every 50% loss began as a 10% or 20% loss. Having the raw courage to sell and cheerfully take your loss is the only way you can protect yourself against the possibility of much greater losses. Decision and action should be instantaneous and simultaneous. To be a big winner, you have to learn to make decisions. I've known at least a dozen educated and otherwise intelligent people who were completely wiped out solely because they would not sell and cut a loss.

What should you do if a stock gets away from you and the loss becomes greater than 10% (which can happen to anyone)? This is an even more critical sign that the stock positively must be sold. The stock was in more trouble than normal so it fell further and faster than normal. Many new investors in the year 2000 lost heavily and some were wiped out . . . lost it all. If they had just followed the simple sell rule discussed above, they would have protected most of their capital.

In my experience, those that get away from you for larger-than-normal losses are the truly awful selections that absolutely must be sold. Something is really going wrong with the stock or the whole market, and it's even more urgent that this stock be sold to avoid a later catastrophe. Remind yourself: "If I ever let a stock drop 50%, I must make a 100% gain on the next stock just to break even! And how often do I buy stocks that double?" You cannot afford to sit with a stock where the loss keeps getting worse.

It is a dangerous fallacy to assume that because a stock goes down, it has to come back up. Many don't. Others take years to recover. AT&T hit a high of $75 in 1964 and took 20 years to come back. Also, when the S&P 500 or Dow declines 20% to 25% in a bear market, many stocks will plummet 60% to 75%. The only way to prevent these types of bad losses is to cut them without hesitation while they're still small. Always protect your account so you can live to invest successfully another day.

In 2000, many new investors incorrectly believed all you had to do was buy high-tech stocks on every dip in price because they would always go back up and there was easy money to be made. This is the amateur's strategy, and it almost always leads to heavy losses. You must remember, semiconductors and other technology stocks are two to three times as volatile and risky as others, so moving rapidly to cut short every loss is even more essential when you're in tech stocks. If your entire portfolio is in nothing but high-tech stocks, or if you're heavily margined in tech stocks, you are asking for serious trouble if you don't quickly cut your losses. You should never invest on margin unless you're willing to cut short all of your losses. You could go belly up in no time. If you happen to get a margin call from your broker (when you're faced with the decision to either sell stock or add money to your account to cover lost equity in a falling stock), don't put good money after bad. Sell some stock, and recognize what the market and your margin clerk are trying to tell you.

Cutting Losses Is Like Buying an Insurance Policy

This policy of limiting losses is similar to paying insurance premiums. You're reducing your risk to precisely the level you're comfortable with. Yes, frequently the stock you sell will often turn right around and go back up. And yes, this can be frustrating, but don't conclude you were wrong in selling when some go back up in price. That is exceedingly dangerous thinking that will eventually get you into big trouble.

Think about it this way: If you bought insurance on your car last year and you didn't have an accident, was your money wasted? Will you buy the same insurance this year? Of course you will!

Did you take out fire insurance on your home or business? If your home hasn't burned down, are you upset that you made a bad financial decision?

No! You don't buy fire insurance because you know your house is going to burn down. You buy insurance just in case, to protect yourself against the remote possibility of a serious loss.

It's exactly the same for the winning investor who cuts all losses quickly. It's the only way to protect against the possible chance of a much larger loss from which it may not be possible to recover.

If you procrastinate and allow a loss to increase to 20%, it will now take a 25% gain just to break even. Wait longer until the stock is down 25% and you'll have to make 33% to get even. Hesitate longer still until the loss is 33% and you'll have to make 50% to get back to the starting gate. The longer you wait the more the math works against you, so don't vacillate. Move immediately to cut out possible bad decisions. Develop the strict discipline to act and to follow your selling rules.

Some people have gone so far as to let losing stocks damage their health. In this situation, it's best to sell and stop worrying. I know a stockbroker who in 1961 bought Brunswick on the way down in price at $60. It had been the market's super leader since 1957, increasing more than 20 times. When it dropped to $50, he bought more, and when it dropped to $40, he added again. When it dropped to $30, he dropped dead on the golf course.

History and human nature continually repeat themselves in the market. In fall 2000, many investors made the identical mistake by buying the prior bull market's leader, Cisco Systems, on the way down at $70, $60, $50, etc., after it had topped at $87. Seven months later it sank to $13, an 80% decline for those that bought at $70. The moral of the story is: Never argue with the market. Your health and peace of mind are always more important than any stock!

Small losses are cheap insurance, and they are the only insurance you can buy on your investments. Even if stocks move up after you sell, which many of them surely will, you will have accomplished your critical objective of keeping all your losses small, and you'll still have money to try again for a winner in another stock.

Take Your Losses Quickly and Your Profits Slowly

There's an old investment saying that the first loss in the market is the smallest loss. In my view, the way to make investment decisions is to always (no exceptions) take your losses quickly and your profits slowly. Yet most investors get emotionally confused and take their profits quickly and their losses slowly.

What is your real risk in any stock you buy under the method we've discussed? It's 8%, no matter what you buy, if you religiously follow this rule. Still, most investors stubbornly ask, "Shouldn't we sit with stocks rather than selling and taking a loss? How about unusual situations where some bad news suddenly hits and causes price declines? Does this loss-cutting procedure apply all the time, or are there exceptions, like when a company has a good new product?"

The answer: *There are no exceptions.* It doesn't change the situation one bit. You must always protect your hard-earned pool of capital. Letting your losses run is the most serious mistake made by almost all investors. You must accept the fact that mistakes in stock selection and timing are going to be made frequently, even by the most experienced of professional investors. I'd go so far as to say that if you aren't willing to cut short and limit your losses, you probably shouldn't buy stocks. Would you drive your car down the street without brakes? If you were a fighter pilot, would you go into battle without a parachute?

Should You Average Down in Price?

One of the most unprofessional things a stockbroker can do is hesitate or fail to call customers whose stocks are down in price. That's when the customer needs help the most. Shirking this duty in difficult periods shows a lack of courage under pressure.

About the only thing that's worse is for brokers to take themselves off the hook by advising customers to "average down" (buy more of a stock that already shows a loss). If I were advised to do this, I'd close my account and look for a smarter broker.

Everyone loves to buy stocks; no one loves to sell them. As long as you hold a stock, you still have hope it might come back up enough to at least get you out even. Once you sell, you abandon all hope and accept the cold reality of temporary defeat.

Investors are always hoping rather than being realistic. The fact that you want a stock to go up so you can at least get out even has nothing to do with the action and brutal reality of the market. The market obeys only the law of supply and demand.

A great trader once noted that there are only two emotions in the market: hope and fear. "The only problem," he added, "is we hope when we should fear and we fear when we should hope."

The Turkey Story

Many years ago, I heard a story by Fred C. Kelly, the author of *Why You Win or Lose,* which illustrates perfectly how the conventional investor thinks when the time comes to make a selling decision:

A little boy was walking down the road when he came upon an old man trying to catch wild turkeys. The man had a turkey trap, a crude device consisting of a big box with the door hinged at the top. This door was kept open by a prop to which was tied a piece of twine leading back a hundred feet or more to the operator. A thin trail of corn scattered along a path lured turkeys to the box. Once inside, the turkeys found an even more plentiful supply of corn. When enough turkeys had wandered inside the box, the old man would jerk away the prop and let the door fall shut. Having once shut the door, he couldn't open it again without going up to the box and this would scare away any turkeys lurking outside. The time to pull away the prop was when as many turkeys were inside as one could reasonably expect.

One day he had a dozen turkeys in his box. Then one sauntered out, leaving 11. "Gosh, I wish I had pulled the string when all 12 were there," said the old man. "I'll wait a minute and maybe the other one will go back."

While he waited for the twelfth turkey to return, two more walked out on him. "I should have been satisfied with 11," the trapper said. "Just as soon as I get one more back, I'll pull the string."

Three more walked out, and still the man waited. Having once had 12 turkeys, he disliked going home with less than eight. He couldn't give up the idea that some of the original turkeys would return. When finally only one turkey was left in the trap, he said, "I'll wait until he walks out or another goes in, and then I'll quit." The solitary turkey went to join the others, and the man returned empty-handed.

The psychology of the normal investor is not much different. They hope more turkeys will return to the box when they should fear that all will walk out and they'll be left with nothing.

How the Typical Investor Thinks

If you're a typical investor, you probably keep records of your transactions; when you think about selling a stock, you probably look at your records to see what price you paid for it. If you have a profit, you may sell, but if you have a loss, you tend to wait. After all, you didn't invest in the market to lose money. However, what you should be doing is selling your worst performing stock first. Keep your flower patch free of weeds.

You may decide to sell your shares in Home Depot, for example, because they show a nice profit, but you'll keep your Kmart because it still has a ways to go before it's back to the price you paid. If this is the way you think, you're suffering from the "price-paid bias" that afflicts 95% of all investors. Suppose you bought a stock two years ago at $30, and it's now worth $34. Most investors would sell it because they have a profit, but what does the price paid two years ago have to do with its worth now? What does that have to do with whether the stock should be held or sold? The key is the relative performance of this stock versus others you either own or could potentially own.

Analyzing Your Activities

To help avoid the price-paid bias, particularly if you are a longer-term investor, I suggest you use a different method of analyzing results. At the end of each month or quarter, compute the percentage change in price of each stock from the last date you did this type of analysis. Now list your investments in order of their relative price performance since your previous evaluation period. Let's say your Caterpillar is down 6%, your Exxon Mobil is unchanged, and General Electric is up 10%. Your list would start with GE on top, then Exxon Mobil, then Caterpillar.

At the end of the next month or quarter, do the same thing. After a few reviews, you will easily recognize the stocks that are not doing well. They'll be at the bottom of the list; those that did best will be at or near the top.

This method isn't foolproof, but it does force you to focus your attention not on what you paid for stocks, but on the relative performance of your investments in the market. It will help you maintain a clearer perspective. Of course, you have to keep records of your costs for tax reasons, but you should use this more realistic method in the longer-term management of your portfolio. Doing this more often than once a quarter can only help you. Eliminating the price-paid bias can be profitable and rewarding.

Any time a commitment in a security is made, you should also determine the potential profit and the possible loss. This is only logical. You wouldn't buy a stock if there were a potential profit of 20% and a potential loss of 80%, would you? But how do you know this is not the situation when you buy a stock if you do not attempt to define these factors and operate according to well-thought-out selling rules? Do you have specific selling rules you've written down and follow, or are you flying blindly?

I suggest you write down the price at which you expect to sell if you have a loss (8% or less below your purchase price) as well as the expected profit potential of all the securities you purchase. For instance, you might consider selling your growth stock when its P/E ratio increases 130% or more from the time the stock originally began its big move out of its initial base pattern. By writing it down, it will be easier to see when the stock has reached one of these levels.

It's bad business to base your sell decisions on your cost and hold stocks that are down in price simply because you can't accept the fact you made an imprudent selection and lost money. In fact, you're making the exact opposite decisions from those you would make if you were running your own business.

The Red Dress Story

The stock market is really no different from running your own business. Investing is a business and should be operated as such.

Assume you own a small store selling women's clothing. You've bought and stocked women's dresses in three colors: yellow, green, and red. The red dresses quickly sell out, half of the green ones sell, and the yellow ones have not sold at all. What do you do about it?

Do you go to your buyer and say, "The red dresses are all sold out. The yellow ones don't seem to have any demand, but I still think they're good. Besides, yellow is my favorite color, so let's buy some more of them anyway,"? Certainly not!

The clever merchandiser who survives in the retail business eyes this predicament objectively and says, "We sure made a mistake. We'd better eliminate the yellow dresses. Mark them down 10%. Let's have a sale. If they don't sell at that price, mark them down 20%. Get our money out of those 'old dogs' no one wants, and put it in more of the hot-moving red dresses that are in demand." This is common sense in a retail business. Do you do this with your investments? Why not?

Everyone makes buying errors. The buyers for department stores are pros, but even they make mistakes. If you do slip up, recognize it, sell, and go on to the next thing. You don't have to be correct on all your investment decisions to make a good net profit.

Now you know the real secret to reducing your risk and selecting the best stocks: Stop counting your turkeys and get rid of your yellow dresses!

Are You a Speculator or an Investor?

There are two often misunderstood words to describe the kind of people who participate in the stock market: speculator and investor.

When you think of the word "speculator," you might think of someone who takes big risks, gambling on the future success of a stock. Conversely, when you think of the word "investor," you might think of someone who approaches the stock market in a sensible and rational manner. According to these conventional definitions, you may think it's smarter to be an "investor."

But Baruch defines "speculator" as follows: "The word speculator comes from the Latin 'speculari,' which means to spy and observe. A speculator, therefore, is a person who observes and acts before [the future] occurs." This is precisely what you should be doing; you should watch the market and individual stocks to analyze what they're doing now, and then act upon that information. Jesse Livermore, another stock market legend, defined "investor" this way: "Investors are the big gamblers. They make a bet, stay with it, and if it goes wrong, they lose it all." After reading this far, you should already know that this is not the proper way to invest. There is no such thing as a long-term investment once a stock drops into the loss column and you're down 8% below your cost.

These definitions are a bit different from those you'll read in Webster's Dictionary, but they are far more accurate. Keep in mind that Baruch and Livermore at many times made millions of dollars in the stock market. I'm not sure about lexicographers.

One of my goals is to get you to question and change many of the faulty investment ideas, beliefs, and methods you have heard about or used in the past. One of these is the very notion of what it means to invest. It's unbelievable how much erroneous information is out there about the stock market, how it works, and how to succeed at it. Learn to objectively analyze all the relevant facts about a stock and how the market is behaving. Stop listening to and being influenced by friends, associates, and the continuous array of experts' personal opinions on daily TV shows.

"I'm Not Worried. I'm a Long-Term Investor, and I'm Still Getting My Dividends."

It's also risky and possibly foolish to say to yourself, "I'm not worried about my stocks being down because they are good stocks, and I'm still getting my dividends." Good stocks bought at the wrong time can go down as much as poor stocks, and it's possible they might not be such good stocks in the first place. It may just be your personal opinion that they're good.

Furthermore, if a stock is down 35% in value, isn't it rather absurd to say you're all right because you are getting a 4% dividend yield? A 35% loss plus a 4% income gain equals a whopping 31% net loss.

To be a successful investor, you must face facts and stop rationalizing and hoping. No one emotionally wants to take losses, but to increase your chances of success in the stock market, you have to do many things you don't want to do. Develop precise rules and hard-nosed selling disciplines, and you'll gain a major advantage.

Never Lose Your Confidence

There's one last critical reason for taking losses before they have a chance to really hurt you: Never lose the courage to make decisions in the future.

If you don't sell to cut your losses when you begin to get into trouble, you can easily lose the confidence you'll need to make buy and sell decisions in the future. Or far worse, you can get so discouraged you finally "throw in the towel" and get out of the market, never realizing what you did wrong, never correcting your faulty procedures, and giving up all future opportunities the stock market has to offer—one of the most outstanding opportunities in America.

Wall Street is human nature on daily display. Buying and selling stocks properly and making a net profit are always a complicated affair. Human nature being what it is, 90% of the people in the stock market—professionals and amateurs alike—simply haven't done much homework. They haven't really studied to learn if what they're doing is right or wrong. They haven't studied in enough detail what makes a successful stock go up and down. Luck has nothing to do with it, and it's not a total mystery. It's certainly not a matter of "random walk" like some inexperienced, university professors believe.

It takes some work to become really good at stock selection, and more still to know how and when to sell. Selling a stock correctly is a tougher job and the one least understood by everyone. To do it right, you need a plan to cut losses and the discipline to do it quickly without wavering.

Forget your ego and pride, stop trying to fight and argue with the market, and don't get emotionally attached to or fall in love with any stock that's losing you money. Remember, there are no good stocks; they're all bad ... unless they go up in price.

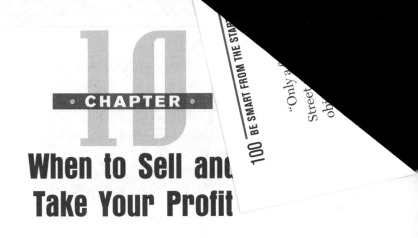

When to Sell and Take Your Profit

This is one of the most vital chapters in this book, covering an essential subject few investors handle well, so study it carefully. Common stock is just like any merchandise. You, as the merchant, must sell your stock if you're to realize a profit, and the best way to sell a stock is when it's on the way up, while it's still advancing and looking strong to everyone else. This way, you won't get caught in the heartrending 20% to 40% corrections that can hit market leaders and put downside pressure on your portfolio. You'll never sell at the exact top, so don't kick yourself if a stock goes still higher after you sell. **If you don't sell early, you'll be late. The object is to make and take significant gains and not get excited, optimistic, or greedy as a stock's advance gets stronger. Keep in mind the old saying: "Bulls make money and bears make money, but pigs get slaughtered."**

The basic objective of every account should be to show a net profit. To retain worthwhile profits, you must sell and take them. The key is knowing when to do just that. Bernard Baruch, the financier who built a fortune in the stock market, said, "Repeatedly, I have sold a stock while it was still rising—and that has been one reason why I have held onto my fortune. Many a time, I might have made a good deal more by holding a stock, but I would also have been caught in the fall when the price of the stock collapsed."

When asked if there was a technique for making money on the stock exchange, Nathan Rothschild, the highly successful international banker, said, "There certainly is. I never buy at the bottom, and I always sell too soon."

ool holds out for the top dollar," said Joe Kennedy, one-time Wall
speculator and the father of former President John F. Kennedy. The
ect is to get out while a stock is up before it has a chance to break and
turn down. Gerald M. Loeb also states, "Once the price has risen into estimated normal or overvaluation areas, the amount held should be reduced
steadily as quotations advance."

One simply must get out while the getting is good. The secret is to hop off
the elevator on one of the floors on the way up and not ride it back down
again.

You Must Develop a Profit-and-Loss Plan

To be a big success in the stock market, you need rules and a profit-and-loss
plan. I developed many of the buy-and-sell rules described in this book in
the early 1960s when I was a young stockbroker with Hayden, Stone. These
rules helped me buy a seat on the New York Stock Exchange and start my
own firm shortly thereafter. When I started out, though, I concentrated on
developing a set of buy rules that would locate the very best stocks, but as
you'll see, I only had half of the puzzle figured out.

My buy rules were first developed in January 1960, when I analyzed the
three best-performing mutual funds of the prior two years. The standout
was the then-small Dreyfus Fund, which racked up gains twice as large as
many of its competitors.

I sent away for copies of every Dreyfus quarterly report and prospectus
from 1957 to 1959. Then I calculated the average cost of each new stock
they purchased. Next I got a book of stock charts and marked in red the
average price that Dreyfus had paid for its new holdings each quarter.

After looking at more than a hundred Dreyfus purchases, I made a stunning discovery: Every stock was bought at the highest price that it had sold
for in the past year. In other words, if a stock bounced from $40 to $50 for
many months, Dreyfus bought as soon as it made a new high in price and
traded between $50 and $51. The stocks had also formed certain chart price
patterns before leaping into new high ground. This gave me two important
clues: buying on new highs was important, and certain chart patterns
spelled big profit potential.

Jack Dreyfus Was a Chartist

Jack Dreyfus was a chartist and a tape reader. He bought all his stocks based
on market action and *only* when the price broke to new highs. He was also
beating the pants off every competitor who ignored the real-world facts of

market behavior and depended only on fundamental, analytical personal opinions.

Jack's research department in those early, big performance days consisted of three young Turks who posted to oversized charts the day's price and volume action on hundreds of listed stocks.

Shortly thereafter, two small funds run by Fidelity in Boston started doing the same thing. They, too, produced superior results. Almost all the stocks the Dreyfus and Fidelity funds bought also had strong increases in their quarterly earnings reports.

So the first buy rules I made in 1960 were as follows:

1. Concentrate on listed stocks that sell for more than $20 a share with at least some institutional acceptance.

2. The company's earnings per share should have increased in each of the past five years, and the current quarterly earnings must be up at least 20%.

3. The stock should be about to make or making a new high in price after emerging from a sound correction and price consolidation period. (See Chapter 12.) This should be accompanied by a volume increase of at least 50% above the stock's average daily volume.

The first stock I bought under this set of buy rules was Universal Match in February 1960. It doubled in 16 weeks, but I failed to make much because I didn't have much money to invest. I was just getting started as a stockbroker and didn't have many customers. I also got nervous and sold it too quickly. Later that year, sticking with my well-defined game plan, I selected Procter & Gamble, Reynolds Tobacco, and MGM. They, too, made outstanding price moves, but I still didn't make much because my money was limited.

About this time, I was accepted to Harvard Business School's first Program for Management Development (PMD). In what little extra time I had at Harvard, I read a number of business and investment books in the library. The best was *How to Trade in Stocks* by Jesse Livermore. From this book, I learned that your objective in the market was not to be right, but to make big money when you were right.

Jesse Livermore and Pyramiding

After reading his book, I adopted Livermore's method of pyramiding, or averaging up, when a stock moved up after purchase. "Averaging up" is a technique where, after your initial stock purchase, you purchase additional shares of the stock as it moves up in price. This is usually warranted when a stock is originally purchased precisely at a correct pivot point and its price has increased 2% or 3% from the original purchase price. Essentially, I followed up what was working with additional but always *smaller* purchases, allowing me to concentrate my buying when I seemed to be right. If I was wrong and the stock dropped a certain amount below my cost, I sold the stock to cut short the loss. This is very different from how most people invest. Most average down, meaning they buy additional shares as a stock declines in price in order to lower their cost per share. But why add more of your hard-earned money to stocks that aren't working?

Learning by Analysis of My Failures

In the first half of 1961, my rules and plan worked great. Some of the top winners I bought that year were Great Western Financial, Brunswick, Kerr-McGee, Crown Cork & Seal, AMF, and Certain-teed, but by summer, all was not well.

I had bought exactly the right stocks at the right time and had pyramided with several additional buys so I had good positions and profits. However, when the stocks finally topped, I held on too long and watched my profits vanish. When you snooze, you lose. It was hard to swallow. I had been dead right on my stock selections for more than a year but had just broken even.

I was so mad that I spent the last six months of 1961 carefully analyzing every transaction made during the prior year. Much like doctors do postmortem operations and the Civil Aeronautics Board conducts postcrash investigations, I took a red pen and marked on charts exactly where each buy and sell decision was made. Then I overlaid the general market averages.

Eventually my problem became clear: I knew how to select the best leading stocks, but I had no plan for when to sell them and take profits. My stocks went up and then down like yo-yos, and my paper profits were wiped out.

For example, the way I handled Certain-teed, a building materials company that made shell homes, was especially poor. I bought the stock in the low $20s, but during a weak moment in the market, I got scared and sold it for only a two- or three-point gain. Certain-teed proceeded to triple in price. I was in at the right time, but I didn't recognize what I had and failed to capitalize on a phenomenal opportunity.

My analysis of Certain-teed and other such personal failures proved to be the critical key in getting me on the right track to future success. Have you ever analyzed every one of your failures so you can learn from them? Most people don't. What a tragic mistake you'll make if you don't carefully look at yourself and the decisions you've made that did not work. This is the difference between winners and losers, whether in the market or in life. If you got hurt in the 2000 bear market, don't get discouraged and quit. Plot out your mistakes on charts, study them, and write some additional rules in order to correct your mistakes and the actions that cost you money. You'll be that much closer to fully capitalizing on the next bull market. You're never a loser until you quit and give up or start blaming other people.

A Revised Profit-and-Loss Plan

As a result of my analysis, I discovered that successful stocks, after breaking out (see Chapter 12), tend to move up 20% to 25%. Then they decline, build new bases, and in some cases, resume their advances. With this new knowledge in mind, I made a rule that I'd buy each stock exactly at the pivot buy point and have the discipline not to pyramid or add to my position more than 5% past that point. Then I'd sell each stock when it was up 20%.

In the case of Certain-teed, however, the stock ran up 20% in just two weeks. This was the type of super winner I was hoping to find and capitalize on the next time around. So, I made an important exception to the "sell at +20% rule": If the stock was so powerful that it vaulted 20% in less than eight weeks, the stock had to be held at least eight weeks. Then it would be analyzed to see if the stock should be held for a possible six-month long-term capital gain. (Six months was the capital gains period at that time.) If stocks fell below their purchase price by 8%, they'd be sold and the loss taken.

So, here was the revised profit-and-loss plan: Take 20% profits when you have them (except with the most powerful of all stocks) and cut losses at a maximum of 8% below the purchase price.

The plan had several big advantages. You could be wrong twice and right once and still not get into financial trouble. When you were right and wanted to follow up with another somewhat smaller buy in the same stock a few points higher, you were frequently forced into a decision to sell one of your more laggard or weakest performers. The money in your slower-performing stock positions was continually force-fed into your best investments. Also, you were putting your money to far more efficient use. You could make two or three 20% plays in a good year, and you didn't have to sit through so many long, unproductive corrections while a stock built a whole new base.

A 20% gain in three to six months is substantially more productive than a 20% gain that takes 12 months to achieve. Two 20% gains compounded in one year equals a 44% annual rate of return; and if, once experienced, you use full margin (buying power in a margin account), your compounded return would be nearly 100%.

How I Discovered the General Market System

Another exceedingly profitable observation I made from analyzing all of my money-losing mistakes was that most of my market-leading stocks that topped had done so because the general market started into a decline of 10% or more. This conclusion led to my developing the system of interpreting the daily general market averages to establish the true trend and crucial changes in the direction of the overall market.

Three months later, by April 1, 1962, following my selling rules automatically forced me out of every stock. I was 100% in cash with no idea the market was headed for a real crash that spring.

About that time, I had just finished reading *Reminiscences of a Stock Operator* by Edwin LeFevre. I was struck by the parallel between the stock market panic of 1907, which LeFevre discussed in detail, and what seemed to be happening in April 1962. Since I was 100% in cash, and my daily Dow analysis said the market was weak at that point, I began to sell short stocks like Certain-teed and Alside (an earlier sympathy play to Certain-teed). For this, I got into trouble with Hayden, Stone's home office on Wall Street. The firm had just recommended Certain-teed as a buy, and here I was going around telling everyone it was a short sale. Later in the year, Korvette was sold short over $40. The profits from both of these short sales were fairly substantial.

By October 1962, during the Cuban missile crisis, I was again in cash. A day or two after the Russians backed down from President Kennedy's naval blockade, the Dow Jones Industrial Average rally attempt followed through signaling a major upturn according to my new system, and I bought the first stock of the new bull market, Chrysler, at $58.

Throughout 1963, I simply followed my rules to the letter. They worked so well that the "worst" performing account I managed that year was up 115%. It was a cash account. Other accounts that used margin were up several hundred percent. There were many individual stock losses, but they were usually small, averaging 5% to 6%. Profits, on the other hand, were awesome because of the concentrated positions we built by careful, disciplined pyramiding when we were right.

Starting with only $4000 or $5000 that I had saved from my salary, plus some borrowed money and use of full margin, I had three back-to-back big winners: Korvette on the short side in late 1962, Chrysler on the buy side, and Syntex, which was bought at $100 per share with the Chrysler profit in June 1963. After eight weeks, Syntex was up 40%, and I decided to play this powerful stock out for six months. By the fall of 1963, the profit topped $200,000, and I decided to buy a seat on the New York Stock Exchange. So don't ever let anyone tell you it can't be done!

Many long evenings of study led to precise rules, disciplines, and a plan that finally worked. Luck had nothing to do with it; it was persistence and hard work. You can't expect to watch television, drink beer every night, or party with all your friends and still find the answers to something as complex as the stock market or the American economy. In America, anyone can do anything by working at it. If you get discouraged, don't ever give up. Go back and put in some detailed extra effort. It's always the study and learning time you put in *after* nine to five, Monday through Friday, that ultimately makes the difference between winning and reaching your goals or missing out on truly great (and profitable!) opportunities.

Two Things to Remember About Selling

Before we examine the key selling rules one by one, keep these two key points in mind:

First, buying right solves most of your selling problems. If you buy exactly at the right time off a proper daily or weekly chart base in the first place, and you do not chase or pyramid a stock when it's extended in price more than 5% past a correct pivot buy point, you will be in position to sit through most normal corrections. Winning stocks very rarely ever drop 8% below a correct pivot buy point. In fact, most big winners don't close below their pivot point. Buying as close as possible to the pivot point is therefore absolutely essential and may let you cut the smaller number of resulting losses quicker than 8%. A stock might only have to drop 4% or 5% before you know something could be wrong.

Second, beware of the big-block selling you see on the ticker tape just after you buy a stock during a bull market. The selling might be emotional, uninformed, temporary, or not as large (relative to past volume) as it appears. The best stocks can have sharp sell-offs for a few days or a week. Consult a stock chart for overall perspective to avoid getting scared or shaken out in what may just be a normal pullback.

Technical Sell Signs

By studying how the greatest stock market winners all topped, as well as the market itself, I came up with the following list of factors that occur when a stock tops and rolls over. Perhaps you noticed that few selling rules involve changes in the fundamentals of a stock. Many big investors get out of a stock before trouble appears on the income statement. If the smart money is selling, so should you. Individual investors don't stand much chance when institutions begin liquidating large positions. You buy with heavy emphasis on fundamentals, such as earnings, sales, profit margins, return on equity, and new products, but many stocks peak when earnings are up 100% and analysts are projecting continued growth and higher price targets. Therefore, you must frequently sell based on unusual market action (price and volume movement).

There are many different signals to look for when trying to recognize when a stock is topping. These include the price movement surrounding climax tops, adverse volume, and other weak action. A lot of this will become clearer to you as you continue to study this information, as well as apply it to your daily decision making. These principles have been responsible for most of my success in the market, but they can seem a bit complicated at first. I suggest you read these selling rules again after you read Chapter 12 on chart reading.

Climax Tops

Many leading stocks top in explosive fashion. They make climax runs (when a stock suddenly advances at a much faster rate for one or two weeks after an advance of many months). In addition, they often end in exhaustion gaps (when a stock's price opens up on a gap from the prior day's close) on heavy volume. These and related bull market climax signals are discussed in detail below:

1. **Largest daily price run-up.** If a stock's price is extended for many months (it's had a significant run-up from its buy point off of a sound and proper base) and closes for the day with a larger price increase than on any previous up days since the beginning of the whole move up, watch out! This usually occurs very close to a stock's peak, or top.

2. **Heaviest daily volume.** The ultimate top might occur on the heaviest volume day since the beginning of the advance.

3. **Exhaustion gap.** If a stock that has been advancing rapidly is greatly extended from its original base many months ago and then opens on a gap up in price from the previous day's close, the advance is near its peak. For example, a two-point gap in a stock's price would occur if it closed at its high of $50 for the day and the next morning opened at $52 and held above $52 during the day. This is called an exhaustion gap.

4. **Climax top activity.** Sell if a stock's advance gets so active that it has a rapid price run-up for two or three weeks on a weekly chart (8 to 10 days on a daily chart). This is called a climax top. The price spread from the stock's low to high for the week will be greater than on any prior week since the beginning of the original move many months ago. In a few cases near the top of a climax run a stock may retrace the prior week's large price spread from the prior week's low to its high point and close the week up a little, with volume remaining very high. I call this "railroad tracks" because on a weekly chart you'll see two parallel vertical lines. This is a sign of continued heavy volume distribution without real additional price progress for the week.

5. **Signs of distribution.** After a long advance, heavy daily volume without further upside price progress signals distribution. Sell your stock before unsuspecting buyers are overwhelmed.

6. **Stock splits.** Sell if a stock runs up 25% to 50% for one or two weeks on a stock split. Stocks tend to top around excessive stock splits. If a stock's price is extended from its base and a stock split is announced, in many cases the stock could be sold.

7. **Increase in consecutive down days.** The number of consecutive down days in price versus up days in price will probably change and increase after most stocks start down from their top. You may see four or five days down, followed by two or three days up whereas before you would have seen four days up and then two or three down.

8. **Upper channel line.** In a few cases, you should sell if a stock hits its upper channel line after a huge run-up. (On a stock chart, channel lines are somewhat parallel lines drawn by connecting the lows of the price pattern with one straight line and then connecting the highs made over several months with another straight line.) Studies show that stocks surging above their upper channel lines should be sold.

9. **200-day moving average line.** Some stocks may be sold when they are 70% to 100% or more above their 200-day moving average price line.

10. **Selling on the way down from the top.** If you didn't sell early while the stock was still advancing, sell on the way down from the peak. After the first break down, some stocks may pull back up in price one time.

Low Volume and Other Weak Action

1. **New highs on low volume.** Some stocks will make new highs on lower or poor volume. As the stock goes higher, volume trends lower, suggesting that big investors have lost their appetite for the stock.

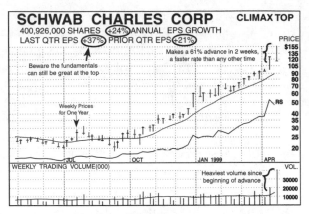

Climax top

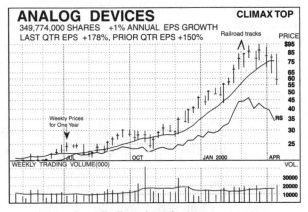

Railroad tracks top

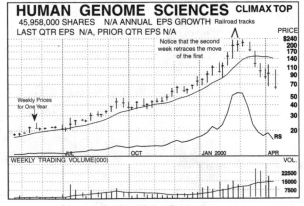

Railroad tracks top

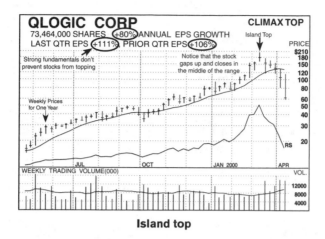

QLOGIC CORP

73,464,000 SHARES (+80%) ANNUAL EPS GROWTH

LAST QTR EPS (+111%) PRIOR QTR EPS (+106%)

CLIMAX TOP

Island Top

Strong fundamentals don't prevent stocks from topping

Notice that the stock gaps up and closes in the middle of the range

Weekly Prices for One Year

PRICE

$210
180
150
120
100
80
60
50
40
30
20

RS

JUL OCT JAN 2000 APR

WEEKLY TRADING VOLUME(000)

VOL.

12000
8000
4000

Island top

2. **Close at/near day's price low.** Tops can also be seen on a stock's daily chart in the form of "arrows" pointing down. That is, the stock will, for several days, close at or near the lows of the daily price ranges, fully retracing the day's advances.

3. **Third/fourth-stage bases.** Sell when your stock makes a new high in price if it's off a third- or fourth-stage base. The third time is seldom a charm in the market. It has become too obvious, and almost everyone sees it. These late-stage base patterns will usually be faulty, appearing more wide and loose.

4. **Signs of a poor rally.** When you see initial heavy selling near the top, the next recovery will follow through weaker in volume, show poor price recovery, or last a shorter number of days. Sell on the second or third day of a poor rally; it may be the last good chance to sell before trend lines and support areas are broken.

5. **Decline from the peak.** After a stock declines 8% or so from its peak, in some cases examination of the previous run-up, the top, and the decline may help determine if the advance may be over or if a normal 8% to 12% correction is in progress. You may occasionally want to sell if a decline from the peak exceeds 12% or 15%.

6. **Poor relative strength.** Poor relative price strength can be a reason for selling. Consider selling when a stock's IBD's Relative Price Strength Rating drops below 70.

7. **Lone Ranger.** Consider selling if there is no confirming price strength by any other important member of the same industry group.

Breaking Support

Breaking support occurs when stocks close the week below established major trend lines as well as other forms of price support.

1. **Long-term uptrend line is broken.** Sell if a stock closes at the end of the week below a major long-term uptrend line or breaks a key price-support area on *overwhelming* volume. An uptrend line should connect at least three intraday or intraweek price lows occurring over a number of months. Trend lines drawn over too short of a time period aren't valid.

2. **Greatest one-day price drop.** If a stock already has made an extended advance and suddenly makes its greatest one-day price drop since the beginning of the move, consider selling if confirmed by other signals.

3. **Falling price/heavy weekly volume.** In some cases, sell if a stock breaks down on the largest weekly volume in its prior several years.

4. **200-day moving average line turns down.** After a prolonged upswing, if a stock's 200-day moving average price line turns down, consider selling the stock. Also, sell on new highs if a stock has a weak base with much of the price work in the lower half of the base or below its 200-day moving average price line.

5. **Living below 10-week moving average.** Consider selling if a stock has had a long advance, then closes below its 10-week moving average and lives for many weeks below that average, unable to rally.

Other Prime Selling Pointers

1. If you cut all losses at 7% or 8%, take a few profits when up 25% or 30%. Compounding three gains like this could give you 100% or more gain. However, don't sell for 25% or 30% gains any market leader with institutional support that's up 20% in only one, two, or three weeks from the pivot buy point on a proper base. Those could be your big leaders and should be held for a potentially greater profit.

2. Big investors must sell when they have buyers to absorb their stock. Therefore, consider selling if a stock runs up and then good news or major publicity (a cover article in *Business Week,* for example) is released.

3. When it's exciting and obvious to everyone that a stock is going higher, sell, because it is too late! Jack Dreyfus said, "Sell when there is an *overabundance* of optimism. When everyone is bubbling over with optimism and running around trying to get everyone else to buy, they are fully invested. At this point, all they can do is talk. They can't push the market up anymore. It takes buying power to do that." Buy when you're scared

to death and others are unsure. Wait until you are happy and tickled to death to sell.

4. In most cases, sell when quarterly earnings percentage increases slow materially for two consecutive quarters.

5. Be careful of selling on bad news or rumors; they may be of temporary influence. Rumors are sometimes started to scare the individual investor, the little fish, out of his or her holdings.

6. Always learn from all of your past selling mistakes. Do your own post-analysis by plotting on charts your past buy and sell points. Study your mistakes carefully and write down additional rules to avoid past mistakes that caused excessive losses.

When to Be Patient and Hold a Stock

Closely related to the decision on when to sell is when to sit tight. Following are some suggestions for doing just that.

Buy growth stocks where you can project a potential price target based on earnings estimates for the next year or two and possible P/E expansion from the stock's original base breakout. Your objective is to buy the best stock with the best earnings at exactly the right time and have the patience to hold it until you have been proven right or wrong. In a few cases you may have to allow 13 weeks after your first purchase before you conclude that a stock that hasn't moved is a dull, faulty selection. This, of course, applies only if the stock did not reach your defensive, loss-cutting sell price first. In a fast-paced market, like the one in 1999, tech stocks that didn't move after several weeks while the general market was moving higher could have been sold earlier, and the money moved into other stocks that were breaking out of sound bases with top fundamentals.

When your hard-earned money is on the line, it's important more than ever to pay attention to the general market and check IBD's "The Big Picture" column, which analyzes the market averages. If you make new purchases when the market averages are under distribution, topping, and starting to reverse direction, you'll have trouble holding the stocks you've bought. (Most breakouts will fail and most stocks will go down, so stay in phase with the general market direction. Don't argue with a declining market.)

After a new purchase, draw a defensive sell line in red on a daily or weekly graph at the precise price level at which you will sell and cut your loss (8% or less below your buy point). In the first 1½ to 2 years of a new bull market, you may want to give stocks this much room on the downside and hold until the price touches the sell line before selling. In some instances, the sell line may be raised but kept below the low of the first normal correction after your initial purchase. If you raise your loss-cutting sell point, don't move it up too close to the current price. This will keep you from being shaken out during any normal weakness. You definitely shouldn't continue to follow a stock up by raising stop-loss orders because you will be forced out near the low of an inevitable, natural correction. Once your stock is 15% or more above your purchase price, you can begin to concentrate on the price where or under what rules you will sell on the way up to nail down your profit.

Any stock that rises close to 20% should never be allowed to drop back into the loss column. If you buy a stock at $50 and it shoots up to $60 (+20%) or more, and you don't take the profit when you have it, there's no intelligent reason to ever let it drop all the way back to $50 or below and create a loss. You may feel embarrassed, ridiculous and not too bright buying at $50, watching it hit $60, and then selling at $50 to $51, but you've already made the mistake of not taking your profit. Avoid making a second mistake and letting it develop into a loss. Remember, one important objective is to keep all of your losses as small as possible.

Also, major advances require time to complete. Don't take profits during the first eight weeks of a move unless the stock gets into serious trouble or is having a two- or three-week "climax" run-up on a stock split. Stocks that show a 20% profit in less than eight weeks should be held through the eight weeks unless they are of poor quality without institutional sponsorship or strong group action. In many cases, dramatic stocks advancing 20% or more in only one to four weeks are the most powerful stocks of all—capable of doubling, tripling, or more. If you own one of these true CAN SLIM™ market leaders, try to hold it through the first couple of times it pulls back in price to, or slightly below, its 10-week moving average price line. Once you have a decent profit, try to hold through the stock's first short-term correction of 10% to 20%. Remember, your objective is not just to be right but to make big money when you are right.

"It never is your thinking that makes big money," said Livermore. "It's the sitting." Investors who can be right and sit tight are rare. It takes time for a stock to make a large gain. The first two years of a new bull market typically provide your best and safest period but require courage, patience, and profitable sitting. If you really know a company and its products well, you'll have the additional confidence required to sit tight through several inevitable but normal corrections. Achieving giant profits in a stock takes time and patience.

You've just read one of the most valuable chapters in this book. If you review it several times and adopt a disciplined profit-and-loss plan for your own investments, it could be worth several thousand times what you paid for this book. You should even make a point to reread this chapter once every year. You can't become a big winner in the market until you learn to be a good seller as well as a good buyer. Those readers who followed these historically proven sell rules during 2000 nailed down most of their substantial gains made in 1998 and 1999. Some made 500% to 1000% or more.

Should You Diversify, Invest for the Long Haul, Buy on Margin, Sell Short, Etc.?

When you decide to participate in the stock market, there are more decisions you are faced with besides which stock to purchase. There's the notion of how you will handle your portfolio, how many stocks you should buy, what types of actions you will take, and what types of investments are better left alone. This and the following chapter will introduce you to the many options and alluring diversions you have at your disposal. Some are very beneficial and worthy of your attention, while many others are overly risky, complicated, or an unnecessary distraction and less-rewarding pursuit. Regardless, it helps to be informed and know as much about the investing business as possible.

How Many Stocks Should You Really Own?

How many times have you been told, "Don't put all your eggs in one basket"? On the surface, it seems like good advice, but my experience is that few people do more than one or two things exceedingly well. Jacks-of-all-trades and masters of none are rarely dramatically successful in any field, including investing.

Would you go to a dentist who did a little engineering or cabinetmaking on the side and who, on weekends, wrote music and worked as an auto mechanic, plumber, and accountant?

This is true of companies as well as people. The best example of diversification in the corporate world is the conglomerate. Most conglomerates don't do well. They're too big, too inefficient, and too spread out in too many businesses to focus effectively and grow profitably.

114

Do you remember when Mobil Oil diversified into the retail business when it bought Montgomery Ward, the struggling national department store chain? It never worked. Neither did Sears Roebuck's move into financial services with the purchases of Dean Witter and Coldwell Banker; nor General Motors's takeover of computer-services giant EDS; nor hundreds of other corporate diversification attempts.

The more you diversify, the less you know about any one area. Many investors overdiversify. The best results are usually achieved through concentration, by putting your eggs in a few baskets you know well and watch very carefully. The more stocks you own, the slower you may be to react and take selling action to raise sufficient cash when a serious bear market begins. You should sell, get off margin, and raise at least some cash when major market tops occur. Otherwise, you will give back most of your profits.

The winning investor's objective should be to have one or two big winners rather than dozens of very small profits. It's much better to have a number of small losses and a few very big profits. Broad diversification is often a hedge for ignorance.

Most people with $20,000 to $100,000 to invest should consider limiting themselves to four or five carefully chosen stocks. Once you own five stocks and a tempting situation comes along that you want to buy, you should muster the discipline to sell off your least attractive investment. If you have $5000 to $20,000 to invest, three stocks might be a reasonable maximum. A $3000 account could be confined to two equities. Keep things manageable. The more stocks you own, the harder it is to keep track of them. Even investors with portfolios over a million dollars need not own more than six or seven well-selected securities.

How to Spread Your Purchases Over Time

It's possible to spread your purchases out over a period of time. When I accumulated a position in Amgen in 1990 and 1991, I bought on numerous days. The buying was spread out and add-on buys were only made when there was a significant gain on earlier buys. If the market price was 20 points over my average cost and a new buy point occurred off a proper base, I bought more.

However, newcomers should be extremely careful in trying this more risky, highly concentrated approach. You've got to do it right, and you positively have to sell or cut back if things don't work as expected.

In a bull market, one way to maneuver your portfolio toward more concentrated positions is to follow up and make one or two smaller additional buys in stocks as soon as they have advanced 2% to 3% above your original or last purchase price. However, don't allow yourself to keep chasing a stock once it's extended too far past a correct buy point. This will also spare you the frustration of owning a stock that goes a lot higher but isn't doing your portfolio much good because you own fewer shares of it than you do of other, less-successful issues. At the same time, sell and eliminate stocks that start to show losses before they become big losses.

Using the follow-up purchasing procedure should keep more of your money in just a few of your best stock investments. No system is perfect, but this one is more realistic than a haphazardly diversified portfolio and has a better chance of achieving important results. Diversification is definitely sound; just don't over do it. Always set a limit on how many stocks you will own and stick to your rules.

Should You Invest for the Long Haul?

If you do decide to concentrate, should you invest for the long haul or trade more frequently? The answer is that the holding period (long or short) is not the main issue. What's critical is buying the right stock—the very best stock—at precisely the right time, then selling it whenever the market or your various sell rules tell you it's time to sell. The time between your buy and your sell could be either short or long. Let your rules and the market decide which one it is. If you do this, some of your winners will be held for three months, some for six months, and a few for one, two, three years or more. Most of your losses will be held for shorter periods, normally from a few weeks to three months. No well-run portfolio should ever have losses that have been carried six months or more. Keep your portfolio clean and in sync with the market. Remember, good gardeners always weed the flower patch and prune weak stems.

Should You Day Trade?

One type of investing I have always discouraged people from doing is day trading, where you buy and sell a given stock on the same day. Most investors lose money doing this. The reason is simple: You're predominantly dealing with minor daily fluctuations that are harder to read than basic trends over a longer time period. Besides, there's generally not enough profit potential in day trading to offset the commissions you generate and the losses that inevitably must occur. Don't try to make money so fast. Rome wasn't built in a day.

There is a new form of day trading that is more like short-term swing trading (buying a stock on the upswing and selling before an inevitable pull-back). It involves buying a stock at its exact pivot buy point off a chart (coming out of a base or price consolidation area) and selling it five or so days later after the breakout. Sometimes pivot points off of patterns such as the cup-with-handle pattern (see Chapter 12) identified on intraday charts of 5-minute intervals can reveal a stock breaking out from an intraday pattern. If done with real skill, this can work for some people, but it requires a lot of time, study, and experience.

Should You Use Margin?

In the first year or two, while you're still learning to invest, it's much safer to operate on a cash basis. It usually takes most new investors at least two to three years to fully gain enough market experience, make several bad decisions, waste time trying to reinvent the wheel, and experiment with unsound beliefs before they are able to make and keep substantial profits. With a few years' experience, a sound plan and a strict set of both buy and sell rules, you might consider buying on "margin" (using borrowed money from your brokerage firm in order to purchase more stock). Generally, margin buying should be done by younger investors who are still working. Their risk is somewhat less because they have more time to prepare for retirement.

The best time to use margin is usually during the first two years of a new bull market. Once you recognize a new bear market, you should get off margin immediately and raise as much cash as possible. You must understand that when the general market declines and your stocks start sinking, you will lose your initial capital twice as fast if you're fully margined than you would if you were invested on a cash basis. This dictates that you absolutely *must* cut all losses quickly and get off margin when major general market deterioration begins. If you speculate in small capitalization or high-tech stocks fully margined, a 50% correction can cause a total loss. This happened to some new investors in 2000 and early 2001.

You don't have to be fully margined all the time. Sometimes you'll have large cash reserves and no margin. At other times, you'll be invested on a cash basis. At still other points, you'll be using a small part of your margin buying power; and in a few instances, when you're making genuine progress in a bull market, you may be fully invested on margin. All of this depends upon the current market situation and your level of experience. I have always used margin and believe it offers a real advantage to an experienced investor who knows how to confine his or her buying to quality market leaders and who has the discipline and common sense to always cut losses short *with no exceptions.*

Your margin interest expense, depending on laws that change constantly, might be tax-deductible. However, in certain periods margin interest rates can become so high that the probability of substantial success may be limited.

Never Answer a Margin Call

If a stock in your margin account collapses in value to a point where your stockbroker asks you to put up money or sell stock, don't put up money; think about selling stock. Nine times out of ten you'll be better off. The marketplace is telling you that you're on the wrong path, you're getting hurt, and things aren't working. So sell and cut back your risk level. Again, why put good money after bad?

To buy on margin you'll need to sign a margin agreement with your broker and have your stock certificates held in "street" (the brokerage company's name). As long as you're dealing with an established New York Stock Exchange firm, this should not create risk for you. In fact, having stock held in street cuts down on the time and paperwork involved in keeping up with stock certificates, dividends, and splits, and it is more common now than ever. In fact, most investors do not have their brokers issue actual stock certificates anymore. This eliminates the time and trouble of taking securities back and forth to your broker each time you make a transaction, and it averts problems and notorious delays with transfer agents, whose job it is to collect, register, transfer, and mail certificates. The itemized account statements that most brokers provide each month are enough for most investors since they serve as complete records for tax purposes.

Should You Sell Short?

I did some research on short selling and wrote a booklet in 1976 (now out of print), but not much has changed on the subject since then. It's still a topic few investors understand and an endeavor at which even fewer succeed, so consider carefully whether it's right for you. More active and seasoned investors might consider limited short selling. However, short selling is far more complicated than simply buying stocks, and most short sellers are run-in and lose money.

What is short selling? Think of short selling as reversing the normal buy and sell process. In short selling, you sell the stock (instead of buy it)—even though you don't own it and therefore must borrow it from your broker—in the hope that it will go down in price (instead of up). If the stock falls in price as you expect, you can "cover your short position" by buying it in the open market at a lower price and pocket the difference as your profit. You would sell short if you think the market is going to drop substantially or that a certain stock is ready to cave in. You sell the stock first, hoping to buy it back later at a lower price.

Sounds easy, right? Wrong. Short selling rarely works out well. Usually the stock you sell short, expecting a colossal price decrease, will do the unexpected and begin to creep up in price. When it goes up, you lose money.

Effective short selling is usually done at the beginning of a new general market decline. This means you have to short based on the behavior of the daily market averages. This in turn requires the ability to (1) interpret the daily Dow, S&P 500, or Nasdaq indices, as discussed in Chapter 7, and (2) select stocks that have had tremendous run-ups and have definitely topped out months earlier. In other words, your timing has to be flawless. You can be right, but if you're too early, you can be forced to cover at a loss.

In selling short you also have to minimize your risk by cutting your losses at 8%. Otherwise, the sky's the limit, and your stock could have an unlimited price increase.

My first rule in short selling: Don't sell short during a bull market. Why fight the overall tide? However, sooner or later you may disregard the advice in this book, try it for yourself, and find out the hard way—the same way one learns that "wet paint" signs usually mean what they say. Save the short selling for bear markets. Your odds will be a little better.

The second rule is: Never sell short a stock with a small number of shares outstanding. It's too easy for market makers and professionals to run up a thinly capitalized stock on you. This is called a "short squeeze" (meaning you could find yourself with a loss and be forced to sell), and it doesn't feel very good when you're in one. It's safer to short stocks trading an average daily volume of 5 to 10 million shares or more.

The two best chart price patterns for selling short are shown on the two accompanying graphs (see page 120).

1. The "head and shoulders" top. The "right shoulder" of the price pattern on the stock chart *must* be slightly lower than the left. The correct time to short is when the third or fourth pullback up in price during the "right shoulder" is about over. (Note the four upward pullbacks in the right shoulder of the Lucent Technologies head and shoulders top.) One of these upward price pullbacks will reach slightly above the peak of a rally a few weeks back. This serves to run-in the premature short sellers. Former big market leaders that have broken badly can have several upward price pullbacks of 20% to 40% from the stock's low point in the right shoulder. The stock's last run-up should cross over its moving average line. In some, but not all, cases the stock will show deceleration in quarterly earnings growth or earnings will have actually turned down. The stock's relative strength line should also be in a clear downtrend for at least 20 weeks up to 34 weeks. In fact, we found through research that

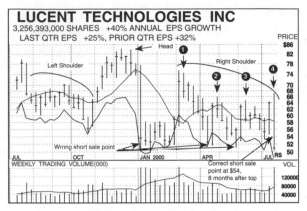

89% decrease in 11 months

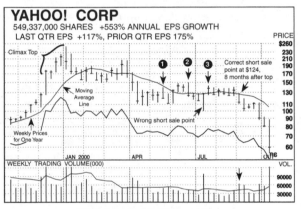

87% decrease in 11 months

almost all sound, short-selling patterns occur five to seven months after a formerly huge market leader has clearly topped. Few people understand this and most short sellers lose money because of premature, faulty, or overly obvious timing.

2. Third- or fourth-stage cup-with-handle or other patterns that have definitely failed after attempted breakouts. The stock should be picking up trading volume and starting to break down below the "handle" area. (See Chapter 12 on chart reading and failed breakouts.)

Typically, short selling must be executed on an "uptick" from the previous trade. (An uptick is any trade that is higher than the previous trade by at least a penny.) Therefore, orders should normally be entered either at the market or at a maximum, with a limit of $0.25 or so *below* the last price. A weak stock could trade down a point or more without having an uptick.

One alternative would be buying put options that don't need an uptick to receive an executed trade. You could also short tracking indices like the QQQs (Nasdaq 100), SMHs (semiconductors), or BBHs (biotech). These also do not require an uptick.

Shorting is done in a margin account, so check with your broker to see if you can borrow the stock you want to sell short. Also, if the stock pays a dividend while you are short, you'll have to pay the dividend to the person who bought the stock you sold. Lesson: Don't short big dividend-paying stocks.

Short selling is treacherous even for professionals, and only the more able and daring should give it a try. One last warning: Don't short an advancing stock just because its price seems too high. You could be "taken to the cleaners."

To summarize, **diversification is good, but don't overdiversify. Concentrate on a smaller list of well-selected stocks, and let the market help determine how long each should be held. Using margin may be okay if you're experienced, but it involves significant extra risk. Lastly, don't sell short unless you know exactly what you're doing. Be sure to use charts for your timing.**

CHAPTER 12

How to Read Charts Like an Expert and Improve Your Stock Picks and Timing

In the world of medicine, X-rays and brain scans are "pictures" doctors study to help diagnose what is going on in the human body. EKGs and ultrasound waves are recorded on paper or TV-like monitors to illustrate what's happening to the human heart.

Similarly, maps are plotted and set to scale to help people understand exactly where they are and how to get where they want to go. Seismic data are traced on charts to help geologists study which structures or patterns seem most likely to contain oil.

In almost every field, there are tools available to help correctly evaluate current conditions and give their users accurate facts. The same is true in investing. Economic indicators are plotted on graphs to assist in their interpretation. A stock's price and volume history are recorded on charts to help determine if a stock is strong, healthy, and under accumulation or if it is weak and behaving abnormally.

Would you allow a doctor to open you up and perform heart surgery if he or she had not utilized the critical necessary tools? Of course not. That's just plain irresponsible. However, many investors do just that when they buy and sell stocks without first consulting stock charts. Just as doctors would be irresponsible not to use X-rays, CAT scans, and EKGs on their patients, investors are just plain foolish if they don't learn to interpret price and volume patterns found on stock charts. If nothing else, charts can tell you when a stock is not acting right and should be sold.

Chart Reading Basics

Charts record the factual price performance of thousands of stocks. Price changes are the result of daily supply and demand in the largest auction marketplace in the world. Investors who train themselves to properly decode price movements on charts have an enormous advantage over those who either refuse to learn or just don't know any better. Would you fly in a plane without instruments or take a long, cross-country trip in your car without a road map? Charts are your investment road map so you always know where you are and where you're headed. In fact, the distinguished economists Milton and Rose Friedman devoted the first 28 pages of their excellent book, *Free to Choose,* to the power of market facts and the unique ability of prices to provide important and accurate information to decision makers.

Chart patterns (or "bases") are simply areas of price correction and consolidation after an earlier price advance. The skill you need to learn in analyzing them is to be able to diagnose whether the price and volume movements are normal or abnormal. Do they signal strength or weakness? Major advances occur off strong, recognizable price patterns (discussed later in this chapter). Failures can always be traced to bases that are faulty or too obvious.

Fortunes are made every year by those who take the time to learn to properly interpret charts. Professionals who don't make use of them are confessing their ignorance of highly valuable measurement and timing mechanisms. To further emphasize this point: I have seen many high-level investment professionals ultimately lose their jobs due to weak performance. Often, their poor records are a direct result of not knowing very much about market action and chart reading. Universities that teach finance or investment courses and dismiss charts as irrelevant or not important demonstrate their complete lack of knowledge and understanding of how the market really works and how the best professionals operate.

As an individual investor, you too need to study and benefit from stock charts. It's not enough to buy a stock simply because it has good fundamental characteristics, like strong earnings and sales. In fact, no *Investor's Business Daily* reader should ever buy a stock based solely on IBD's proprietary *SmartSelect*® Ratings or the yellow-highlighted (top fundamentals) small- or mid-cap stocks shown in IBD's stock tables. A stock's chart must always be checked to determine if the stock is in a proper position to buy, or if it is a sound, leading stock but too far extended in price above a sound basing area and should be avoided.

As the number of investors in the market has increased over recent years, simple price and volume charts have become more readily available. (*Investor's Business Daily* subscribers have free access to 10,000 daily and weekly charts on the Web at investors.com.) Chart books and online chart services help you follow hundreds and even thousands of stocks in a highly organized, time-saving way. Some are more advanced than others, offering both fundamental and technical data in addition to price and volume movement. Subscribe to one of the better chart services, and at your fingertips you'll have valuable information not easily available elsewhere.

History Repeats Itself: Learn to Use Historical Precedents

As mentioned in earlier chapters, our system for selecting winning stocks is based on how the market actually operates, not on my or anyone else's personal opinions or theories. We analyzed the greatest winning stocks of the past to discover they all had seven common characteristics, represented by the acronym CAN SLIM™. We also discovered there were several successful price patterns and consolidation structures that repeated themselves over and over again. In the stock market, history repeats itself. This is because human nature rarely changes. Price patterns of the great stocks of the past can serve as models for future selection. There are several price patterns you'll want to look for when analyzing a stock for purchase. I'll also go over some signals to watch out for that indicate when a price pattern may be faulty and unsound.

The Most Common Chart Pattern: "Cup With Handle"

One of the most important price patterns looks like a cup with a handle when the outline of a cup is viewed from the side. Cup patterns can last from 7 weeks to as long as 65 weeks, but most are three to six months. The usual correction from the absolute peak (top of the cup) to the low point (bottom of the cup) of most of the price patterns varies from around the 12% to 15% range to upwards of 33%. A strong price pattern of any type should always have a clear and definite price uptrend prior to the beginning of its base pattern. You should look for at least a 30% increase in price in the prior uptrend, together with improving relative strength and a very substantial increase in volume at some points in the prior uptrend.

In most, but not all, cases, the bottom part of the cup should be rounded and give the appearance of a "U" rather than a very narrow "V." This characteristic allows the stock time to proceed through a needed natural correction with two or three final little weak spells around the lows of the cup. The

"U" area is important because it scares out or wears out the remaining weak holders and takes other speculators' attention away from the stock. A more solid foundation of strong owners who are much less apt to sell during the next advance is thereby established. The accompanying chart from Daily Graphs Online® shows the daily price and volume movements for Harley Davidson.

It's normal for growth stocks to create cup patterns during intermediate general market declines and correct 1½ to 2½ times the market averages. Your best choices generally are stocks with base patterns that deteriorate the least during an intermediate market decline. Whether you're in a bull or bear market, stock downturns exceeding 2½ times the market averages are usually too wide and loose and must be regarded with suspicion. Dozens of former high-tech leaders, such as JDS Uniphase, formed wide, loose, and deep cup patterns in the second and third quarter of 2000. They were almost all faulty, failure-prone patterns signaling that the stocks should have been avoided when they attempted to break out to new highs.

A very few volatile leaders can plunge as much as 40% or 50% in a bull market. Chart patterns correcting over this amount during bull markets have a higher rate of failure if they try to make new price highs and resume their advance. The reason? A downswing over 50% from a peak to a low means the stock must increase 100% from its low to get back to its old high. Historical research has shown that stocks making new price highs after such huge moves also tend to fail 5% to 15% beyond their breakout prices. Stocks coming straight off the bottom into new highs off cups are also frequently more risky.

Sea Containers was a glowing exception. It descended about 50% during an intermediate decline in the 1975 bull market. It then formed a perfectly shaped cup-with-handle price structure and proceeded to increase 554% in the next 101 weeks. This stock, with its 54% earnings growth rate and its latest quarterly results up 192%, was one of several classic cup-with-handle stocks I presented to Fidelity Research & Management in Boston during a monthly consulting meeting in early June 1975. Upon seeing such big numbers, one of the portfolio managers was instantly interested.

As you can see by this example, some patterns that have corrected 50% to 60% or more coming out of an intermediate bull market decline or a major bear market can succeed. (See the charts for Sea Containers and The Limited.) In these cases, the percent of decline is a function of the severity of the general market and the tremendous extent of the stock's prior price run-up.

For all cup-with-handle patterns illustrated in this book, the following symbols apply: A = left side of cup; B = bottom of cup; C = right side of cup; D = handle.

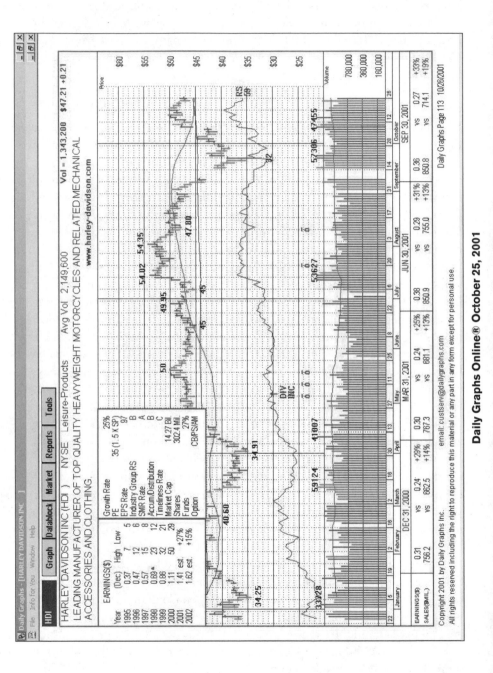

email: custserv@dailygraphs.com

Daily Graphs Online® October 25, 2001

Daily Graphs Page 113 10/26/2001

126

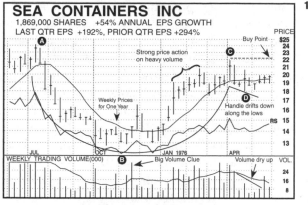

563% increase in 23 months

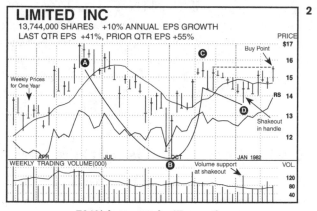

701% increase in 17 months
The cup area is from Ⓐ to Ⓒ in each of these two figures (1 and 2).

Basic Characteristics of Handle Areas

The formation of the handle area generally takes more than one or two weeks and has a downward price drift or shakeout (where the price drops below a prior low point in the handle made a few weeks earlier) near the end of its down-drifting price movement. Volume will dry up noticeably near the lows in the handle's price pullback phase.

There are a few exceptions: Cups without handles have a somewhat higher failure rate, although many stocks do successfully advance without forming a handle. Also, some of the more volatile technology names in 1999 formed handles of only one or two weeks before they began their major price advances.

When handles do occur, they must always form in the upper half of the overall base structure, as measured from the absolute peak of the entire base to the absolute low of the cup. The handle should also be above the stock's 200-day moving average price line. Handles forming in the lower half of an overall base or completely below the stock's 200-day line are weak and failure-prone. Demand up to that point has not been strong enough to enable the stock to recover more than half its prior decline.

Additionally, handles that consistently wedge up (drift upward along their price lows or just go straight sideways along their lows rather than drift down) have a much higher probability of failing when they break out to new highs. This upward-wedging behavior along low points in the handle doesn't let the stock undergo the needed shakeout or sharp price pullback after having advanced from the low of the base into the upper half of the pattern. This high-risk trait tends to occur in third- or fourth-stage bases, in laggard stock bases, or in very active market leaders that become too widely followed and therefore too obvious. You should beware of wedging handles.

A price drop in a proper handle should be contained within 10% to 15% of its peak unless the stock forms a very large cup, as in the unusual case of Sea Containers in 1975. Downturns in handles exceeding this percentage during bull markets look wide and erratic and are, in most cases, improper, and risky. However, if you are in a bear market bottom's last shakeout area, the unusual general market weakness will cause some handle areas to quickly decline around 20% to 30%, but the price pattern can still be sound.

Constructive Patterns Have Tight Price Areas

There should also be some tight areas in the price patterns of stocks under accumulation. On a weekly chart, tightness is defined as small price variations from high to low for the week, with several consecutive weeks' prices closing unchanged or remarkably near the previous week's close. If every week in the base pattern has a wide spread from each week's high to low point, it's been constantly in the market's eye and will frequently not work when it breaks out. However, amateur chartists will not notice the difference and the stock can run up 5% to 15%—drawing in less discriminating traders—before it breaks badly and fails.

Find Pivot Points and Watch "Volume Percent Change"

When a stock forms a proper cup-with-handle chart pattern and then charges through an upside buy point, which Jesse Livermore referred to as the "pivot point" or "line of least resistance," the day's volume should increase at least 50% above normal. It's not uncommon for new market leaders to show volume spikes up 500% to 1000% during major breakouts.

In almost all cases, it is professional buying that causes the big, above-average volume increases in the better-priced, better-quality stocks at pivot breakouts. Ninety-five percent of the general public is usually afraid to buy at such points because it's scary and seems risky and rather absurd to buy stocks at their highest prices. The object isn't to buy at the cheapest price or near the low but to begin buying at exactly the right time, when your chances are greatest for success. This means you have to learn to wait for a stock to move up and trade at your buy point before making an initial commitment. If you work and cannot watch the market constantly, small quote devices or quotes available on cell phones and Web sites will help you stay on top of potential breakout points.

The winning individual investor waits to buy at these precise pivot points. This is where the real move starts and all the exciting action begins. If you try to buy before this point, you might be premature. In many cases the stock will never get to its breakout point, leaving you with a stock that has stalled or may actually decrease in price. You want a stock to prove its strength to you before you invest in it. Also, if you buy more than 5% to 10% past the precise buy point, you are buying late and more than likely, you will get caught in the next price correction. Your automatic 8% loss-cutting rule will force you to sell because the stock was extended in price and didn't have enough room to go through a perfectly normal minor correction.

Pivot buy points in correct chart base patterns are not necessarily at a stock's old high. Most occur 5% to 10% below the former peak. The peak price in the handle area is where most buy points occur, and this is almost always somewhat below the base's actual high point. This is an important point to remember. If you wait for an actual new high price you often buy too late. Sometimes you can get a slight head start by drawing a down trendline across certain peak points in the stock's price pattern (including the handle area) and begin your purchase as the trendline is broken. However, you have to be right in your chart and stock analysis to get away with this.

Look for Volume Dry-Ups Near Lows of a Price Pattern

Nearly all proper bases will show a dramatic dry-up in volume for one or two weeks along the very low of the base pattern and in the low area of the handle. This means that all of the selling has been exhausted and there is no more stock coming into the marketplace. Healthy stocks under accumulation almost always show this symptom. The combination of tightness in prices (daily or weekly price closes being very near each other) and dried-up volume is generally quite constructive.

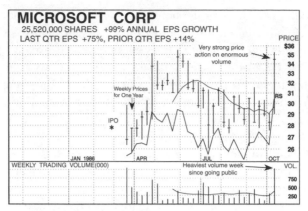

MICROSOFT CORP
25,520,000 SHARES +99% ANNUAL EPS GROWTH
LAST QTR EPS +75%, PRIOR QTR EPS +14%

Very strong price action on enormous volume

Weekly Prices for One Year

IPO
*

JAN 1986   APR   JUL   OCT
WEEKLY TRADING VOLUME(000)

Heaviest volume week since going public

PRICE $36 35 34 33 32 31 30 29 28 27 26

VOL. 750 500 250

Big volume clue (350% increase in 12 months)

Big Volume Clues Are Valuable

Another valuable clue to the trained chart reader is the occurrence of big daily and weekly volume spikes. Microsoft is an example of an outstanding stock that flashed heavy accumulation just before a huge run-up (see chart).

Weeks of advancing prices on heavy volume, followed in other weeks by extreme volume dry-ups, are also a very constructive sign. If you use a daily chart service in conjunction with weekly graphs, you'll be able to see unusual trading activity that sometimes happens on only one day.

Volume is a remarkable subject worthy of careful study. It can help you recognize if a stock is under accumulation (institutional buying) or distribution (institutional selling). Once you acquire this skill, you won't have to rely on the personal opinions of analysts and experts. Big volume at key points is indispensable.

Volume is your best measure of supply and demand and institutional sponsorship—two vital ingredients in successful stock analysis. Learn how to use charts to time your purchases correctly. It's simply too costly making buys at the wrong time, or worse, buying stocks that are not under accumulation or have unsound, faulty price patterns.

The next time you consider buying a stock, check its weekly volume. It's a constructive sign when the number of weeks the stock closes up in price on above average weekly volume outnumber the number of weeks it closes down in price on above average volume while still in its chart base.

The Value of Market Corrections

Price patterns are almost always (80% of the time) created during periods of market corrections, so you should never get discouraged and give up on the stock market's potential during intermediate term sell-offs or bear markets.

Bear markets can last as short as three or six months or, in more rare cases, up to two years. If you carefully followed the sell rules in this book, you will have sold and nailed down most of your profits, cut short any losses, raised significant cash, and moved off margin.

Even if you sold out completely and moved entirely to cash, you never want to throw in the towel because bear markets create new bases on new stocks that could be the next cycle's 1000% winners. You don't foolishly give up while the greatest opportunities of a lifetime are setting up and just around the corner.

A bear market is the time to do a postanalysis of prior decisions. Plot on daily or weekly charts exactly where you bought and sold all of your stocks in the past year. Study your decisions and write out some new rules to avoid the mistakes you made in the past cycle. Then study several of the biggest winners you missed or mishandled. Develop some rules to make sure you buy real leaders in the next bull market cycle. They will be there, and this is the time to be watching them as they begin to form bases. The question is whether you will be there with a plan to capitalize on them.

Other Price Patterns to Look for:

How to Spot a "Saucer-With-Handle" Price Pattern

A saucer with handle is a price pattern similar to the cup with handle except that the "saucer" part tends to stretch out over a longer period of time, making the pattern more shallow. If the names "cup with handle" or "saucer with handle" sound unusual, consider that for years you have recognized and called certain constellations "the big and little dipper."

The General Electric chart below shows an example of a saucer-with-handle price structure.

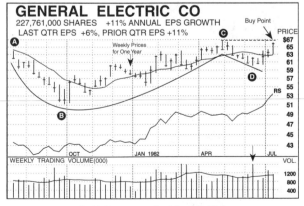

74% increase in 11 months

Recognizing a "Double-Bottom" Price Pattern

A double-bottom price pattern looks like the letter "W." This pattern does not occur as often as the cup with handle. It is usually important that the second bottom of the "W" match the price level (low) of the first bottom or, as in most cases, undercut it by one or two points, thereby creating a shake-out of weaker investors.

Double bottoms may also have handles, although this is not essential. Depth and horizontal length are similar to that of the cup formation. In theory, a double bottom may not be quite as powerful as a proper cup with handle, since the stock had to fall back twice to its low point to make the double bottom. The pivot buy point in a double bottom is located on the top right side of the "W" where the stock is coming up after the second leg down. The pivot point should be equal in price to the top of the middle peak of the "W." If the double bottom has a handle, then the peak price of the handle is the pivot buy point. See the accompanying charts for Dome Petroleum, Texas Oil & Gas, Price Co., and Cisco Systems for outstanding examples of double-bottom price patterns found during 1977, 1978, 1982, and 1990. The buy points are $42, $32, $20, and $32.

For double-bottom patterns (see pages 132–133), the following symbols apply: A = beginning of base; B = bottom of first leg; C = middle of "W" which sets the buy point; D = bottom of second leg. If the double-bottom pattern has a handle, then E = top of the handle (sets the buy point) and F = bottom of the handle.

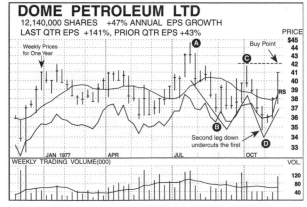

Double-bottom price pattern. 918% increase in 44 months.

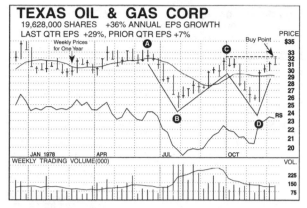

Double-bottom price pattern. 532% increase in 23 months.

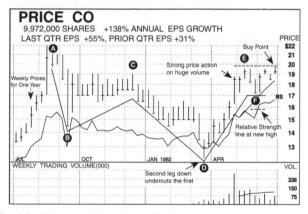

Double-bottom price pattern. 110% increase in 11 months.

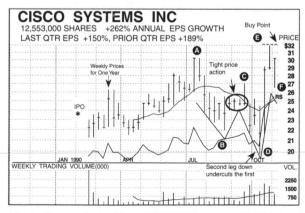

Double-bottom price pattern. 74445% increase in 113 months.

Definition of a "Flat-Base" Price Structure

A flat base is another rewarding price structure. It is usually a second-stage base that occurs after a stock has advanced 20% or more off a cup with han-

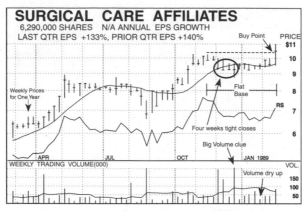

Flat-base price pattern. 1833% increse in 33 months.

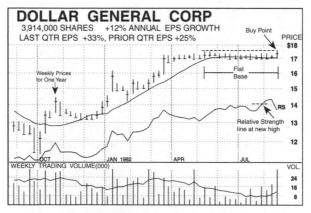

Flat-base price pattern. 705% increase in 34 months.

dle, saucer with handle, or double bottom. The flat base moves straight sideways in a fairly tight price range for at least five or six weeks, and it does not correct more than 10% to 15%. Standard Oil of Ohio in May 1979, Smith-Kline in March 1978, Dollar General in 1982, and Surgical Care Affiliates in 1989 are good examples of flat bases (see some of these in the above charts). Pep Boys in March 1981 formed a longer flat base. If you miss a stock's initial breakout from a cup with handle, you should keep your eye on it. In time it may form a flat base and give you another opportunity to buy.

High, Tight Flags Are Rare

A high, tight flag price pattern is rare and occurs in no more than one or two stocks during a bull market. It begins by moving approximately 100% to 120% in a very short period of time (four to eight weeks) and then corrects sideways, usually in three, four, or five weeks, no more than 10% to 20%. This is the strongest of patterns, but it's also very risky and difficult to interpret correctly. Many stocks can skyrocket 200% or more off this formation. (See the charts for E. L. Bruce, June 1958; Certain-teed, January 1961; Syntex, July 1963; Rollins, July 1964; Emulex, October 1999; and Qualcomm, December 1999.)

The E. L. Bruce pattern in the second quarter of 1958, at around $50, provided a perfect chart pattern precedent for the Certain-teed advance that occurred in 1961. Certain-teed in turn became the chart model I used to buy my first big winner, Syntex, in July 1963.

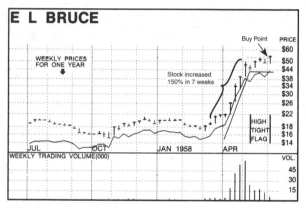

High-tight flag price pattern. Over 200% increase in 2 months.

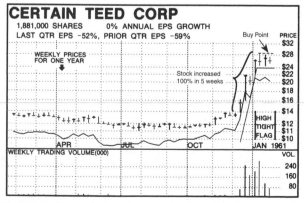

High-tight flag price pattern. 482% increase in 12 months.

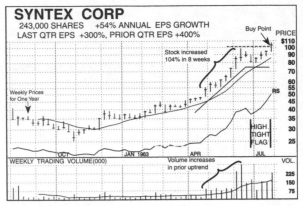

High-tight flag price pattern. 482% increase in 6 months.

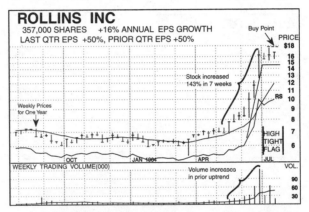

High-tight flag price pattern. 89% increase in 2 months.

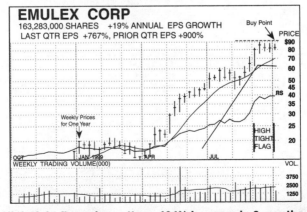

High-tight flag price pattern. 404% increase in 6 months.

What Is a Base on Top of a Base?

During the latter stages of a bear market, a seemingly negative condition flags what may be aggressive new leadership in the new bull phase. I call this unusual case a "base on top of a base."

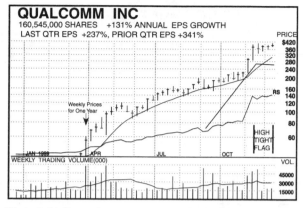

High-tight flag price pattern. 96% increase in 1 month.

What happens is that a powerful stock breaks out of its base and advances but is unable to increase a normal 20% to 30% because the general market begins another leg down. The stock, therefore, pulls back in price and builds a second back-and-forth price consolidation area just on top of its previous base while the general market averages keep making new lows.

When the bearish phase in the overall market ends, as it always does, this stock is more apt to be one of the first to emerge at a new high en route to a huge gain. It's like a spring being held down by the pressure of a heavy object. Once the object (in this case, a bear market) is removed, the spring is free to do what it wanted to do all along. This is another example of why it is foolhardy to get upset and emotional with the market or lose your confidence. The next big race could be just a few months away.

Two of our institutional services firm's best buy recommendations in 1978 (M/A-Com and Boeing) showed base-on-top-of-a-base patterns. One advanced 180%; the other 950%. Ascend Communications and Oracle (see graphs on the next page) were other examples of a base on top of a base. After breaking out at the bear market bottom of December 1994, Ascend Communications bolted almost 1500% in 17 months. Oracle repeated the same base-on-base pattern in October 1999 and zoomed nearly 300%.

Ascending Bases

Ascending bases, like flat bases, occur midway along a move up after a stock has broken out of a cup-with-handle or double-bottom base. It has three pullbacks from 10% to 20% with each low point during the sell-off in price being higher than the preceding, which is why I call it an ascending base. Each of the pullbacks usually occurs due to the general market declining at that time. (See points 1, 2, and 3 on the charts for Redman Industries and America Online on page 139.)

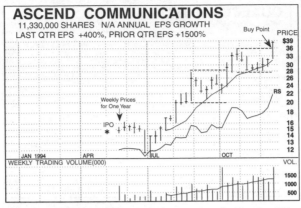

Base on top of a base. 1496% increase in 17 months.

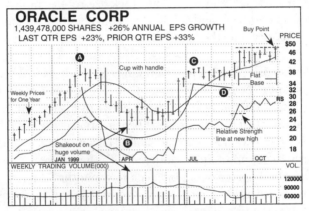

Base on top of a base. 274% increase in 5 months.

Boeing formed a 13-week ascending base in the second quarter of 1954 and afterward doubled in price. Redman Industries, a builder of mobile homes, had an 11-week ascending base in the first quarter of 1968 and proceeded to increase 500% in just 37 weeks. America Online created the same type of base in the first quarter of 1999 and resumed what turned out to be a 500% run-up from the breakout of a 14-week cup with handle in October 1998. So you see, history does repeat itself. The more historical patterns you know and come to recognize, the more money you should be able to make in the market. (Chart examples E-1 and E-2 are on the next page.)

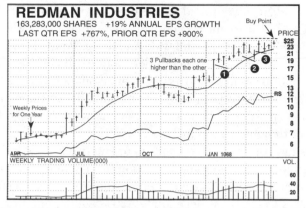

Ascending base price pattern. 503% increase in 9 months.

Ascending base price pattern. 91% increase in 1 month.

Wide-and-Loose Price Structures Are "Failure Prone"

Wide and loose looking charts usually fail but can tighten up later.

New England Nuclear and Houston Oil & Minerals are two cases of stocks that tightened up following wide, loose, and erratic price movements. I cite these two examples because I missed both of them at the time. It's always wise to review big winners you missed to find out why you didn't recognize them when they were exactly right and ready to soar.

New England Nuclear formed a wide, loose, and faulty price pattern that looked like a double bottom from points A, B, C, D, and E (see the chart on page 141). It declined about 40% from the beginning at point A to point D. That was excessive, and it took too much time—almost six months—to hit bottom. Note the additional clue provided by the declining trend of its relative strength line (RS) throughout the faulty pattern. Buying at point E was wrong. The handle was also too short and did not drift down to create a shakeout. It wedged up along its low points.

New England Nuclear formed a second base from points E to F to G, but if you tried to buy at point G, you were wrong again. It was premature because the price pattern was still wide and loose. Points E to F saw a prolonged decline with relative strength deteriorating badly. The rise straight up from the bottom at point F to its bogus breakout point G was too fast and erratic, covering only three months. Three months of improving relative strength versus the prior 17 months of decline wasn't enough to turn the previous poor trend into a positive one.

The stock then declined from points G to H to form what appeared to be a handle area for the possible cup formation from points E to F to G. If you bought at point I on the breakout attempt, the stock failed again. Reason: the handle was too loose; it degenerated 20%. However, after failing that time, the stock at last tightened up its price structure from points I to J to K, and 15 weeks later, at point K, broke out of a tight, sound base and nearly tripled in price afterwards. Note the stock's strong uptrend and materially improved relative strength line for 11 months from point K back to point F.

There really is a right time and a wrong time to buy a stock, but understanding the difference requires some study. It isn't easy at first, but it can be very rewarding.

Some faulty, wide-and-loose patterns that faked people into buying during the prolonged bear market that began in March 2000: Veritas Software on October 20, 2000; Anaren Microwave on December 28, 2000; and Comverse Technology on January 24, 2001 (see page 142).

Houston Oil & Minerals mentioned above is an even more dramatic example of the handle correction from points F to G being a wide-and-loose pattern that later tightened up into a constructive price formation (see the accompanying chart). A to B to C was extremely wide, loose, and erratic (percent decline is too much). B to C was straight up from the bottom without any pullback in price. Points C and D were false attempts to break out of a faulty price pattern, and so was point H, which tried to break out of a wide and loose cup with handle. Afterward, a tight nine-week base formed from points H to I to J. (Note the extreme volume dry-up along the December 1975 lows—see page 143.)

An alert stockbroker in Hartford, Connecticut, called this structure to my attention. However, I'd been so conditioned by the two prior years of poor price patterns and less-than-desirable earnings that my mind was slow to change when the stock suddenly altered its behavior in only nine weeks. I was also probably intimidated by the tremendous price increase that occurred in Houston Oil in the earlier 1973 bull market (see page 143). This proves that opinions are frequently wrong, but markets seldom are.

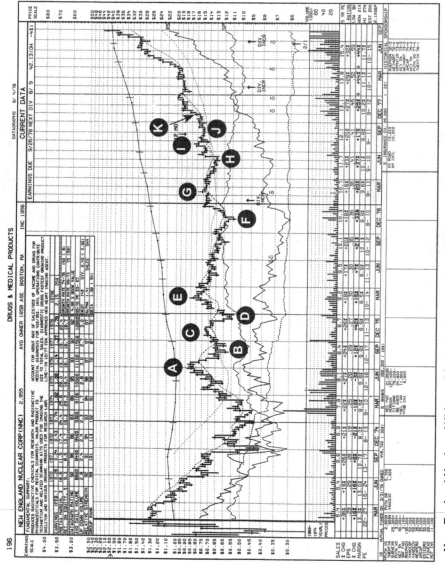

New England Nuclear. Wide-and-loose price structure tightening into a constrictive price formation.

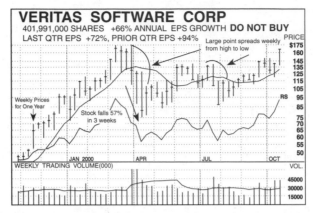

Wide and loose faulty pattern. 90% decrease in 11 months.

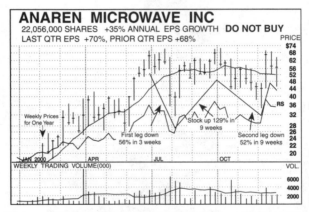

Wide and loose faulty pattern. 83% decrease in 3 months.

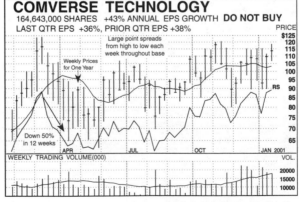

Wide and loose faulty pattern. 87% decrease in 9 months.

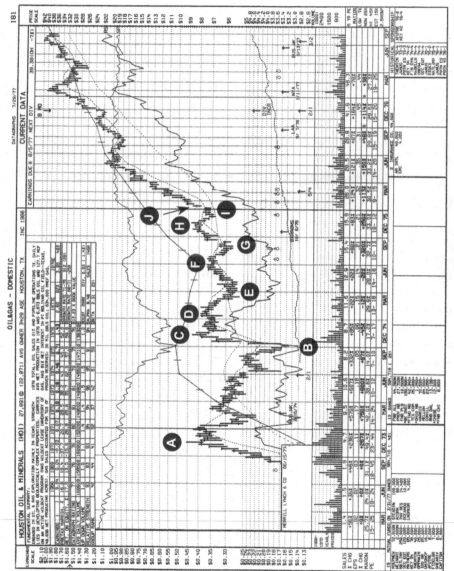

Wide-and-loose price structure tightening into a constructive price formation.

143

It also points out a very important principle. It takes time for all of us to change opinions that we have built up for a substantial period. In this instance, the current quarterly earnings turning up 357% after three down quarters didn't even change my incorrect bearish view of the stock to a bullish one. The right buy point was in January 1976.

Peoplesoft in August 1994 repeated the New England Nuclear and Houston Oil patterns. Peoplesoft failed in its breakout attempt from a wide, loose, wedging-upward pattern in September 1993. It then failed a second time in its breakout attempt in March 1994, when its handle area formed in the lower half of its cup-with-handle pattern. Finally, when the chart pattern and general market was right, it skyrocketed starting in August 1994.

Detecting Faulty Price Patterns and Base Structures

Unfortunately, there has not been any original or thorough research done on price pattern analysis in the last 70 years. In 1930, Richard Schabacker, a financial editor of *Forbes,* wrote a book, *Stock Market Theory and Practice.* In it he discussed many patterns, such as triangles, coils, and pennants. Our detailed model-building and investigations of price structure over the years have shown these patterns to be unreliable and risky. They probably worked in the latter part of the "Roaring '20s," when most stocks ran up in a wild, climactic frenzy. Something similar happened in 1999 and the first quarter of 2000 when many loose faulty patterns seemed to work. These periods were like the Dutch tulip bulb craze of the seventeenth century during which rampant speculation caused variations of tulip bulbs to skyrocket to astronomical prices.

Our studies show that, with the exception of high, tight flags, which are extremely rare and hard to interpret, and flat bases of five or six weeks, the most reliable base patterns must have a minimum of seven to eight weeks of price consolidation. Most coils, triangles, and pennants are simply weak foundations without sufficient time or price correction to become proper bases. One-, two-, three-, and four-week bases are very risky. In virtually all cases, they should be avoided.

In 1948 John McGee and Robert D. Edwards wrote *Technical Analysis of Stock Trends.* The book discusses many of the same faulty patterns presented in Schabacker's earlier book.

In 1962, William Jiler wrote an easy-to-read book, *How Charts Can Help You in the Stock Market,* which explains many of the correct principles behind technical analysis. However, it too seems to have continued the display and discussion of certain failure-prone patterns of the pre-Depression era.

Triple bottoms and head-and-shoulder bottoms are also patterns widely mentioned in several books on technical analysis. We have found these to be weaker patterns as well. A head-and-shoulders bottom may succeed in a few instances, but it has no strong prior uptrend, which is essential for most powerful market leaders.

However, when it comes to signifying a top in a stock, head-and-shoulder top patterns are one of the more reliable. Be careful: With just a little knowledge of charts, you can misinterpret what is a correct head-and-shoulders top. Many pros don't interpret the pattern properly. The right (second) shoulder must be slightly below the left shoulder (see the chart for Alexander & Alex).

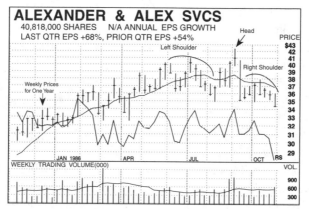

Head-and-shoulder top price pattern. 53% decrease in 13 months.

A triple bottom is a looser, weaker, and less-attractive base pattern than a double bottom. The reason is that the stock corrects and falls back sharply to its absolute low three times rather than twice, as with a double bottom, or one time, as in the strong cup with handle. As mentioned earlier, a cup with a wedging handle is also usually a faulty, failure-prone pattern, as you can see in the Global Crossing Ltd. Chart example. A competent chart reader would have avoided or sold Global Crossing, which later became bankrupt.

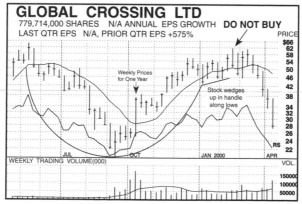

Wedging handle failure-prone pattern. 99% decrease in 20 months from end of handle.

How to Use Relative Price Strength Correctly

Many fundamentalist securities analysts think technical analysis means buying stocks with the strongest relative price strength. Others think technical research refers only to the buying of high "momentum" stocks. Both are incorrect.

It's not enough to just buy stocks that show the highest relative price strength on some list of best performers. You should buy stocks that are performing better than the general market just as they are beginning to emerge from sound base-building periods. The time to sell is when the stock advances rapidly, is extended materially from its base, and is showing extremely high relative price strength. To recognize the difference, you have to use daily or weekly charts.

What Is Overhead Supply?

A critically important concept to learn in analyzing price movements is the principle of overhead supply. Overhead supply is when there are areas of price resistance in a stock as it moves up after experiencing a downtrend. These areas of resistance represent prior purchases of stock and serve to limit and frustrate a stock's upward movement because the investors who made these purchases are motivated to sell when the price returns to their entry point. (See the chart for At Home.) This is so they can end the pain by selling at breakeven. For example, if a stock advances from $25 to $40, then declines back to $30, most of the people who bought late in the upper $30s and at $40 will have a loss in the stock unless they were quick to sell and cut their loss (which most people don't do). Therefore, if the stock later climbs

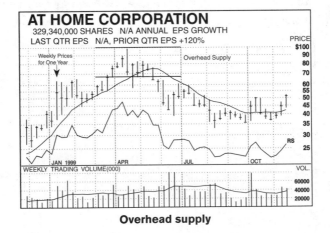

Overhead supply

back to the high $30s or $40 area, all the investors that had losses can now get out and break even.

These are the holders that made the promise to themselves: "If I can just get out even, I will sell." Human nature is pretty consistent. So it is normal that a number of these people will sell when they see a chance to get their money back after having been down a significant amount.

Good chartists know how to recognize the price areas that represent heavy areas of overhead supply. They will never make the fatal mistake of buying a stock that has a large recent amount of overhead supply. This is a serious mistake many analysts concerned solely with fundamentals sometimes make.

However, a stock that's able to fight its way through its overhead supply may be safer to buy, even though the price is a little higher. After all, it has proved to have sufficient demand to absorb and move past the level of resistance. Supply areas more than two years old create less resistance. Of course, a stock that has just broken out into new high ground for the first time has no overhead supply to contend with, which adds to its appeal.

Excellent Opportunities in Unfamiliar, Newer Stocks

Alert investors should have a way of keeping track of all the new stock issues that have emerged over the last one to eight years. This is important because some of these newer and younger companies will be among the most stunning performers of the next year or two. The Nasdaq section in your newspaper will help you stay current.

Some new issues move up a small amount and then retreat to new price lows during a bear market. This creates a rather unimpressive record. When the next bull market begins, a few of these forgotten newcomers will sneak back up unnoticed, form base patterns, and suddenly take off and double or triple in price.

Most investors miss these outstanding price moves because they occur in new names that are largely unknown to most people. A charting service can help you spot these unfamiliar, newer companies, but make sure your service follows a large number of stocks (not just one or two thousand.)

Successful, young, high-tech growth stocks tend to enjoy their fastest earnings growth between their fifth and tenth years in business, so keep an eye on them during their early growth periods.

To summarize, improve your stock selection by learning to read and use charts; they provide a gold mine of information. While it will take some time and study on your part to become good at it, interpreting them is easier than you think.

⬤A Loud Warning to the Wise About Bear Markets!!!

Let me offer one last bit of judicious guidance. If you are new to the stock market or the historically tested and proven strategies outlined in this book, or more importantly, you are reading this book for the first time near the beginning or middle of a bear market, do not expect the presumed buy patterns to work. Most will definitely be defective. **You absolutely do not buy breakouts during a bear market.**

The price patterns will be too deep, wide, and loose in appearance compared to earlier patterns. They will be third- and fourth-stage bases; have wedging or loose, sloppy handles; have handles in the lower half of the base; or show narrow "V" formations moving straight up from the bottom of a base into new highs, without any handle forming. Some patterns may show laggard stocks with declining relative strength lines and price patterns with too much adverse volume activity or every week's price spread wide.

It isn't that bases, breakouts, or the method isn't working anymore; it's that the timing and the stocks are simply all wrong. The price and volume patterns are phony, faulty, and unsound. The general market is turning negative. It is selling time. Be patient, keep studying, and be 100% prepared. Later, at the least expected time, when all the news is terrible, winter will ultimately pass and a great new bull market will suddenly spring to life. The practical techniques and proven disciplines discussed here should work for you for many, many future economic cycles.

· PART ·
III

Investing Like a Professional

Models of the Greatest Stock Market Winners: 1952–2001

Throughout this book I've made mention of the greatest winning stocks of the past. Now that you've been introduced to the CAN SLIM™ method of investing, you should know that a number of these same companies were actually recommended to clients through our institutional services firm or we bought them ourselves.

It's possible to make your dreams come true using the CAN SLIM™ method. You may have heard or read about the many individuals who have changed their lives using this book. It really happens, and it can happen to you, no matter how large or small your account.

This chapter will introduce you to a few early examples of success using this system. There are many, many others. In addition, it will also introduce to you some of the greatest winning stocks since 1952. Study this chapter closely; you'll find that these patterns repeat over and over again throughout time. If you learn to recognize them early, you could get in on some future big profits.

Tracing the Growth of a Small Account

In 1961, with $10 from each of my classmates at Harvard's Program for Management Development (PMD), we started the first PMD Fund with the grand total of $850. It was mostly for fun. Each classmate began with one $10 share in the fund.

Marshall Wolf, then with National Newark & Essex Bank, and later an executive vice president at Midatlantic National Bank, had the thankless job of secretary-treasurer, keeping the records, informing the gang, and filing and paying taxes each year. I got the easy job of managing the money.

It's an interesting account to study because it proves you can start very small and still win the game if you stick with sound methods and give yourself plenty of time. On September 16, 1986 (some 25 years later), after all prior taxes were paid, the account was worth $51,653.34. The profit, in other words, was more than $50,000 and each share was worth $518. That is nearly a 50-fold after-tax gain.

The actual buy and sell records in the accompanying table illustrate in vivid detail the execution of the basic investment methods we have discussed up to this point.

Note that while there were about 20 successful transactions through 1964, there were also 20 losing transactions. However, the average profit was around 20% while the average loss was about 7%. If losses had not been cut in Standard Kollsman, Brunswick, and a few others, later severe price drops would have caused much larger losses. This small cash account concentrated in only one or two stocks at a time. Follow-up buys were generally made if the security moved up in price.

The account made no progress in 1962, a bad market year, but was already up 139% by June 6, 1963, *before* the first Syntex buy was made. By the end of 1963, the gain had swelled to 474% on the original $850 investment.

The year 1964 was lackluster. Worthwhile profits were made in 1965, 1966, and 1967, though nothing like 1963, which was a very unusual year. I won't bore you with 20 pages of stock transactions. Let me just say that the next 10 years showed further progress, despite losses in 1969 and 1974.

Another period of interesting progress started in 1978 with the purchase of Dome Petroleum. All decisions beginning with Dome are shown in the next table.

Dome offers an extremely valuable lesson on why most stocks sooner or later have to be sold. Bought, as you can see, at $77 and sold near $98, it eventually fell below $2! History repeated itself in 2000 and 2001 as many Internet big winners like CMGI dropped from $165 to $1. Note also that the account was worn out of Pic'n'Save on July 6, 1982, at $15, but we bought it back at $18 and $19, though at a higher price, and made a large gain by doing so.

The U.S. Investing Championship

Another engaging example of the CAN SLIM™ principles being properly applied is the story of one of our associates, Lee Freestone. Lee participated in the U.S. Investing Championship in 1991, when he was just

Shares	Stock	Date Bought	Price Paid	Date Sold	Price Sold	Gain or Loss
5	Bristol Myers	1/1/61	64.88	2/21/61	78.75	
7	Bristol Myers	1/4/61	67.25	2/21/61	78.75	149.87
18	Brunswick	2/21/61	53.75	3/10/61	68.00	223.35
29	Certain-teed	3/10/61	42.13	4/13/61	39.75	(104.30)
24	Stan. Kollsman	4/13/61	45.75	6/27/61	45.00	
	Stan. Kollsman		45.75	6/27/61	43.38	(82.66)
25	Endevco Corp.	4/26/61	13.00	5/25/61	17.50	102.96
10	Lockheed	6/13/61	44.88			
10	Lockheed	6/27/61	46.38			
5	Lockheed	7/25/61	48.50	8/29/61	48.25	7.55
6	Crown Cork	9/1/61	108.50			
5	Crown Cork	9/1/61	110.00	10/2/61	103.25	(100.52)
20	Brunswick	10/11/61	64.25	10/24/61	58.13	
	Brunswick			11/1/61	54.00	223.49
3	Polaroid	10/31/61	206.75			
3	Polaroid	11/1/61	209.00	2/21/61	180.00	(191.68)
30	Korvette	2/28/62	41.00	3/30/62	47.88	
30	Korvette	4/5/62	52.25	4/13/62	54.25	183.96
10	Crown Cork	5/28/62	99.25	5/22/62	97.25	(50.48)
30	Lockheed	6/15/62	41.25	6/2/62	39.75	(81.02)
5	Xerox	6/20/62	104.75			
5	Xerox	6/25/62	105.25	7/12/62	127.13	190.30
10	Homestake Mining	7/16/62	59.50	7/24/62	54.25	
10	Homestake Mining	7/16/62	58.75	7/24/62	54.25	(87.66)
10	Polaroid	7/31/62	105.00	7/19/62	97.88	(101.86)
30	Korvette (Short)	10/24/62	21.88	9/28/62	35.13	385.94
10	Chrysler	10/30/62	59.00			
15	Chrysler	11/1/62	60.34	1/15/63	83.63	545.40
15	RCA	1/16/63	62.50			
15	RCA	1/18/63	65.25	2/28/63	62.00	(111.02)
25	Coastal States	2/28/63	31.38	3/14/63	32.13	(8.46)
14	Chrysler	2/27/63	92.50			
8	Chrysler	3/14/63	93.00	4/16/63	109.13	300.03
25	Control Data	4/23/63	44.13	5/13/63	49.63	102.55
25	Intl. Minerals	5/6/63	52.88	5/15/63	54.88	11.47
22	Chrysler	5/13/63	54.38	6/10/63	61.75	
25	Chrysler	5/17/63	55.63	6/10/63	61.75	211.30
15	Syntex	6/11/63	89.25	9/23/63	146.13	
10	Syntex	8/7/63	114.50	9/23/63	146.13	
15	Syntex	10/9/63	149.13	10/22/63	225.00	2,975.71
15	Control Data	7/9/63	69.13	7/17/63	67.25	(59.62)
15	RCA	1/8/64	102.02	2/11/64	105.68	53.98
15	RCA	1/9/64	106.19	2/11/64	105.68	(8.49)
15	RCA	1/10/64	107.33	2/11/64	105.68	(25.54)
50	Pan Am	2/17/64	65.53	3/9/64	68.00	123.29
25	McDonnel Air	3/11/64	62.17	5/11/64	60.00	(54.26)
25	Chrysler	3/12/64	47.88	4/7/64	43.87	(100.35)
25	Chrysler	3/13/64	49.27	4/7/64	43.87	(135.06)
30	Chrysler	3/17/64	50.21	4/30/64	46.08	(123.83)
30	Consol. Cigar	3/19/64	49.35	4/20/64	47.25	(62.87)
25	Greyhound	4/7/64	55.47	5/1/64	57.63	53.88
20	Greyhound	4/8/64	58.55	5/1/64	57.63	(18.52)
15	Xerox	4/21/64	95.23	5/1/64	93.00	(33.41)
15	Xerox	4/29/64	98.53	5/5/64	95.00	(52.95)
30	Chrysler	5/13/64	52.14	7/8/64	48.75	(101.69)
50	Chrysler	5/13/64	52.32	6/11/64	46.50	(290.79)
50	Chrysler	5/13/64	52.34	6/30/64	49.00	(166.82)
50	Cerro Corp.	7/2/64	49.00	9/16/64	56.00	349.51
20	Cerro Corp.	7/6/64	50.68	9/16/64	56.00	106.50
50	NY Central RR	7/8/64	41.65	11/16/64	49.05	369.89

PMD Fund Transactions, 1961–1964

Shares	Stock	Date Bought	Price Paid	Date Sold	Price Sold	Gain or Loss
100	Dome Petroleum	12/28/78	77.00			
20	Dome Petroleum			2/26/79	97.88	14,226.72
320	4/1 split on 6/6/79			10/17/80	63.00	(3,165.82)
300	Fluor	10/17/80	56.50	2/9/81	48.25	
50	Fluor	10/17/80	56.88			
100	Pic 'N' Save	6/4/81	55.00			
300	3/1 split 6/29/81			7/6/82	15.00	(1,094.00)
100	Espey Mfg.	11/19/81	46.75	6/8/82	38.00	
50	Espey Mfg.	11/19/81	47.00	4/23/82	46.00	(1,313.16)
100	MCI Comm.	4/23/82	37.00	8/20/82	36.38	(123.50)
96	MCI Comm.	7/6/82	45.50			
	2/1 split on 9/20/82			1/3/83	38.25	2,881.92
200	Pic 'N' Save	8/20/82	18.50	7/16/84	19.25	3,892.00
45	Hewlett Packard	9/10/82	53.00	8/11/83	82.88	1,307.35
100	Pic 'N' Save	8/27/82	19.50			
185	Pic 'N' Save	1/3/83	38.13			
	2/1 split on 12/1/83			2/1/85	23.25	4,115.02
200	Price Co.	7/6/84	39.25			
326	Price Co.	2/1/85	53.75			
8	Price Co.			3/25/85	57.00	
	2/1 split on 2/11/86			6/17/86	49.88	26,489.87
15	Price Co.			3/20/86	43.25	

PMD Fund Transactions, 1978–1986

24 years old. Using the CAN SLIM™ technique, he came in second for the year with a result of 279%. In 1992, he gained a 120% return and again came in second. The U.S. Investing Championship is not some paper transaction derby. Real money is used and actual transactions are made in the market. Lee continued to invest successfully with even larger returns in the late 1990s.

Examples of Great Winners to Guide You

Graphs for a selected group of the greatest stock market winners follow. They are models of the most successful investments in the United States from 1952 through 2001. Study them carefully and refer to them often. They are examples of what you must look for in the future. The thin wavy line with an RS at the end and shown below the prices is a relative price strength line.

Study the price patterns. History will repeat itself. All models show the stock's chart pattern just before the point where you want to take buying action.

Texas Instruments, for example, broke out of its 36-week cup-with-handle base at $30 in March 1958. If you bought it when it traded at $30, you would have enjoyed Texas Instruments's 760% advance to $258 in the next 26 months.

If you think you're just looking at a bunch of charts, think again. What you are seeing are pictures of the price accumulation patterns of the greatest winning stocks—just before their enormous price moves began. The charts are presented in five configurations: cup-with-handle pattern, cup-without-handle pattern, double-bottom pattern, flat-base pattern, and base-on-top-of-a-base pattern.

Cup-With-Handle Pattern

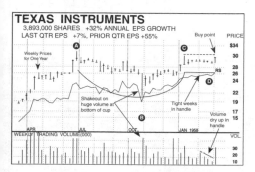

728% increase in 28 months

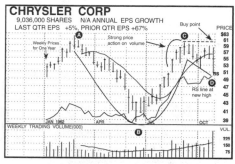

353% increase in 23 months

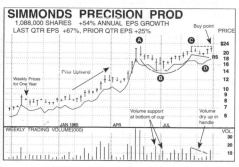

757% increase in 9 months

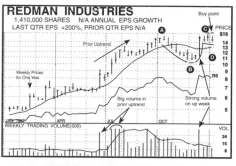

767% increase in 12 months

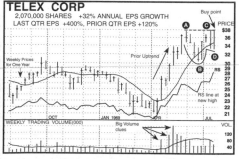

268% increase in 6 months

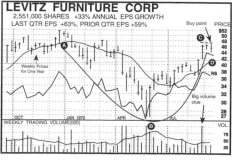

679% increase in 20 months

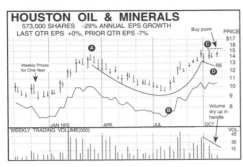

900% increase in 12 months

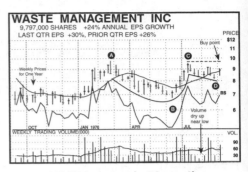

1100% increase in 56 months

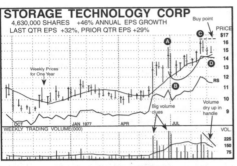

429% increase in 13 months

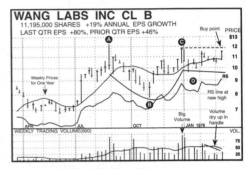

1543% increase in 34 months

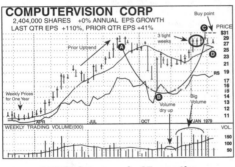

1233% increase in 27 months

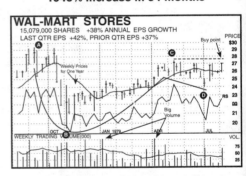

7250% increase in 131 months

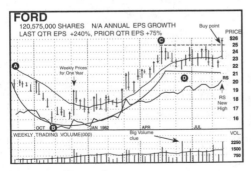

879% increase in 60 months

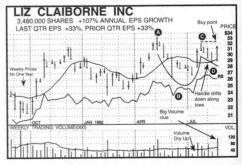

2820% increase in 58 months

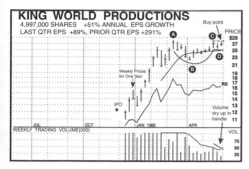

KING WORLD PRODUCTIONS
4,997,000 SHARES +51% ANNUAL EPS GROWTH
LAST QTR EPS +89%, PRIOR QTR EPS +291%

700% increase in 29 months

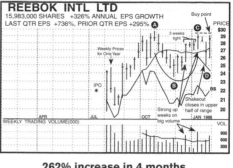

REEBOK INTL LTD
15,983,000 SHARES +326% ANNUAL EPS GROWTH
LAST QTR EPS +736%, PRIOR QTR EPS +295%

262% increase in 4 months

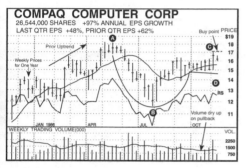

COMPAQ COMPUTER CORP
26,544,000 SHARES +97% ANNUAL EPS GROWTH
LAST QTR EPS +48%, PRIOR QTR EPS +62%

378% increase in 11 months

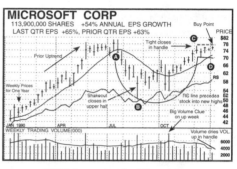

MICROSOFT CORP
113,900,000 SHARES +54% ANNUAL EPS GROWTH
LAST QTR EPS +65%, PRIOR QTR EPS +63%

152% increase in 12 months

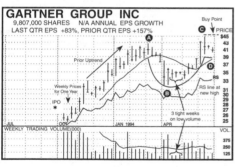

GARTNER GROUP INC
9,807,000 SHARES   N/A ANNUAL EPS GROWTH
LAST QTR EPS +83%, PRIOR QTR EPS +157%

667% increase in 23 months

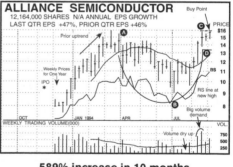

ALLIANCE SEMICONDUCTOR
12,164,000 SHARES   N/A ANNUAL EPS GROWTH
LAST QTR EPS +47%, PRIOR QTR EPS +46%

589% increase in 10 months

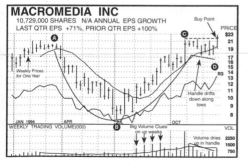

MACROMEDIA INC
10,729,000 SHARES   N/A ANNUAL EPS GROWTH
LAST QTR EPS +71%, PRIOR QTR EPS +100%

522% increase in 11 months

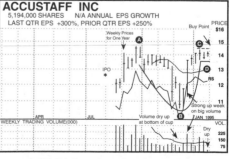

ACCUSTAFF INC
5,194,000 SHARES   N/A ANNUAL EPS GROWTH
LAST QTR EPS +300%, PRIOR QTR EPS +250%

1486% increase in 16 months

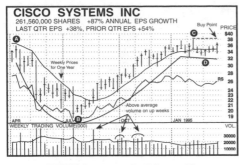

CISCO SYSTEMS INC
261,560,000 SHARES +87% ANNUAL EPS GROWTH
LAST QTR EPS +38%, PRIOR QTR EPS +54%

3797% increase in 60 months

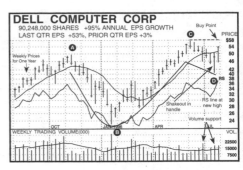

DELL COMPUTER CORP
90,248,000 SHARES +95% ANNUAL EPS GROWTH
LAST QTR EPS +53%, PRIOR QTR EPS +3%

2973% increase in 30 months

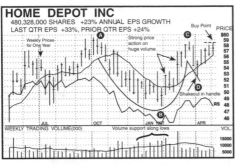

HOME DEPOT INC
480,328,000 SHARES +23% ANNUAL EPS GROWTH
LAST QTR EPS +33%, PRIOR QTR EPS +24%

431% increase in 32 months

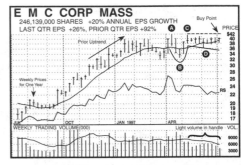

E M C CORP MASS
246,139,000 SHARES +20% ANNUAL EPS GROWTH
LAST QTR EPS +26%, PRIOR QTR EPS +92%

1249% increase in 33 months

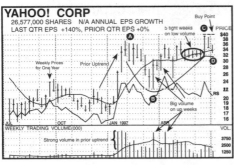

YAHOO! CORP
26,577,000 SHARES N/A ANNUAL EPS GROWTH
LAST QTR EPS +140%, PRIOR QTR EPS +0%

7443% increase in 30 months

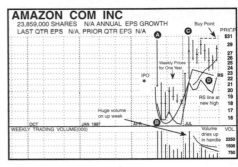

AMAZON COM INC
23,859,000 SHARES N/A ANNUAL EPS GROWTH
LAST QTR EPS N/A, PRIOR QTR EPS N/A

3805% increase in 16 months

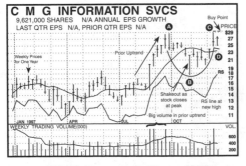

C M G INFORMATION SVCS
9,621,000 SHARES N/A ANNUAL EPS GROWTH
LAST QTR EPS N/A, PRIOR QTR EPS N/A

8958% increase in 24 months

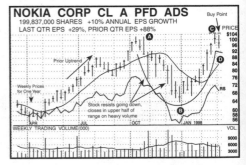

NOKIA CORP CL A PFD ADS
199,837,000 SHARES +10% ANNUAL EPS GROWTH
LAST QTR EPS +29%, PRIOR QTR EPS +88%

800% increase in 24 months

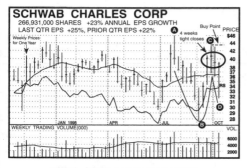

439% increase in 6 months

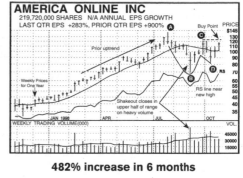

482% increase in 6 months

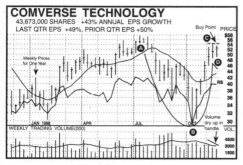

606% increase in 16 months

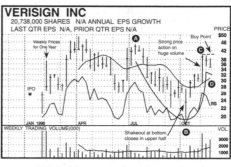

2543% increase in 15 months

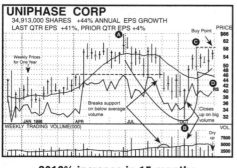

2016% increase in 15 months

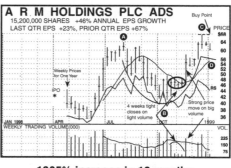

1385% increase in 13 months

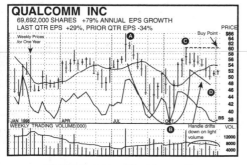

2567% increase in 12 months

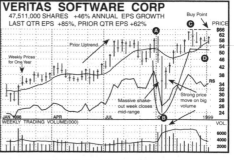

1097% increase in 14 months

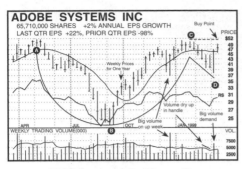

596% increase in 20 months

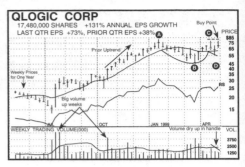

919% increase in 10 months

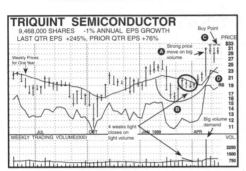

1078% increase in 9 months

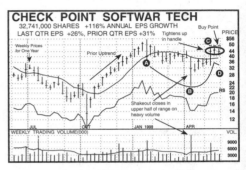

1142% increase in 9 months

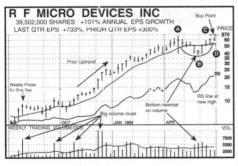

444% increase in 8 months

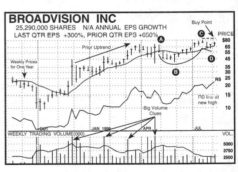

949% increase in 7 months

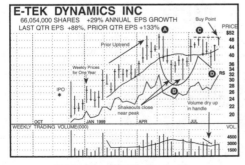

507% increase in 6 months

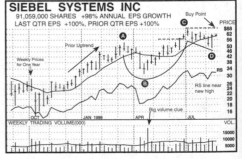

420% increase in 7 months

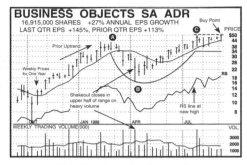

535% increase in 8 months

1495% increase in 6 months

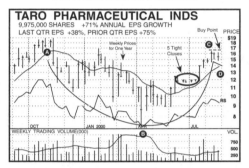

503% increase in 11 months

Cup-Without-Handle Pattern

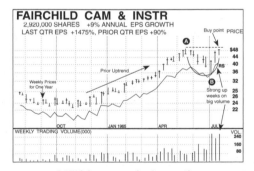

347% increase in 8 months

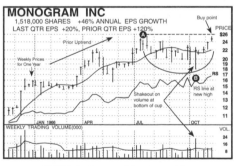

775% increase in 15 months

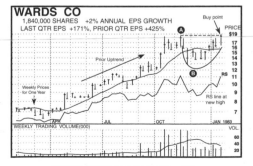

233% increase in 8 months

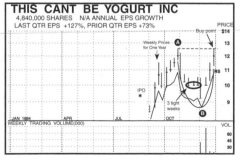

1557% increase in 54 months

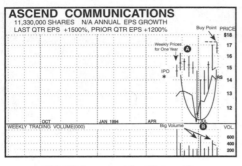

3206% increase in 22 months

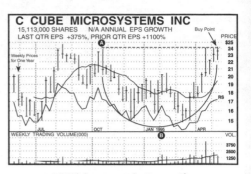

494% increase in 9 months

1949% increase in 16 months

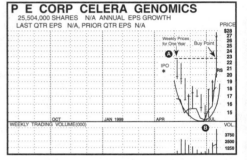

2281% increase in 7 months

Double-Bottom Pattern

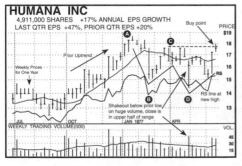

1275% increase in 47 months

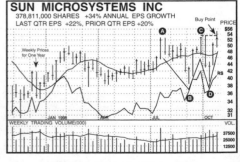

688% increase in 17 months

Flat-Base Pattern

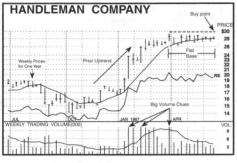

332% increase in 32 months

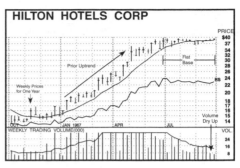

235% increase in 14 months

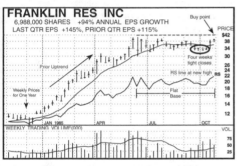

3596% increase in 109 months

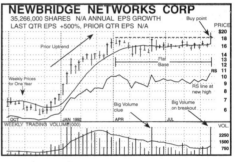

699% increase in 11 months

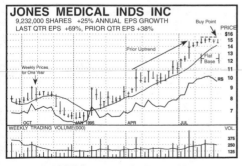

483% increase in 8 months

839% increase in 9 months

Base-on-Top-of-a-Base Pattern

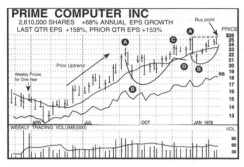

1500% increase in 40 months

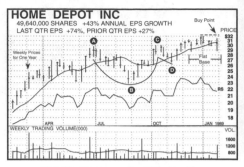

2640% increase in 115 months

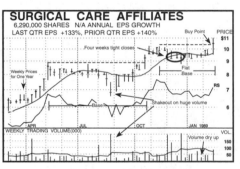

1833% increase in 33 months

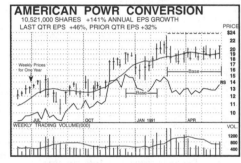

2100% increase in 46 months

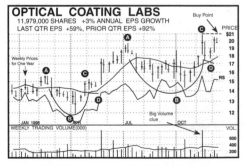

1957% increase in 13 months

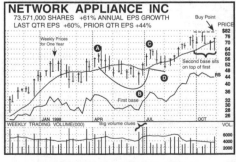

517% increase in 4 months

How to Find Winning Stocks Using Investor's Business Daily

Why We Created *Investor's Business Daily*

For decades, professional money managers were the only ones with access to the in-depth data most critical to finding winning stocks. In effect, they had a monopoly on the most relevant investment information. That's why I started *Investor's Business Daily* in April 1984: to bring this needed information to all investors.

Known for its investing capabilities as far back as the 1960s, William O'Neil + Co. built the first computerized daily stock market database in the United States to track and compare stock performance. Detailed tracking uncovered remarkable insights into what constitutes a major stock market winner, particularly its characteristics *before* making a major price move. Most of this information is now available through *Investor's Business Daily*, which offers everyone—professional and individual investors alike—an opportunity to profit from the detailed analysis previously available only to institutional investors. Because our primary concern is interpreting the national business economy utilizing our comprehensive research database, *Investor's Business Daily* is an information provider first and a newspaper second.

If you are serious about becoming a more successful investor, it is positively within your grasp. If you can commit to studying the proven strategies outlined in this book, being disciplined and focusing on daily learning, you're halfway there. IBD's proprietary research tools are the other half of the equation. For many of you, this will mean familiarizing yourself with data, methods, and concepts that are different from those you're accustomed to seeing and using. For example, according to our historical study of the greatest winning stocks, if you'd been relying on P/E ratios, you would've missed almost every major winner dating back to 1952. The information in IBD is based on the characteristics found in the most successful companies of all time before their major price moves. Following these valid models for success has helped me and many others achieve success since the 1960s.

Investor's Business Daily began in April 1984 with only 15,000 subscribers. In the years prior to our launch, *The Wall Street Journal* grew steadily to reach its peak of 2.1 million domestic circulation by our 1984 introduction date. Since that time, *Investor's Business Daily* has increased its market share versus *The Journal* nearly every year, reaching 302,400 circulation, according to the March 31, 2001, Audit Bureau of Circulations report. In key, high-population areas such as southern California, Florida, and Long Island, NY, IBD's share of regular paid subscribers and newsstand sales is 20% to 30%. While many of our readers were former *Wall Street Journal* subscribers, there is little current duplication of readership, since several surveys show only 18% of IBD subscribers also take The Journal.

How *Investor's Business Daily* Is Different

So what is it exactly that distinguishes IBD from other sources? Let's take a closer look.

- **IBD makes it easy to search for winning stocks.** With over 10,000 publicly traded stocks to choose from, IBD provides performance lists and proven proprietary fundamental and technical ratings that help narrow your choices to only the very best opportunities.

- **It offers a quicker, easier way to understand the general market.** The key elements of the day's trading action are numbered on market index charts and explained with commentary to give you a sound perspective on the health of the overall market and improve your timing of buy and sell decisions.

- **It provides investing education and support.** IBD's entire focus is on solid database research and extensive model-building . . . facts, *not* opinion. There is a multitude of sources outlined in this chapter that can help you learn and understand how the market really works, based on years of historical precedent.

A New Way to Find Winning Stocks

At *Investor's Business Daily,* we've developed an entirely different way to search for winning stocks. That's because after more than four decades of research, we know that top stocks show definite signs of strength well before they become winners. That confuses many people who instead would prefer a bargain: the low-priced, unknown stocks they hope will take off and surprise us all. As we've said before, cheap stocks are cheap for a reason; they show deficiencies that don't allow the stock to progress. For a stock to move higher, it needs earnings growth, strong sales, and several other factors to demonstrate that it's emerging as a leader. If you catch it at the early stages, you will be able to capitalize on its enormous moves.

Remember that the greatest winners of all time like Cisco Systems and Home Depot began their biggest price moves after they'd gained leadership positions in earnings and sales growth and the other factors described in this chapter. Some of the most critical data you will need to start your search can be found in the IBD stock tables.

The unique ratings in IBD are an easy way to catch those winners *before* they actually take off, so it's important to review them each day. IBD stock tables are completely different from anything you'll see elsewhere. Our proprietary *SmartSelect*™ Corporate Ratings speak volumes about each stock's performance and how a stock compares to all the others in our database. The elements in these ratings, which are numbered 1 through 9 in the accompanying chart, are explained in detail below.

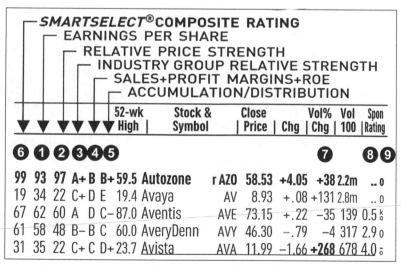

Investor's Business Daily®
November 1, 2001

Sample IBD's *SmartSelect*® Corporate Ratings

The IBD SmartSelect® Corporate Ratings

The one line of information in the IBD *SmartSelect*® Corporate Ratings is much more powerful and meaningful than anything you'll find in standard price tables. These ratings, proven to be the most predictive measurements of a stock's future value, will narrow your search from over 10,000 stocks to the top investment ideas.

You'll find it's like a condensed financial report that looks at the fundamental strength or weakness of a stock. It is also a well-rounded evaluation of each company's general health. Most importantly, along with daily and/or weekly charts, these ratings will help you find winning stocks. Let's examine each element.

Earning Per Share Rating Indicates a Company's Relative Earnings Growth

Strong earnings growth is essential to a stock's success and has the greatest impact on its future price performance. The first absolutely vital component of the *SmartSelect*® Ratings is the Earnings Per Share (EPS) Rating, which is labeled ❶ in the chart on the prior page.

EPS Rating calculates the growth and stability of each company's earnings over the last three years, giving added weight to the most recent few quarters. The result is compared with all other common stocks in the price tables and is rated on a scale from 1 to 99, with 99 being the best.

Example: An EPS Rating of 90 means that a company's bottom-line earnings results over the short and long term are in the top 10% of the roughly 10,000 stocks being measured.

This one number gives you the relative earnings performance of publicly held companies and the prospects for their stocks. It's an objective measure by which you can compare the audited results of one company to any other; for example, the earnings growth of IBM to that of Hewlett Packard, Lockheed, Loews Companies, Wal-Mart, or Merrill Lynch. Earnings estimates are not used in the calculation because they are personal opinions, which, as you know, might be wrong and do change.

Since earnings power and growth are the most basic measures of a company's success, the EPS Rating is invaluable for separating the true leaders from the poorly managed, deficient, and lackluster companies in today's tougher worldwide competition.

The EPS Rating is also more meaningful than the widely followed Fortune 500 lists that rank corporations by company size. Size alone rarely guarantees innovation, growth, or profitability. Most large companies that are anywhere from 50 to 100 years old may have a well-known brand image, but often they are losing market share to younger, more innovative companies that have created newer, better products.

Relative Price Strength Rating Shows Emerging Price Leaders

Since we've learned that the best stocks are strong price performers even before their major moves, you should look for stocks with price leadership. Relative Price Strength (RS) Rating shows you which stocks are the best price performers, measuring a stock's performance over the previous 12 months. That performance is then compared against all other publicly traded companies and given a 1 to 99 rating, with 99 being best. Look at the column labeled ❷ in the chart.

Example: An 85 RS Rating means the stock's price movement has outperformed 85% of all other common stocks in the last year. The greatest winning stocks since 1952 showed an average RS Rating of 87 when they broke out of their first price consolidation areas (bases). In other words, the greatest stocks were already outperforming nearly 90%, or nine out of 10, of all other stocks in the market *before* they made their biggest price gains.

Even in poor markets, a Relative Price Strength Rating that breaks below 70 can forewarn you of a possible problem situation. When you compare these fact-based performance ratings to the old, unscientific methods typically based on faulty opinions, academic theories, stories, promotions, and tips, it becomes inarguable that IBD's unique ratings can give you a clear edge up in the market.

You Need Both Strong EPS and RS Ratings

The implication of both Earnings Per Share Rating and Relative Price Strength Rating is considerable. So far, you've been able to determine the top leaders in earnings and relative price strength. The vast majority of superior stocks will rank 80 or higher on *both* EPS and RS Ratings *before* their major moves. Since one is a fundamental measurement and the other is a marketplace valuation, insisting on both numbers being strong should, in positive markets, materially improve your selection process.

Of course, there's no guarantee that a company's terrific past or current record can't suddenly turn sour in the future. That's why you must always use a loss-cutting strategy, such as the sell rules discussed in Chapters 9 and 10. It's also prudent and essential to check the stock's daily or weekly chart to see if it's in a proper base or is extended in price too far above its most recent area of consolidation. (For a review of common chart patterns to watch for, refer to Chapter 12.)

As previously discussed, models of the best-performing companies over the last half-century showed that both earnings growth for the last three years and percent increase in earnings per share for the latest two quarters were the two most common fundamental characteristics.

With hard data like that available to you, it naturally begs the question, why would you ever invest your hard-earned dollars in a sluggish stock that sports a 30 EPS Rating or a 40 RS Rating when there are literally thousands of companies with higher ratings, including hundreds with superlative numbers?

It's not that companies with poor ratings can't perform. It's just that a greater percentage of them turn out to be disappointments. Even when a low-rated company has a decent price move, you'll find that the better-rated stocks in the same industry have probably done much better.

In a way, the combined use of EPS Rating and RS Rating is similar to A. C. Nielsen's viewer ratings for TV shows. Who wants to continue sponsoring a TV show that gets poor ratings?

Now, pretend for a minute you're the manager of the New York Yankees. It's off-season, and you're going to pick new players for next year's team. Would you trade for, recruit, or sign only .200 hitters? Or would you select as many .300 hitters as possible?

The .300 hitters cost you more money; their P/Es are higher and they sell nearer to their price high. It's true the .200 hitters are available at a cheaper price, but how many games will you win with nine players in your lineup averaging .200? When the bases are loaded in the ninth inning and the score is tied, who would you rather see step up to the plate: a .200 hitter or a .300 hitter? How often does an established .200 hitter blossom into a batting champion?

Selecting and managing a portfolio of stocks is no different than baseball when it comes to performance. To win consistently and finish first in your division, you need a roster of the very best players available—those with proven records of excellence. You won't do as well in your investing if you insist on buying poorer performers and "cheaper stocks" in the hope of "discovering" a winner. Hope never works in the market unless you start with a quality stock that's begun to build steam. It's the "steam" (earnings and price strength) that is the key prerequisite to future growth. Don't be fooled by bargain-basement thinking. Replace your hopes and personal opinions with proven measurable facts.

It's also interesting to note that these practical, no-nonsense ratings have helped to wake up corporate board members and put pressure on management teams producing second-rate results. A consistently low IBD relative performance rating should be a serious wake-up call to any top management team or board of directors.

Stock Winners Are in Leading Industry Groups

High EPS and RS Ratings are just a part of the stock-picking puzzle. Studies show that the majority of market leaders were also part of a leading industry group. The Industry Group Relative Strength Rating, the column labeled ❸ in the chart, will tell you if your stock's industry group is leading or lagging the market. Even if your stock is doing well, be wary if the overall industry group is underperforming the market. It could be a warning sign.

Industry Group Relative Strength Rating compares the six-month price performance of a stock's industry group to all other industry groups. IBD rates them on an A+ to E scale. The strongest are rated A+, A, or A– (top 24% of industry groups) or B+, B or B–; the weakest have D or E ratings. The real market leaders usually have Industry Group Relative Strength Ratings in the A or B range.

Example: An Industry Group Relative Strength Rating of A puts a stock in the top 16% of companies in terms of its industry group's performance.

For instance, when America Online blasted out of a 14-week price base in October 1998, en route to a 557% gain in just six months, its Industry Group Relative Strength Rating was a bullish A.

Strong Sales, Profit Margins, and Return on Equity Are a Big Clue

Cutting costs may boost a company's earnings for a quarter or two, but powerful, sustained profit increases require healthy sales growth. It's also important to buy companies that make the most of their sales growth. How much profit do they generate from each dollar of sales? How well do they use their capital? The Sales + Profit Margins + Return On Equity (SMR™) Rating combines these important factors and is the fastest way to identify truly outstanding companies with real sales growth and profitability. These are the factors widely followed by analysts. SMR Rating™ is on an A to E scale, with A and B being the best. You want to avoid stocks with an SMR Rating™ of D or E. See the column labeled ❹ on the chart.

Example: An SMR Rating™ of A puts a stock in the top 20% of companies in terms of sales growth, profitability, and return on equity.

During the brief rally that followed the Nasdaq's bear market plunge from March to May 2000, SDL Inc. shot ahead as a leading performer. The maker of components for fiber-optic networks broke out to new highs just as the market confirmed a new uptrend, the most ideal situation for buying a stock. SDL Inc. ran up 112% in just eight weeks. Among its many strong qualities was an SMR Rating™ of A.

Accumulation/Distribution—The Influence of Professional Trading on Stocks

Professional investors wield huge influence over a stock's price. Thus, it's essential to buy the better stocks that mutual funds are buying and sell what they are selling on a heavy basis. Trying to go against this monumental trading will only hurt your results. A quick way to keep track of professional trading is to use the Accumulation/Distribution Rating (the column labeled ❺ on the chart), which is based on daily price and volume changes. It tells you if your stock is under accumulation (professional buying) or distribution (professional selling). This thoroughly tested, complex, and proprietary formula is accurate and not based on simple up/down volume calculations. Stocks are rated on an A to E scale, each letter represents the following:

A = heavy accumulation (buying) by institutions

B = moderate accumulation (buying) by institutions

C = equal (or neutral) amount of buying and selling by institutions

D = moderate distribution (selling) by institutions

E = heavy distribution (selling) by institutions

When a stock receives an A or B rating in *Investor's Business Daily*, it means that the stock is being bought on balance. However, this does not guarantee that it must go up. The buying activity is being picked up, but maybe the funds are buying into a questionable position and could be wrong in what they are doing. Stocks rated as D and E, in most cases, should be avoided. C-rated stocks are neutral and may be OK.

You needn't feel you've missed out on the trading action if you spot heavy buying or selling. Many funds take weeks and even months to complete their positions in a stock or rid themselves of it, which gives you time to capitalize on that action. However, be sure to check a daily or weekly stock chart to see if the stock is in the early, beginning stage of a move, or if it is overextended in price and too risky or late to buy.

Composite Rating: An Overview

The rating in the first column of the IBD stock tables is the *SmartSelect*® Composite Rating, which combines all five *SmartSelect*® Ratings into a summary rating for quick review of overall performance. Look at the column labeled ❻. The *SmartSelect*® Composite Rating formula is simple:

- Because of the impact of earnings and previous price performance on stock price, double weighting is given to both Earnings Per Share and Relative Price Strength Ratings. Normal weight is given to each of the other three *SmartSelect*® Ratings: Industry Group Relative Strength, SMR™, and Accumulation/Distribution (ACC/DIS Rating™).

- The percent off the stock's 52-week high is also used in the *SmartSelect*® Composite Rating.

- The results are then compared to the entire database, and a 1 to 99 rating—with 99 being best—summarizes the five most predictive measurements we've just discussed.

In some stocks, the *SmartSelect*® Composite Rating may be higher than the five individual *SmartSelect*® Ratings. This is because the formula is weighted and includes the stock's percent off its 52-week high.

When reviewing the stock tables, this simple rating gives you an enormous time-saving edge. Work your way down the columns and look for *SmartSelect*® Composite Ratings of 80 or better to spot the strong opportunities. The next step is to review all five individual *SmartSelect*® Ratings: EPS, RS, Industry Group Relative Strength, SMR™, and Accumulation/Distribution. With a quick scan of the stock tables, you're now that much closer to being sure you are selecting better stocks.

Volume Percent Change Tracks the Big Money Flow

Another important measurement IBD created is Volume Percent Change (see the column labeled ❼). Most newspapers and information providers on TV and the Web only provide a stock's trading volume for the day, which doesn't tell the entire, meaningful story. Based on the volume information they provide, how would you know if the volume for all the stocks in your portfolio and those you're looking at for purchase is normal, abnormally low, or abnormally high? In order to know this, you'd have to keep in your head or on paper what the average daily volume is for each stock under review. Instead, you can rely on IBD to keep track of this for you. IBD was the first to provide investors with a Volume Percent Change that monitors what the normal daily trading level has been for every stock over the most recent 50 trading days.

Stocks trade at many different volume levels, and any major changes in volume can give you significant clues. One stock may trade on average 10,000 shares a day, while another trades 100,000 shares a day, and still another trades 1 million shares a day. The key is not how many shares were traded, but whether that volume activity is unusual or not. For example, if a stock with an average trading volume of 10,000 shares suddenly trades 70,000 shares, while its price jumps one point, the stock has increased in price on a 600% increase in volume, generally a positive sign. The Volume

Percent Change column will show a +600% that quickly alerts you to emerging professional interest in the stock. (In this case, the stock is trading 600% above its normal volume, and if the price is up substantially all of a sudden, this is a major tip-off.) Volume Percent Change is like having a computer in your pocket to carefully monitor changing supply and demand for every single stock.

Volume Percent Change is one of the main reasons so many specialists on the floor of the New York Stock Exchange, professional portfolio managers, top-producing stockbrokers, and savvy individual investors use IBD's stock tables. There isn't a better way to track the flow of money in and out of companies.

Other Ways to Find Potential Leaders in IBD's Tables

- Stocks making new highs tend to go higher, so another item money managers review is the boldfaced stocks up one point or more or hitting new price highs in IBD's stock tables. Stocks down one point or more or making new price lows are underlined. It's easy to scan the tables rapidly and be aware of just the key market action for the day.

- Preferred stocks are displayed in a separate area, along with low-priced stocks under $10 a share, to save you time. Lower-priced stocks have been separated out because 50 years of computer modeling show that 97% of all the greatest Nasdaq stocks broke out of their initial sound chart patterns at prices of $15 and higher and NYSE stocks $20 and higher. So why waste your valuable time wading through hundreds of less successful, low-priced laggards, and potential losers. If you insist on looking at lower quality, low-priced stocks, at least they're all in one place for easier scanning.

- IBD screens its powerful database to bring your attention to the best potential investments. So you can easily identify them, they are highlighted in yellow. Based on a proprietary formula, these stocks meet certain growth stock characteristics found in our models of the winning stocks of the last 50 years.

- Another helpful tool in the stock tables is the Institutional Sponsorship Rating (SPON RATING™), based on an A to E scale, with A being best (see the column labeled ❽). This proprietary gauge averages the three-year performance rating of all mutual funds owning a stock, plus the trend in recent quarters of the total number of fund owners. This rating appears once a week in the rotating column of the tables.

- In the far right column, labeled ❾, it is noted if the company has repurchased its own stock in the last year (r) (frequently a positive sign). You'll also find notations for ex-dividend or ex-rights (x); earnings due in the next four weeks (k); earnings report in the current issue of IBD (–); and options on stocks (o).

- Price-earnings ratios and dividend yields are shown on a rotating basis. They honestly don't change too much, and our research of successful stocks consistently proves that P/Es and dividend yields have little to do with what makes a stock a winner. So, in spite of their widespread popularity in past years, these measurements are somewhat less important than the other vital factors discussed previously.

Be Alert to Stocks With the Greatest Percent Change in Volume

Most newspapers and other information providers show the 15 most active stocks. Their lists usually include securities like General Electric and AT&T, which trade millions of shares a day. *Investor's Business Daily* invented a special daily list, "Where the Big Money's Flowing," to highlight stocks with the biggest percentage changes in their trading volume for the day versus their average daily volume over the prior 50 days. Stocks closing up for the day are separated from those closing down, allowing you to see exactly which stocks the big money is flowing into and out of each day.

"Where the Big Money's Flowing" is more relevant than most active lists because our computer surveillance picks up on the more innovative, entrepreneurial organizations of small to medium size that have significant increases in volume. These stocks would never reach the total volume large enough to make the more common lists that show big volume stocks like AT&T. You can easily miss important emerging stocks overlooked in standard lists.

Stocks appearing in "Where the Big Money's Flowing" that rate 80 or above in both Earnings per Share and Relative Price Strength Ratings are boldfaced. Pay close attention to these names; with high ratings, and increases in price and volume, they may deserve further research. Other information providers also list the stocks with the best percentage gains in price. These lists are almost worthless because they will highlight, for example, a $2 stock up $0.38—a big percentage gain—but as you know by now, you rarely get rich prospecting in the junk pile. Concentrate instead on IBD's meaningful list of 25 of the more significant securities priced $16 or higher for Nasdaq and $20 or higher for NYSE. As mentioned before, cheap stocks are cheap for a reason.

Where The Big Money's Flowing

Stocks $18 and higher, with at least 1/2 point price change & trade 60,000 shares (if Vol % Chg is +300% or more, must trade 75,000 shares). For stocks up in price, the EPS+RS must be 110 or more and next year's earnings estimate 17%+. Stocks without estimates are included. Stocks rated 80 EPS and 80 Relative Strength or higher are **boldfaced.**

Rel	Grp		Acc		52-Wk		Stock	Closing	Price	PE	Float	Vol	Vol%
EPS	Str	Rtg	SMR	Dis	High	Stock Name	Symbol	Price	Chg	Ratio	(mil)	(1000s)	Chg
51	95	A+	C	B	18.07	United Industrial	UIC	19.90	+1.90	34	9.1	462	+682
80	**91**	**B+**	**C**	**A**	**33.38**	**WilsonGreatbtch Tc**	**GB**	**30.00**	**+1.22**	**83**	**8.5**	**135**	**+241**
62	86	A–	B	C	28.06	SovranSelf Storage	SSS	27.90	+1.20	15	11	82	+174
91	**92**	**A**	**B**	**A**	**93.40**	**General Dynamics** o	**GD**	**94.99**	**+2.39**	**22**	**181**	**3,455**	**+165**
93	**90**	**A+**	**A**	**B**	**49.40**	**HilbRogal Hamilton**	**HRH**	**50.50**	**+1.60**	**30**	**12**	**227**	**+143**
66	91	A	D	B	36.68	Raytheon B o	RTN	36.30	+1.33	23	234	6,037	+126
74	68	A–	B	D	33.50	Equity Office Pptys o	EOP	31.00	+0.61	21	384	3,688	+120
69	93	A	D	A	47.85	Lockheed Martin o	LMT	49.11	+1.38	40	430	5,550	+110
94	63	A	B	D	77.25	Varian Medical Sys o	VAR	61.68	+1.18	31	32	390	+74
62	68	A–	B	B	31.50	CBL & Assoc Pptys	CBL	28.32	+0.52	12	17	129	+63
59	94	A–	D	B	22.25	Supervalu o	SVU	22.74	+1.22	14	128	1,104	+42
81	79	A–	A	B	25.28	Washingtn R E I T	WRE	24.72	+0.52	19	37	128	+41
71	95	A	C	B	43.17	Pediatrix Medical o	PDX	33.71	–5.54	33	20	1,516	+521
24	46	E	C	D	56.50	Nucor o	NUE	36.52	–4.22	13	76	2,202	+325
90	60	B	A	C	35.50	LNR Property Corp o	LNR	27.52	–0.55	8	22	387	+272
80	51	B+	C	D	37.20	ComntyHealth Sys o	CYH	26.12	–0.54	77	39	705	+205
96	88	B+	A	B	39.50	Ninety–Nine Cts o	NDN	32.70	–2.36	40	27	748	+162

Investor's Business Daily®
October 9, 2001

Sample IBD's Where the Big Money's Flowing

Always Check Stocks Making New Highs Daily

An important step in finding winning stocks is to search out companies making new price highs. The "Stocks in the News" mini-charts zero in on 20 better-performing NYSE and 20 better-performing Nasdaq companies every day. They are quality stocks that either:

- Hit new price highs (name will be boldfaced)
- Are near a new high (regular type face for company name)
- Show the greatest increase in volume for $15-and-above stocks, with at least a 50-cent per share increase (underlined).

These mini weekly basis charts show you the number of shares outstanding, EPS Rating, company description, stock symbol, annual earnings growth rate, Accumulation/Distribution Rating, percent owned by management, percent company debt, Industry Group Relative Strength Rating, relative strength line and RS Rating, average daily trading volume, price-earnings ratio, current quarterly earnings, high and low prices for the prior two years,

Investor's Business Daily® October 18, 2001

Sample IBD's Stocks in the News

return on equity, Sponsorship Rating, percentage changes in earnings and sales for recent quarters, and if the stock has options.

This is a great way to search for emerging leaders just as they appear on the radar screen. While almost all eventual leaders will surface on these graphs, you must remember that not all companies in "Stocks in the News" will be successful and work out.

The investor without "Stocks in the News" will generally overlook fascinating companies worth paying attention to. This is particularly true of the lesser-known issues that trade on the Nasdaq, but it is these unfamiliar names that might blast off and become the year's biggest winners. Here is an example:

In June 1986, I randomly selected a June 1985 issue of *Investor's Business Daily* and checked all the mini-charts shown in the Nasdaq "Stocks in the News" section. In the 12 months that followed, 90% of the stocks had advanced in price by an average 75% while the general market rose 25% over the same period.

Listen to the General Market for Investing Success

To really do well in stocks, you simply have to know how to interpret the direction of the daily general market averages. It's easier than you might think.

To do this properly, you can't merely view one average, such as the Dow, to get the complete perspective. That is why *Investor's Business Daily* shows all three major indices together: the S&P 500, the Nasdaq Composite, and the Dow Jones Industrials.

There's an important reason these three indices are stacked one on top of the other. At most major market tops and bottoms, subtle divergences in the indices can more easily be detected. Many investors miss these signs if they aren't viewing the indices in this way.

Learn to recognize these market variations on a day-to-day basis. Studying the general market once a week is not enough. Do you think great piano players get that way by practicing only once a week? All the market information you need is on the "General Markets & Sectors" pages every day in IBD. "The Big Picture" commentary on the "General Markets" page provides a step-by-step, numbered analysis of the daily action in the three major indices. If you get in the habit of following this column each day, you should see your market timing improve dramatically.

What really separates "The Big Picture" from other market commentary is that you won't get a roundup of what Wall Street strategists think the market *should* be doing; they've had unusually poor records, especially in 2000 and 2001, of catching major turns in the general averages. Instead, this commentary reviews what the market itself is saying by its very action. You'll learn more about the market's health by studying and recognizing correctly what it's doing *right now*. Here are some examples:

- In 1999, "The Big Picture" market column noted emerging signs of the big October 1999 rally, in which the Nasdaq nearly doubled in less than five months. Investors who read about this were able to get in on some historical market gains.

- In March 2000, long before most of Wall Street conceded the bull market was dead, there were numerous "Big Picture" columns citing signs of distribution and breakdown in the market. Those unaware suffered unnecessary losses while those who recognized and followed these important signs sold stock and preserved their capital.

- "The Big Picture" is also on record for spotting the confirmation of a fresh but limited rally in late May and early June 2000. Some of these rallies are fleeting, so you must be prepared to capitalize on them at exactly the right time.

- The column also clearly documented the market distribution on the Nasdaq Composite in the first two weeks of September 2000. This was a crucial top that Wall Street analysts and strategists completely missed in their TV commentary and in their written reports. If you are an investor short on time, never miss IBD's "The Big Picture" column.

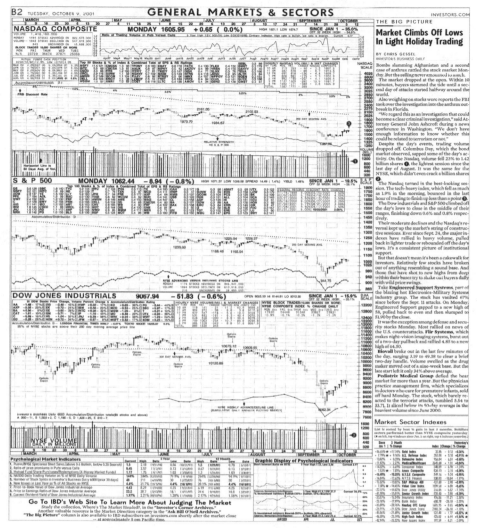

Investor's Business Daily®
October 9, 2001

Sample IBD's General Markets & Sectors Page

Be sure to reread Chapter 7, which shows you how to spot market tops and when the market comes out of a moderate to serious correction. Since the majority of stocks follow the course of the general market, pay close attention to this lesson so that you learn to spot these key market turns. As you start to review market action on a daily basis, you'll begin to recognize the key signs of emerging new trends.

Psychological Market Indicators Can Also Be Important

Psychological market indicators are definitely secondary in importance, but they can, in some cases, be helpful in anticipating or confirming market direction. Some of the better ones are:

- The percentage of investment advisory services that are bearish or bullish (The more bullish they are, the less positive it is for the market.)
- The put/call volume ratio (An extreme increase in put activity is considered a bullish sign. This occurred at the market bottom in 2001.)

Both are presented on IBD's "General Markets" page.

Remember that when most people are finally onto a trend (as psychological market indicators illustrate), the opposite market action is likely to occur.

Key Market Sector Graphs Let You Hone in on Leadership

Once you've looked at the general market action, it's time to zero in on which sectors are leading. Ten smaller major sector graphs appear daily on IBD's "Industry Groups" page. They divide the economy and market into broad categories such as high tech, junior growth stocks, consumer companies, health care securities, and even new issues.

The percentage change in each index is quoted every day in the market sector box so you can separate the leading sectors from the laggards. The New York Stock Exchange Composite and the Dow transportation and utilities are among the 24 indices shown daily.

In early 1994, using data in this market sector box, you could easily see that the high-tech sector was the leading market segment, with junior growth stocks next in strength and utilities seriously underperforming. Conversely, in March 2000, signs of weakening within the high-tech sector were apparent. Never miss reviewing sector performance if you want to be a more successful investor.

What's the Market's Bias?

The market favors small-capitalization stocks at times and then switches to big-caps. How do you know its current preference? Just look at the accompanying IBD chart comparing big-cap growth funds to small-cap growth funds. When big-cap funds hold the upper hand, it makes sense to concentrate your buying on big-cap stocks. The reverse holds true for when small-caps are in favor.

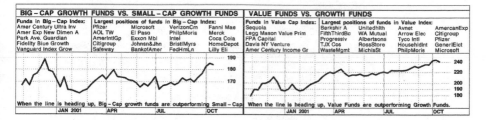

| BIG – CAP GROWTH FUNDS VS. SMALL – CAP GROWTH FUNDS | VALUE FUNDS VS. GROWTH FUNDS |

Funds in Big – Cap Index:	Largest positions of funds in Big – Cap Index:				Funds in Value Cap Index:	Largest positions of funds in Value Index:			
Amer Century Ultra Inv	Pfizer	Microsoft	VerizonCm	Fanni Mae	Sequoia	Berkshir A	UnitedhIth	Avnet	AmercanExp
Amer Exp New Dimen A	AOL TW	El Paso	PhilpMoris	Merck	Legg Mason Value Prim	FifthThirdBc	WA Mutual	Arrow Elec	Citigroup
Park Ave. Guardian	AmerIntlGp	Exxon Mbl	Intel	Coca Cola	FPA Capital	Progressiv	Albertsons	Tyco Intl	Pfizer
Fidelity Blue Growth	Citigroup	Johnsn&Jhn	BristlMyrs	HomeDepot	Davis NY Venture	TJX Cos	RossStore	HousehldInt	GenerlElct
Vanguard Index Grow	Safeway	BankofAmer	FedHmLn	Lilly Eli	Amer Century Income Gr	WasteMgmt	MichlsSt	PhilpMoris	Microsoft

When the line is heading up, Big – Cap growth funds are outperforming Small – Cap | When the line is heading up, Value Funds are outperforming Growth Funds.
JAN 2001   APR   JUL   OCT | JAN 2001   APR   JUL   OCT

Investor's Business Daily®
October 9, 2001

Sample IBD's Market Graphs: Big Cap vs. Small Cap; Value vs. Growth

Next to the "Big-Cap Growth Funds vs. Small-Cap Growth Funds" chart is the "Value Funds vs. Growth Funds" chart. The market at times rotates from a "value" bias to a "growth" bias. Value stocks tend to have lower price-earnings ratios than growth stocks. As a powerful rally ages, some professionals may start moving into supposedly safer, more defensive stocks. A shift from a growth to a value bias, which occurred in March 2000 as the Nasdaq topped, helped confirm what the general averages were saying about the topping market at that time.

How to Spot the Hottest Industries

We mentioned earlier that the biggest winners are usually leading stocks in leading industry groups. How do you search for the best industries efficiently? Check "IBD's 197 Industry Groups Rankings," a daily industry group evaluation, to find the leading groups.

Industries are broken down into 197 industry groups based on six-month price action. This is a more detailed breakdown than normally seen, but you only need to consider a group such as the computer sector in 1999 to understand exactly why having so many industry groups makes sense. This is really one of the best ways to see where the big money is being traded. For example, in 1999 the Computer-Local Networks group gained an average of 195%, while the Software-Medical group was up only 27%. These more detailed groups will steer you to the real market leadership.

For added perspective, industry group rankings from the prior week and six months are also shown in the chart. This gives you an idea of which groups are rapidly moving up (under accumulation) or moving down (under distribution).

Daily and year-to-date changes compiled for each group are shown, along with the number of stocks in each group. The day's best-performing groups are boldfaced; the worst performers are underlined.

Rank 6 This Wk	Last Fri	Mo Ago	Industry Name	No of Stocks In Grp	%Chg Since Jan 1	Daily % Chg
1	1	60	Comml Svcs-Security/Sfty	52	+35.7	+3.7
2	2	24	Retail/Whsle-Auto Parts	16	+66.2	−0.2
3	6	76	Metal Ores-Gold/Silver	55	+60.1	+0.9
4	5	15	Elec-Military Systems	22	+66.6	+1.8
5	3	150	Medical-Generic Drugs	14	+22.5	0.0
6	4	119	Retail/Whlse Office Supl	7	+55.5	−0.7
7	8	105	Funeral Svcs & Rel	8	+38.8	−0.5
8	7	6	Retail-Misc/Diversified	78	+44.7	+0.1
9	10	152	Insurance-Brokers	11	+9.6	−0.4
10	12	72	Medical-Whsle Drg/Sund	16	+16.0	−0.8
11	13	108	Medical/Dental/Serv	62	−1.0	−0.3
12	9	12	Medical-Nursing Homes	17	+27.2	−0.5
13	21	22	Banks-Northeast	157	+25.0	−0.6
14	16	92	Cosmetics/Personal Care	48	+8.5	+0.4
15	20	20	Banks-Southeast	133	+25.5	−0.8
16	18	90	Retail-Super/Mini Mkts	44	+6.9	−0.4
17	14	125	Medical-Products	135	−8.3	−0.8
18	24	58	Banks-West/Southwest	97	+7.7	−1.3
19	11	25	Comml Serv-Business Svcs	16	−0.7	−5.2
20	26	133	Food-Dairy Products	10	+27.0	−1.7

Investor's Business Daily®
October 9, 2001

IBD's Industry Group Rankings

"52-Week Highs & Lows"

Historically, winning stocks usually come from the top 40 groups and/or from the top five broad sectors showing the most stocks making new price highs in IBD's unique "52-Week Highs & Lows" list. It's vital to understand that stocks hitting new highs for the first time are worth researching. This is especially true of those that trade on the Nasdaq because few sources provide new high lists for Nasdaq securities. IBD groups stocks making new highs by sector and includes each stock's symbol, price, and EPS Rating. This is definitely a shopping list worth researching. Those that appear on the "New Price Lows" list are ones you'll want to temporarily avoid.

At the top of IBD's one-of-a-kind "New Price Highs" list will be the sector with the most stocks making new price highs. This gives you perspective on where money is flowing. Our historical studies show when you're in a positive market with many stocks making new highs, you should look for the top five or six sectors. These will show you the strongest stock leaders. In a bull market, your portfolio should have a representation in these sectors.

Key Futures Graphs for Traders and Economic Perspective

Twenty-four important futures are presented Monday through Thursday in graphic form, with the list expanding to 36 on Fridays. All charts track prices

52-Week Highs & Lows
46 New Price Highs
70 New Price Lows

NYSE (n)-14 Highs, 36 Lows
NASDAQ-26 Highs, 27 Lows
AMEX (a)-6 Highs, 7 Lows

Based on a study of stock market winners, most stocks on the New Highs list tend to go higher. You can also use our unique New Highs list to spot new groups asserting market leadership. Stocks listed within each group are in order of stocks showing the greatest % increase in trading volume. Closing price and Earnings Per Share (EPS) Rating are also shown. For more information consult our free education modules on IBD's web site at www.investors.com. Nasdaq stocks over $2 only. †See Graphs in NYSE or NASDAQ "Stocks In The News"

Name	Symbol	Price	EPS
New Highs			
MEDICAL (11)			
RightchcCr(n)	RIT	62.10	72
Immucell	ICCC	4.36	43
Interpore	BONZ	8.28	70
Curative	CURE	13.45	43
NMT Med	NMTI	6.50	80
SangstMd	SANG	23.40	62
Atrion	ATRI	27.12	97
SmithNphw(n)	SNN	55.66	44
StJudeMed(n)	STJ	73.35	91†
Johnsn&Jhn(n)	JNJ	58.08	90†
Langer	GAIT	6.70	19
FINANCE (5)			
VnKmPAVal(n)	VPV	14.99	...
EatnVPA(a)	EVP	12.85	...
BlkInvQtyTr(n)	BQT	9.28	...
NatHlthRty(a)	NHR	16.10	44
FedAgricA(n)	AGMA	32.05	96
RETAIL			
TractorSupl	TSCO	27.25	66

Name	Symbol	Price	EPS
TuesMrng	TUES	14.25	13†
ACMreArt	ACMR	18.76	73
FOOD/BEV			
MeritgH(a)	MHG	2.80	60
Friendly(a)	FRN	3.90	36
RalstonPr(n)	RAL	32.82	69
COMPUTERS			
OSISystem	OSIS	14.30	8†
BTG	BTGI	12.40	28
MomntBs	MMTM	18.70	12
BUSINESS PRD			
Flanders	FLDR	2.50	10
CecoEnv	CECE	3.25	40
IMCORecy(n)	IMR	8.01	21
TRANSPORT			
MtrCargo	CRGO	12.95	81
Kirby Corp(n)	KEX	26.25	92†
SVGS & LN			
Flag Fncl	FLAG	8.00	72
FirstIndep	FFSL	14.50	85
ELECTRONICS			
AndrsnGp	ANDR	10.25	28
SyprisSol	SYPR	11.00	46
TELECOMM			
Covista	CVST	7.75	19
PRINT/PUB			
MultiColor	LABL	21.03	80
MISC			

Name	Symbol	Price	EPS
SensormtcEl(n)	SRM	25.6	
5			44
LEISURE			
SingingMch(a)	SMD	8.73	32
INSURANCE			
HilbRogal(n)	HRH	54.80	95
ENERGY			
ShamrockLg(n)	UDL	37.95	75
BUSINESS SVC			
Corvel	CRVL	27.01	92
BUILDING			
Dectron Intl	DECT	7.45	73
AUTO&PARTS			
DscntAuto(n)	DAP	16.50	83
APPAREL			
LeslieFay	LFAY	4.80	20
AIRCRAFT			
Simula(a)	SMU	5.33	80
INDUSTRY GROUP N/A			
ChartrFnl	CHFN	14.32	3
New Lows			
MEDICAL (7)			
Isomet		2.65	49
Ortec		4.75	12

Investor's Business Daily®
October 19, 2001

Sample IBD's New Highs List

back 3½ months and include stochastic price momentum lines. This is helpful not only to commodity traders but to corporate officials and students of the economy as well. The price of crude oil, for instance, may influence inflation rates as well as the health of airline stocks; lumber prices give a hint of the building industry's health. To invest well, it's important to stay tuned to everything from currencies to corn and understand what's leading and lagging. Spot (cash) and future price tables are also furnished for a variety of commodities.

Check "Up" Versus "Down" Corporate Earnings Reports Daily

When corporations announce their quarterly earnings results, IBD separates the reports into those showing increases and those showing decreases. Percentage changes in both earnings and sales are also shown. The company's stock, its symbol, closing price, EPS and RS Ratings are provided as well. There are also separate lists of "Best Ups" and "Worst Downs."

Earnings News

The ★ means quarter is up 30% or more & sales & earnings gain accelerated from the prior quarter. ↑ or ↓ means % chg is higher or lower than prior quarter. Stock price, relative strength, group & EPS Rating reflect prior day's data.

Best Ups

Company	Symbol	Last Qtr % Chg	Last Qtr Earnings	Last Qtr Sales	A. Tax Margin
CHOLESTECH CORP	CTEC	+ 550% ↑	0.13 vs 0.02 +	39% ↑ +	13.3% ↑
CAPSTEAD MORTGAGE CORP	CMO	+ 383%	1.45 vs 0.30 +	0% +	0.0%
ITRON INC	ITRI	+ 317% ↑	0.25 vs 0.06 +	45% ↑ +	6.4% ↑
GENESIS MICROCHIP INC	GNSS	+ 220% ↑	0.32 vs 0.10 +	140% ↑ +	18.4% ↑
K L A TENCOR CORP	KLAC	+ 207% ↑	0.46 vs 0.15 +	31% ↑ +	17.2% ↓
TRANSALTA CORP	TAC	+ 186%	0.20 vs 0.07 +	73% +	6.2%
WOLOHAN LUMBER CO	WLHN	+ 174% ↑	0.63 vs 0.23 –	20% ↑ +	2.8% ↑
TARO PHARMACEUTICAL INDS	TARO	+ 162% ↓	0.34 vs 0.13 +	52% ↑ +	17.7% ↑
DIAL CORP	DL	+ 160%	0.26 vs 0.10 +	12% +	5.6%
BANCORPSOUTH INC	BXS	+ 136%	0.26 vs 0.11 +	0% +	0.0%
WELLS FINANCIAL CORP	WEFC	+ 136%	0.85 vs 0.36 +	0% +	0.0%
T H Q INC	THQI	+ 133%	0.14 vs 0.06 +	28% ↓ +	4.7% ↓
KINDER MORGAN INC	KMI	+ 126%	0.52 vs 0.23 +	69% +	25.6%
PEOPLESOFT INC	PSFT	+ 113%	0.17 vs 0.08 +	15% +	9.9%
SMITH INTERNATIONAL	SII	+ 105%	0.84 vs 0.41 +	27% +	4.6%

Investor's Business Daily®
October 9, 2001
Sample IBD's Earnings News Summary

Smart Mutual Fund Price Tables Reveal Past Performance

Many investors buy mutual funds. *Investor's Business Daily's* unique mutual fund tables can help you make sounder evaluations because every Friday they show each fund's year-to-date total return and the last 52 weeks' percentage change plus the prior three years' rating of total results and five-year after-tax return. IBD was the first newspaper to show performance data in its fund tables. In addition, different graphs are shown each day of outstanding funds and their most recent, publicly available stock buys and sells. Some of their top new buys could be ideas for you to research further. Mutual fund managers are not only some of the biggest investors, but they are usually well informed about the stocks they buy. They have teams of analysts that do reviews of each company's financial reports, and you may want to capitalize upon their research efforts. Also, mutual funds pack more power into any purchase or sale of stock. The earlier you catch the moves they make that are sound, the better your potential.

The 10% of funds that rise the most each day are boldfaced in IBD's fund tables. Check out "Mutual Funds," which features interviews with top money managers, to find what stocks they're buying and their market perspective. Each month, the "Funds & Personal Finance" special section also lists the "New Buys of Top-Rated Mutual Funds" with 130 top-performing stocks the best-performing funds are buying.

New Issues, Corporate Offerings, and New Listings

Pending new issues are listed showing you the dollar amount, indicated price, type of security offered, business description of each company, and the underwriter's name.

Yield-Curve Graphic Display Plus Selected Interest Rates

Interest rates impact everyone. The Fed Funds Rate, FRB Discount Rate, rate of three-month Treasury Bills, the prime rate, rates of 30-year Treasury

MUTUAL FUND PERFORMANCE

36 Mos Performance Rating | Fund	2001 % Chg	12wk % Chg	5 Yr After Tax%	Net Asset Value	NAV Chg
For Thursday, October 18, 2001					
—A—					
AAL A					
$ 6.5 bil 800–553–6319					
C+ Balanced b	−7	−3	..	11.54	−.06
C+ Bond	+8	+4	+27	10.14	..
C− Capital Gr	−20	−9	+66	29.39	−.28
D− Equity Income	−15	−9	+36	12.34	−.16
E High Yield Bd	−2	−1	..	6.27	..
E International	−30	−10	−15	8.26	−.15
A− Mid Cap Stk	−24	−15	+8	11.45	−.10
D Muni Bond	+7	+3	+23	11.39	..
A Small Cap Stk	−6	−10	+28	12.44	−.14
AAL B					
$ 265 mil 800–553–6319					
D Capital Gr	−20	−9	..	28.36n	−.27
AAL Instl					
$ 166 mil 800–553–6319					
Bond	+9	+4	..	10.15n	+.01
Capital Gr	−20	−9	..	29.44n	−.28
AARP Investment					
$12.7 bil 800–322–2282					
Scud PthwyGr	−18	−10	..	11.86n	−.09
E Scudder Bal	−10	−6	+20	16.76n	−.06
Scudder Glbl	−19	−7	..	21.52n	−.33
B− Scudder GNMA	+8	+3	+26	15.37n	..
Scudder Gr&In	−18	−11	..	19.56n	−.14
E Scudder Inc	+7	+2	..	12.81n	−.01
Scudder Mgd	+6	+3	..	9.24n	..
Scudder ShTrm	+6	+2	..	10.81n	..
D− ScudderCapGr	−27	−13	+35	41.62n	−.21
ScudderS&P500	−19	−11	..	14.22n	−.11
ScudPthwyCn	−5	−4	..	10.98n	−.04

36 Mos Performance Rating | Fund	2001 % Chg	12wk % Chg	5 Yr After Tax%	Net Asset Value	NAV Chg
D− Muni Bond m	+4	+1	+13	8.08n	..
C− Select Eq	−34	−16	+26	13.96n	−.15
A+ SmCapOpp m	−19	−10	..	11 71n	−13
A+ Sml Cap Gr m	−26	−15	..	21.09n	−.22
E Strat Inc m	0	−1	−10	8.63n	..
D− Value m	−19	−11	+37	9.68n	−.11
Value II m	−26	−16	..	6.36n	−.08
E Weingarten m	−38	−13	−3	12.00n	−.13
AIM Funds C					
$ 4.9 bil 800–554–1156					
Aggress Gr m	−32	−17	..	8.44n	−.10
E Balanced b	−16	−8	..	24.92n	−.17
Basic Value m	−10	−13	..	24.93n	−.16
E Blue Chip m	−29	−12	..	10.95n	−.07
A− Cap Dvlp m	−20	−15	..	14.02n	−.12
E Charter m	−29	−14	..	10.33n	−.08
E Constellatn m	−32	−15	..	18.97n	−.14
Dent Demo m	−41	−19	..	7.48n	−.06
E Glbl Growth m	−34	−11	..	14.09n	−.13
E High Yield b	−7	−3	..	4.60n	+.01
E Intl Equity m	−28	−14	..	13.96n	−.15
E Intl Value m	−20	−9	+10	12.21n	−.13
Lg Cap Opp m	−31	−14	..	8.76n	−.09
Lrg Cap Gr m	−42	−12	..	8.68n	−.06
MdCapOpp m	−29	−12	..	15.73n	−.19
C− Select Eq m	−34	−16	..	13.94n	−.15
D− Value m	−19	−11	..	9.68n	−.12
E Weingarten m	−38	−13	..	12.01n	−.13
AIM Glb Theme					
$ 2.3 bil 800–347–4246					
A+ Finl Svcs A b	−17	−12	+84	20.71	−.20
A+ Finl Svcs B m	−18	−12	+79	20.01n	−.20
A+ Hlth Care A b	−1	−4	+92	30.32	−.19
A+ Hlth Care B m	−1	−4	+87	28.40n	−.18

Investor's Business Daily®
October 19, 2001
Sample IBD's Mutual Fund Tables

Bonds and tax-exempt bonds, rate of Moody's AA utilities, and 90-day CD interest rates are shown graphically each day. A yield curve of U.S. Treasury issues is also available daily. These important rates should help you better plan your business financing, personal financing, and investing.

Separate Convertible Bond Tables With Key Data

Convertibles are shown in their own table with key data such as S&P ratings, yield to maturity, volume, conversion ratio, and premium or discount calculated to save you time.

"Your Weekend Graphic Review"

Every Friday, you'll see charts of companies that are within 15% of their price highs and have both EPS and RS Ratings of 85 or more. It's a great prospect list closely followed by many serious investors.

"Investor's Corner"

Ongoing education for both new and experienced investors is essential to successful investing. "Investor's Corner" is a daily column with insights and lessons to help build solid investing skills. It's on the front page.

You will find over time that most of your investing questions will be answered in this column. A wide variety of topics are covered to build your knowledge, and pertinent lessons are offered during critical market turns. In addition, the full-page, twice-weekly feature, "The Smart Investor," is devoted to further educating investors of all levels.

"The New America": Innovation and Leadership

Another place to search for new stock ideas and possible leaders is "The New America" column, focusing on entrepreneurial companies with new products and services or those that are changing the way we live or do business. The real leaders are often companies with the most innovative products and the best management.

Each day, you can study companies growing rapidly and creating or competing in new markets. This will provide you with ideas for further research.

Internet and Technology Insights

An extensive, two- or three-page section, "Internet & Technology," focuses on this area because so many great companies in the past have been in this category: Microsoft, Dell, Intel, Cisco, and AOL, to name a few. You can learn about new innovations at leading technology companies and the important new products and technologies coming from this industry in the future. IBD is where many technology company managers go to stay on top of rapid changes as they emerge.

THE NEW AMERICA

Broadening Its Reach
FTI's expansion into new areas has helped boost its sales, cash flow and payroll.

Annual revenue

Annual cash flow

Personnel

Source: Company reports; Datamonitor Capital Markets; I.T.R. Securities

FTI CONSULTING INC. *Annapolis, Maryland*

Shift In Business Focus Lifts Consultant's Sales

BY ALAN R. ELLIOTT
INVESTOR'S BUSINESS DAILY

Forensics once was the art of argument. Today the term describes a growing number of expert fields. Each investigates, prepares and supports complex technical issues, often for use during trial or litigation.

Those fields are the stomping grounds of FTI Consulting Inc. A hothouse for trial-based engineering research, the firm recently expanded to handle bankruptcy, restructuring and turnaround consulting for banks and other corporations.

Three years ago, financial consulting contributed less than 5% of the

"We determined the fastest-growing part of our marketplace was financial consulting," he said. "So we decided to get into that business."

The change didn't come cheap. Three acquisitions in 1998 helped grow revenue 33% that year to $58.6 million. But earnings dropped 27%, and long-term debt jumped to $46 million.

"We were a micro-cap company," Dunn said. "We decided to pursue our strategy of growth even though we didn't have stock to use as capital. So we had to go borrow."

FTI is a talent-based operation. Its assets aren't tied up in facilities or equipment. Its manufacturing takes place between the ears of its staff.

The firm significantly increased

ADVANCED TECHNICAL PRODUCTS INC. *Roswell, Georgia*

After A Tough Start, Supplier Hits Its Stride

BY AMY REEVES
INVESTOR'S BUSINESS DAILY

Getting a new company off the ground is always a tough, exhilarating job. But for Advanced Technical Products Inc., the first few years were more exciting than anyone wanted.

The firm was formed in 1996 for the express purpose of buying three units of Brunswick Corp. that made military gear. Brunswick today makes pleasure boats, billiards and bowling balls.

But the three units Advanced Technical eyed made products such as chemical and biological agent detectors, camouflage, fuel tanks and missile-launch tubes.

For two years the firm was private. But in 1997 it went public by merging with Lunn Industries, maker of structures like aircraft doors, floors, bulkheads and tail cones.

For a while, things seemed to go humming along. In 1999 the company drew the attention of Veritas Group, leading to another merger agreement.

'Out Of Control'

In January 2000, the trouble started. Authorities discovered that managers of Alcore Inc., a Lunn unit, had been overstating results to drive up the firm's stock. They then sold shares for their own profit.

No one charged officers in the parent company or other units, but the damage was done. The stock plunged, investors fled and Veritas bailed out of the merger deal.

"It was like management was out of control," said Roger Favale, president.

Guarding The Future

Advanced Technical Products' monitors for chemical and biological weapons, like this new vehicle-mounted model, are taking the firm into a new era

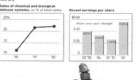

Sales of chemical and biological defense systems, as % of total sales

Recent earnings per share

Source: Company reports

ing the banks elsewhere. Frankly, there was a point where I got disgusted."

Nowadays, Favale sees a lot of promise in Advanced Technical. A new chief executive, Garrett Dominy, took over last year. In June, the firm finally unloaded Alcore on M.C. Gill Corp. for $5 million.

cent order.

In August, Advanced Technical got a $2.5 million order for petroleum-analysis shelters and a $5 million order for camouflage gear and chemical monitors. It also has a long-term contract to supply gear for F-16 and F-22 fighter planes and the B-17 cargo plane.

It's developing a chemical detector that can be mounted on a truck or helicopter.

Dominy sees a possible spike in that business, as well as in missile defense. Advanced Technical makes motor cases for the PAC-3 system, which can strike down oncoming missiles.

Fueling Growth

Although the military makes up 80% of Advanced Technical's business, Dominy and Favale also see promise in the firm's products for alternative-fuel vehicles. It uses composite materials to make natural-gas tanks big enough for buses but so lightweight they can be mounted on top of the vehicle.

On Oct. 1, it introduced what it called the world's largest natural-gas fuel tank, measuring 21.2 inches in diameter. The tank is designed to overcome a major problem with alternative-fuel vehicles: how far they can go without refueling.

All this is paying off in the company's financial results. In the second quarter it earned 56 cents a share, double the prior-year figure. Sales rose 16% to $52 million.

Among the deals highlighted in Advanced Technical's second-quarter earnings statement: contract options for additional Lightweight Camouflage Screen Systems by the U.S. Army's Communications-Electronic command.

The firm also got a contract from Honeywell Engines and Systems for the production of a jet engine fan duct using the resin transfer molding process.

Despite the fact that cash is flow-

Investor's Business Daily®
October 9, 2001

Sample IBD's New America

INTERNET & TECHNOLOGY

Clean Niche: Remaking Cartridges For Printers

BY GARY M. STERN
FOR INVESTOR'S BUSINESS DAILY

Anyone who owns an inkjet printer, fax machine or copier likely uses print cartridges. But what happens when the toner dries up and the cartridges can no longer be used?

Usually they're thrown away. According to Nabil Nasr, director of the National Center for Remanufacturing and Resource Recovery at Rochester (N.Y.) Institute of Technology, used toner cartridges create 38,000 tons of waste annually.

"It's a big environmental problem, given the volume," he said.

More than 10,000 start-up cartridge remanufacturers employ 65,000 people in the U.S., generating $160 million in annual revenue, according to Nasr.

At one end of the scale is 500-employee GRC in Chatsworth, Calif. GRC says its sales topped $50 million in 2000 — about a third of total revenue for the remanufactured cartridge industry.

At the opposite end are companies like one-person Magnolia Ink, formed in 1998 in Lucedale, Miss.

"These companies are filling a niche," Nasr said. "You don't need heavy equipment, margins are good and the technology is easy."

When Donna Davis saw how pricey new print cartridges were,

Video On Demand
The U.S. market for movies bought and downloaded via the Internet could top $1.3 billion in 2005

Sales, in millions

Consumers initially would download movies, such as "Stuart Little," to their PCs. They could connect their PC to their TV with a special cable or wireless device

Source: Cahners In-Stat Group

Video-On-Demand's On Deck
Hollywood studios set to bring movies to homes via Web

BY PATRICK SEITZ
INVESTOR'S BUSINESS DAILY

The major Hollywood studios have come out with fuzzy plans to deliver movies online to consumers early next year. They have many hurdles to clear before people can download the latest Julia Roberts film.

Analysts don't expect the ventures to get off to a slow start. The reason? There are few broadband Internet

and SeaChange International Inc. could benefit as well. Other companies would provide billing systems and content delivery networks.

Assembling the right technology is only one hurdle. The two ventures also have to structure themselves in a way that will please their partners and government regulators.

People can link their PCs to their TVs with a special cable or radio frequency device.

Eventually, studios hope to deliver their movies to cable set-top boxes and other consumer products that are easier for people to use.

Key early markets for video on demand will include college students with high-speed Internet access in their dorms and workers with broadband at their offices.

With New Benchmark, AMD Aims To Prove It Measures Up To Intel

Gauge Compares Rival Chips

Chipmaker also to release a new line of processors, AMD's fastest chips ever

BY JAMES DETAR
INVESTOR'S BUSINESS DAILY

Advanced Micro Devices Inc. is out to tackle a growing problem: There's no accurate way to compare rival microprocessors.

AMD, the No. 2 maker of personal computer processors, will propose a new industry benchmark on Tuesday. The rating scheme will make it easier to compare one PC processor with another, the company says.

Back when AMD and Intel Corp. design, megahertz was an accurate measure, says AMD Chief Executive Jerry Sanders. But when AMD went its own way in the mid-1990s, the old rules went out the window.

"When they made a 386 and we made a 386, the guy that had the fastest clock speed had the fastest part, because the architectures were the same," Sanders said. "But when we went to the K5 and then the K6 and K7 (Athlon), we had our own architecture."

Sanders says AMD's current de-

In the past, consumers got used to rating microprocessors by clock speed. Today's average PC, for example, runs at a clock rate of about 800 megahertz. That means it can do 800 million operations a second.

The fastest clock speed today is the Intel 2-gigahertz Pentium 4 — that's 2,000 megahertz. AMD's fastest processor is the 1.53-gigahertz Athlon XP.

Unfair Edge?

Sanders says the megahertz rating unfairly favors Intel, which touts its clock speeds. Some analysts agree.

"We've used megahertz as a default measurement" for many years, said analyst Mike Feibus at Mercury Research Inc. of Scottsdale, Ariz.

"It was the best thing we had. But when you compare two different platforms like the Intel Pentium 4 and AMD Athlon, it's not much good," Feibus said.

Even Intel officials admit that raw clock speed is no longer as important.

"For 20 years, we have been focused religiously on delivering and taking advantage of that next megahertz," Paul Otellini, an Intel vice president, said at a conference in August.

"As we go forward and start focusing on the compute experience, we

Investor's Business Daily®
October 9, 2001

Sample IBD's Internet & Technology

National Economic Analysis

Policy decisions in Washington, D.C., can have a real financial impact on your investments, and IBD is committed to writing editorials that can influence public policy and change. After an editorial in a September 1985 issue of *Investor's Business Daily* outlining the rationale for further discount rate cuts, we received a short, to-the-point letter from Don Regan, Chief of Staff to former President Reagan. The letter said, ". . . rest assured this will get to all the right places and something will be done about it." The next month Paul Volker, then Federal Reserve Board Chairman, in a speech in Canada, mentioned that money supply was only one of a number of causes of inflation, and the following February the Fed began the first of several discount rate cuts during the subsequent six months.

Investor's Business Daily penned more than 60 editorials on the serious defects and errors in our government's 1993 proposed reform and takeover of the American healthcare system. These editorials were bound into a booklet (now out of print) that was purchased by hundreds of business, political, and media leaders. One daily reader, former Congressman Jack Kemp, said *Investor's Business Daily* carried the most informative coverage on this critical national issue.

Our full-page ad entitled "Enough Is Enough" appeared in *Investor's Business Daily* on the first day off the market bottom in September 2001. It listed many positive actions for Congress and the country to take at a time when there was widespread fear. The ad also ran in *The New York Times*. (See ad at the beginning of this book.)

How to Get the Most Out of IBD Power Tools on Investors.com

Investors.com is the online companion to *Investor's Business Daily's* print edition. This online research tool will take you to the next level by evaluating your investment ideas and selections and generating many new ones.

We discussed the ways *Investor's Business Daily* starts the research process with an efficient assessment of the market, industry groups, and stocks. Here are some additional ways to dig deeper in your research with IBD's specially designed screening tools and charts.

If you're reading this book to hone your investing skills, going through these tools in the following manner will help you develop an easy daily system to review the market, top industries, and, finally, the top stocks. This method will help you find the best stocks, know the right time to buy and sell, and materially improve your results.

The key is to take some time to become familiar with investors.com and learn to navigate the IBD Power Tools. The CAN SLIM™ chapters in this book will help you understand the rationale for the IBD Power Tools, which are programmed to search for companies with the performance characteristics typical of emerging stock market winners.

Tools to Validate Your Ideas

First, let's look at how you can evaluate any stocks you already own or are thinking of buying. There are many questions that should first be answered:

- Is this the right stock to own? Or are there better ones in its group?
- Is the stock in a leading industry group or a laggard one?
- If you own a stock, have you held it too long?
- If the stock looks fundamentally strong and you want to invest in it, is it too soon or too late?

These are just a few questions that need answers before you make your move. The following IBD Power Tools will help you sort through the stock-picking puzzle.

IBD Stock Checkup℠

IBD Stock Checkup℠ evaluates and compares almost 10,000 publicly traded companies and assigns an Overall Rating to put your ideas in the proper perspective. It's essentially a research report with a summary letter grade. There are several components to this report. They include:

- Overall Rating
- Stock's Diagnosis
- Stock's Rank Within Its Industry Group
- Top 5 Companies in the Group
- *SmartSelect*® Ratings

Overall Rating—Grading Your Stock. Does It Pass or Fail?

The Stock Checkup℠ Overall Rating is a quick way to know whether you should move ahead or not. It's like a traffic light that tells you whether to go, slow down, or stop in your research, and it will guide you toward only the very best companies.

Based on the key characteristics of winning stocks, the Overall Rating (A to E, with A being the best and E being the worst) combines the five key

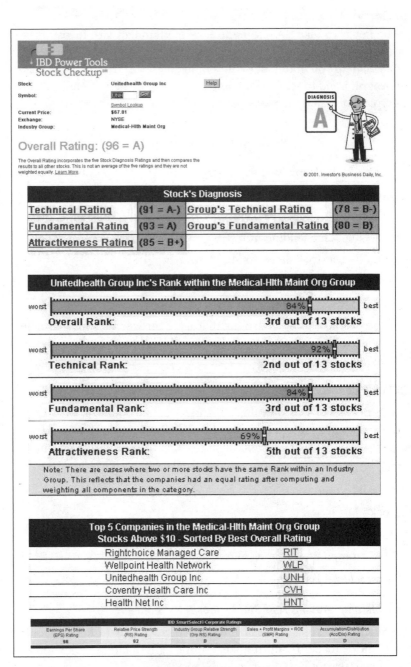

IBD Power Tools
Stock Checkup℠

Stock:	Unitedhealth Group Inc	Help
Symbol:	UNH Go!	
	Symbol Lookup	
Current Price:	$67.81	
Exchange:	NYSE	
Industry Group:	Medical-Hlth Maint Org	

DIAGNOSIS
A

Overall Rating: (96 = A)

The Overall Rating incorporates the five Stock Diagnosis Ratings and then compares the results to all other stocks. This is not an average of the five ratings and they are not weighted equally. Learn More.

© 2001. Investor's Business Daily, Inc.

Stock's Diagnosis			
Technical Rating	(91 = A-)	Group's Technical Rating	(78 = B-)
Fundamental Rating	(93 = A)	Group's Fundamental Rating	(80 = B)
Attractiveness Rating	(85 = B+)		

Unitedhealth Group Inc's Rank within the Medical-Hlth Maint Org Group

worst ———————————————— 84% ———— best
Overall Rank: 3rd out of 13 stocks

worst ———————————————— 92% ———— best
Technical Rank: 2nd out of 13 stocks

worst ———————————————— 84% ———— best
Fundamental Rank: 3rd out of 13 stocks

worst ———————— 69% ———————— best
Attractiveness Rank: 5th out of 13 stocks

Note: There are cases where two or more stocks have the same Rank within an Industry Group. This reflects that the companies had an equal rating after computing and weighting all components in the category.

Top 5 Companies in the Medical-Hlth Maint Org Group	
Stocks Above $10 - Sorted By Best Overall Rating	
Rightchoice Managed Care	RIT
Wellpoint Health Network	WLP
Unitedhealth Group Inc	UNH
Coventry Health Care Inc	CVH
Health Net Inc	HNT

IBD SmartSelect Corporate Ratings				
Earnings Per Share (EPS) Rating	Relative Price Strength (RS) Rating	Industry Group Relative Strength (Grp RS) Rating	Sales + Profit Margins + ROE (SMR) Rating	Accumulation/Distribution (Acc/Dis) Rating
96	82	B	B	D

www.investors.com
October 16, 2001

Sample Investors.com Stock Checkup℠

190

factors shown in the Stock's Diagnosis. It gives you a summary of both the fundamental and technical performance of a company. An A indicates a stock is performing in the top 20% of all stocks.

Stock Diagnosis—Determining the Health of Your Stock

The Stock's Diagnosis includes five of the most critical factors influencing a stock. It tells you how your stock compares to the rest of the market in these critical areas. It also alerts you to what the industry group is doing as a whole, both fundamentally and technically. Historically, the best stocks are found in the leading industries. Always check the strength of the industry group. Typically, you should look for stocks in the top 40 industries (the top 20%).

Stock's Rank Within Its Industry Group—Buy the Best Stocks in the Top Groups

If you scan down the Stock Checkup^sm, you can see how the stock specifically performs against the rest of the stocks in its industry group. This will help you determine if you're making the right choices. It's easy to be swayed by news or TV tips, but this will give you a major edge by sticking to the facts.

Top Five Stocks in the Group—Pointing You Toward Real Potential Leadership

No matter what you've bought or are thinking about buying, this screen shows you where the real leadership is. These are the stocks exhibiting the necessary performance that might propel them further.

IBD SmartSelect® Corporate Ratings

Further down the screen are the IBD *SmartSelect*® Corporate Ratings conveniently displayed for still more perspective.

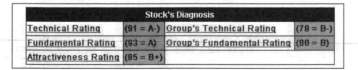

Stock's Diagnosis			
Technical Rating	(91 = A-)	Group's Technical Rating	(78 = B-)
Fundamental Rating	(93 = A)	Group's Fundamental Rating	(80 = B)
Attractiveness Rating	(85 = B+)		

www.investors.com
October 16, 2001
Sample Stock Checkup^SM Diagnosis

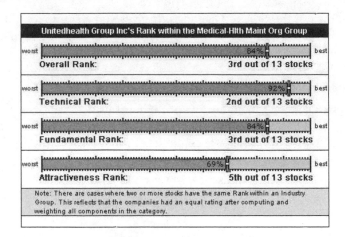

www.investors.com
October 16, 2001

Top 5 Companies in the Medical-Hlth Maint Org Group Stocks Above $10 - Sorted By Best Overall Rating	
Rightchoice Managed Care	RIT
Wellpoint Health Network	WLP
Unitedhealth Group Inc	UNH
Coventry Health Care Inc	CVH
Health Net Inc	HNT

www.investors.com
October 16, 2001

IBD SmartSelect® Corporate Ratings				
Earnings Per Share (EPS) Rating	Relative Price Strength (RS) Rating	Industry Group Relative Strength (Grp RS) Rating	Sales + Profit Margins + ROE (SMR) Rating	Accumulation/Distribution (Acc/Dis) Rating
96	82	B	B	D

www.investors.com
October 16, 2001

(Above) Three sample Stock Checkup^{SM} Diagnoses

IBD Charts—Show You the *Right Time* to Buy or Sell

You never want to buy any highly rated or yellow-highlighted stock in IBD's tables without first checking a chart, and it pays to review both daily and weekly charts regularly on any stocks you own. This is a vital step that will help you spot emerging trends and track a stock's movement so you know the exact time to buy or sell. IBD Charts are designed to make it easier and faster for both new and experienced chart readers to get the real picture. These daily and weekly charts are made available free to IBD subscribers.

For those who feel intimidated by charts, think of a stock chart as a "picture worth a thousand words." It will tell you some vital things about the progress (or lack of progress) for any company. In time, you will find your review is quite automatic. Daily charts can also help you spot possible future winners. IBD Daily Charts include the following:

- Up days in price in blue; down days in red
- Continually updated price and volume data
- EPS and RS Ratings
- Relative Price Strength Line
- 50- and 200-day moving averages of price

Refer again to Chapter 12 to learn to recognize chart patterns. You may also want to consult the IBD Learning Center on investors.com for a course

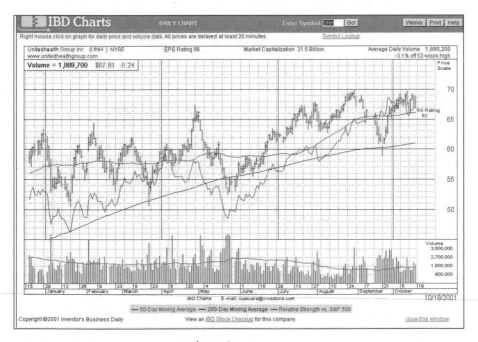

www.investors.com
October 16, 2001
Sample IBD Daily Chart

on chart analysis. Also remember that the majority of stocks tend to follow the overall trend of the market, so be sure to consult the general market indices in *Investor's Business Daily* (The Dow, Nasdaq, and S&P 500) plus IBD's "The Big Picture" daily market interpretation column to make sure your general market timing is correct.

Weekly Charts–Tip-Off to Institutional Trading

IBD Weekly Charts will help you gauge institutional buying. Since mutual funds typically take days, if not weeks (and sometimes longer), to build (or unload) their positions, any heavy volume on the chart may tell you if they're possibly moving in or out of a stock in a major way.

Weekly charts include the same information that appears on the daily charts, with the addition of Shares Outstanding. These charts span nearly two years of price and volume movements.

To capture the biggest gains, it's important to use both daily and weekly charts since they offer varying views on a stock. You will get more exact timing indications from the dailies and the big picture from the weeklies.

Idea-Generating Online Tools

Here are additional tools that may offer you new investment ideas.

"Where the Big Money's Flowing Now"–Learn What the Institutions May Be Buying and Selling as It Happens

This is the online version of the IBD print edition feature, and it appears on the investors.com home page. As we've mentioned earlier, just looking at typical most-active lists won't give you the whole picture. You need to know about the emerging institutional trades that are beginning to show promise. These stocks will appear on this radar screen that is updated continuously throughout the trading day. You can quickly spot the stocks that institutions may be moving into—or out of—in a major way as it happens. Remember that institutional buyers that are taking a position in a stock usually buy in huge quantities that may create major volume in the stock.

Nearly every winning stock will show this type of activity at the onset of its price advance. You don't want to miss this screen if you are searching for emerging leaders. Remember that not all stocks shown on this list will be winners. It's important to check further to make sure the stock's chart looks sound and the ratings show leadership potential. This is a good way to spot the breakout of a stock as it is happening or shortly thereafter.

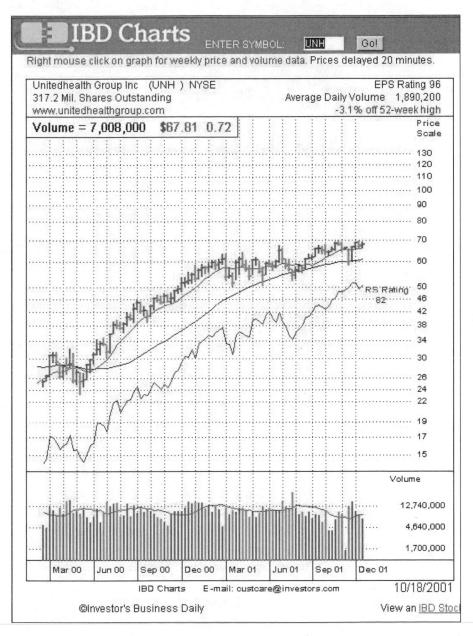

Right mouse click on graph for weekly price and volume data. Prices delayed 20 minutes.

Unitedhealth Group Inc (UNH) NYSE
317.2 Mil. Shares Outstanding
www.unitedhealthgroup.com

EPS Rating 96
Average Daily Volume 1,890,200
-3.1% off 52-week high

Volume = 7,008,000 $67.81   0.72

Price Scale

130
120
110
100
90
80
70
60
50
46
42
38
34
30
26
24
22
19
17
15

RS Rating 82

Volume

12,740,000
4,640,000
1,700,000

Mar 00   Jun 00   Sep 00   Dec 00   Mar 01   Jun 01   Sep 01   Dec 01

IBD Charts   E-mail: custcare@investors.com   10/18/2001

©Investor's Business Daily   View an IBD Stock

www.investors.com weekly chart
October 16, 2001
Sample IBD Weekly Chart

IBD's 'Where The Big Money's Flowing Now'

10/18/2001

Help

These stocks are experiencing unusually high volume. Click "Get Ratings" for a company analysis.

Stock Symbol	Price (20 min. delay)	Price Change	Volume (1000s)	Volume % Change	SmartSelect® Ratings
Up					
RIT	62.35	+17.24 ⬆	3,249	+5,316	Get Ratings
ICUI	44.15	+5.35 ⬆	232	+537	Get Ratings
ESI	36.23	+2.00 ⬆	524	+214	Get Ratings
HRH	54.61	+4.31 ⬆	300	+171	Get Ratings
SANG	23.25	+0.95 ⬆	754	+144	Get Ratings
AMSG	23.90	+0.80 ⬆	502	+124	Get Ratings
SYK	56.15	+0.77 ⬆	1,092	+117	Get Ratings
Down					
ESITZ	79.75	-9.67 ⬇	554	+3,802	Get Ratings
CSRX	39.97	-8.06 ⬇	19,605	+1,218	Get Ratings
CPWM	16.37	-6.44 ⬇	4,456	+879	Get Ratings
BREL	25.40	-2.10 ⬇	617	+643	Get Ratings
ACAM	34.22	-2.13 ⬇	521	+604	Get Ratings
WST	24.00	-1.35 ⬇	124	+547	Get Ratings
ASW	29.60	-3.26 ⬇	1,217	+535	Get Ratings

TIP: Click the Stock Symbols to view Detailed Quotes. Click your browser's refresh or reload button to update this page.

www.investors.com
October 16, 2001

Sample IBD Where the Big Money's Flowing Now

"Screen of the Day"–Sorting for Leadership and Ideas

Each day, there's a different list that sorts the entire stock database looking for potentially superior stocks based on important performance criteria. This is a quick way to find leaders and the better possible ideas in different categories. Lists change daily and include categories such as Top Relative Price Strength Stocks, *SmartSelect*® All Stars, and Top Acceleration in Earnings.

Intraday "Volume Percent Change"–Another Way to Spot Possible Winners

A stock needs support from institutional buying to propel it further. Volume percentage changes on an intraday basis will tell you if a stock is trading above or below its average daily volume of the last 50 trading days. You can find the intraday "Volume Percent Change" under Quotes.

Continuing Education–The Key to Investing Success

The IBD Learning Center

For most investors, not a day goes by without questions. A complete stock investment course to help you improve your knowledge and skill can be found at investors.com. It outlines every aspect of buying and selling stocks as well as chart reading and many other important topics.

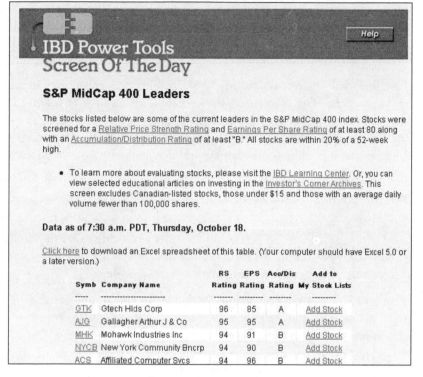

www.investors.com
October 16, 2001
Sample IBD Screen of the Day

Ask Bill O'Neil

It's important that you get all your questions answered, so IBD designed an area on the site to discuss your concerns on topics such as investing principles, chart reading, and how to use IBD's important tools in your research. From the home page, just click on "Ask Bill O'Neil" to read through the extensive archived questions and answers. This is a formidable knowledge base that can be of tremendous value to you. If you still have questions, go to www.askibd.com to access our large database of frequently asked questions.

Daily Graphs Online® Tools and Charts at www.dailygraphs.com

Investor's Business Daily also offers a sophisticated charting service available by subscription only. Daily Graphs® (print edition) and Daily Graphs

Online® are research and reference tools that will further your search for great stocks. These services are available at www.dailygraphs.com, and they provide additional information that should deepen your search still further.

Here's what you'll find online:

- Detailed daily charts on NYSE, AMEX, and Nasdaq stocks updated throughout the day. Shown on these charts are the five years and four quarters of EPS data, profit margins, return on equity, sales growth, annual earnings estimates, shares outstanding and the float, earnings stability, percent held by funds, banks, and management, and much more!
- Special Reports that screen the database for specific criteria that will lead you to top performers.

Both the screens and daily charts will help in your stock selection and market timing. This is a tool you could consider reviewing every day, following your basic research in IBD and on investors.com. Here are just a few of the screening reports that instantly narrow your search:

- **Top 100 Stocks by EPS Rating.** With current and annual earnings playing a major role in a stock's success, you should look at this report every day to find emerging opportunities.
- **Top 100 Stocks by RS Rating.** This list will help you focus on the strongest price performers.
- **Stocks at or Near New Highs.** Focus only on those stocks at or near new highs. Remember that stocks making new highs in a bull market tend to go higher. Look for stocks forming sound bases that are not too far extended in price. This feature zeroes in on stocks at or near their 52-week highs and that also have both EPS and RS Ratings of 80 or higher. This screen could help you catch stocks as they break out into new high ground.

These reports can be sorted in ascending or descending order. You can also minimize the report size and use the space bar on your keyboard to go through the charts on these stocks. This gives you a good view of both the company's fundamental and technical characteristics and helps you determine whether the stock is worth further research. Before purchasing a stock, ask yourself these questions:

1. Is the chart formation sound?
2. Are the quarterly earnings and sales strong?
3. Are the annual earnings and earnings estimates showing growth?
4. Are the *SmartSelect*® Ratings high enough?

The Daily Graphs Online® charts will also show you with the click of a button:

- The five stocks with the highest Relative Price Strength Ratings in the group
- News items on the company
- Percent-off a stock's price high
- Floating number of shares outstanding

IBD Custom Screens at Investors.com

Investor's Business Daily will also offer custom screening of its powerful database. Subscribers to IBD Custom Screens can filter through nearly 10,000 companies. What separates IBD's screening tool from others is its expansive stock database and proprietary screening parameters. The IBD Database can be screened by *SmartSelect*® Ratings, IBD Industry Groups, Earnings, Sales and much more.

In summary, all these time-tested tools combined will give you the most powerful research you can find anywhere, including the Internet or any other publication. Don't forget that the market can turn quickly. With careful daily screening of stocks, industries, and the general market, you will be ready to capitalize at the right time and protect your portfolio when necessary. In addition, keep your eye out for new and exciting features being continually added to these services.

How to Pick the Best Market Sectors, Industry Groups, and Subgroups

The majority of leading stocks are usually in leading industries. Studies show that 37% of a stock's price movement is directly tied to the performance of the industry group the stock is in. Another 12% is due to strength in its overall sector. Therefore, roughly half of a stock's move is due to the strength of its respective group. Because specific industry groups lead each market cycle, you can see how critical it is to consider a stock's industry group before making a purchase.

For the purposes of this discussion, there are three terms we will use: sector, industry group, and subgroup. A *sector* is a broad grouping of companies and industries. These include, for example, basic industries (or "cyclicals"), consumer goods and services, transportation, finance, and high technology. An *industry group* is a smaller, more specific grouping of companies; you normally have several industry groups within one sector. A *subgroup* is even more specific, dividing the industry group into several, very precise subcategories. For example, if we were to look at a company like Viacom, it could be described according to the following:

Sector: Leisure and Entertainment

Industry Group: Media

Subgroup: Radio/TV

For clarity and ease of use, industry group and subgroup names are combined into one description and simply called "industry groups." For example, the industry group for Viacom is known as "Media—Radio/TV."

Why Track 197 Industry Groups?

Why does IBD divide securities into 197 industry groups rather than the 52 groups categorized, say, by Standard & Poor's? It's simple really. All stocks in a given sector do not perform at the same rate. Within a given sector, even if the sector itself is outperforming other sectors, there may be segments of that sector that perform extremely well and others that lag the market. It's important to be able to recognize what's acting better, since this knowledge can mean the difference between superior and mediocre results.

Early on in our study of the market we realized that many of the investment services available at the time did not adequately dissect the market into enough industry groups. It was therefore difficult to determine the specific part of a group where the true leadership was. So we created our own industry groups, breaking down the market into 197 different sub-categories and providing investors with more detailed insights into the makeup of an industry.

How to Determine Which Industry Groups Are Leading the Market

When analyzing industries, we've found some to be so small that signs of strength in the group might not be relevant. If only two small, thinly traded companies make up a sector, it may not be enough to call them a group. On the other hand, there are industries with too many companies, such as the chemical and savings-and-loan industries. This excessive supply does not add to their attractiveness, unless some extremely unusual changes occur in industry conditions.

The 197 industry groups mentioned above can be found each business day in *Investor's Business Daily*. There we rank each group according to its six-month price performance so that you can easily determine which industries are the true leaders. Buyers operating on the "undervalued" philosophy love to do their prospecting in the worst-ranked groups, but analysis has shown that, on average, stocks in the top 50 or 100 groups perform better than those in the bottom 100. To increase your odds of finding a truly outstanding stock in an outstanding industry, concentrate on the top 40 groups.

Both the newspaper and the charting services offer an additional, proprietary source of information to help determine if the stock you're thinking about buying is in a top industry group. Industry Group Relative Strength Rating assigns a letter grade from A+ to E to each publicly traded company that we follow, with A+ being best. A stock with a rating of A+, A, or A– means it is in the top 24% of all industry groups in terms of price performance. (Refer to page 181 for more on Industry Group Relative Strength Rating.)

Every day I also quickly check the "New Price Highs" list in IBD. It is organized in order of the broad industry sectors with the most individual stocks that made new price highs the previous day. You can't find this list in other business publications. Just note the top five or six sectors; they are usually the true leaders.

Another way to find out what industry groups are in or out of favor is to analyze the performance of a mutual fund family's industry funds. Fidelity Investments, one of the nation's successful mutual fund managers, has more than 35 industry mutual funds. A glance at their performance provides yet another good perspective on which industry sectors are doing better.

For William O'Neil + Co. institutional clients, a weekly Datagraph service is provided that arranges 197 industry groups in order of their group relative price strength for the past six months. Stocks in the strongest categories are shown in Volume 1 of the O'Neil Database® books and stocks in the weaker groups are in Volume 2.

The Importance of Following Industry Trends

If economic conditions in 1970 told you to look for an improvement in housing and a big upturn in building, what stocks would have been included in your definition of the building sector? If you acquired a list of them, you'd find that there were hundreds of companies in that sector at the time. So how do you narrow down your choices to the ones that are performing best? The answer: Look at them from the industry group and subgroup levels.

There were actually 10 industry groups within the building sector for investors to consider during the 1971 bull market. That meant 10 different ways you could have played the building boom. Many institutions bought stocks ranging from lumber producer Georgia Pacific to wallboard leader U.S. Gypsum to building-products giant Armstrong Corp. You could have also gone with Masco in the plumbing group, a homebuilder like Kaufman & Broad, building material retailers and wholesalers like Standard Brands Paint and Scotty's Home Builders, or mortgage insurers like MGIC. Then there were manufacturers of mobile homes and other low-cost housing, suppliers of air-conditioning systems, and makers and sellers of furniture and carpets.

Do you know where the traditional building stocks were during 1971? They spent the year in the bottom half of all industry groups, while newer, building-related subgroups in better-performing industry groups more than tripled! On August 14, 1970, the mobile home group crossed into the top

100 industry groups and stayed there until February 12, 1971. The group returned to the top 100 on May 14, 1971, and then fell into the bottom half again on July 28, 1972. In the prior cycle, mobile homes were in the top 100 groups in December 1967 and dropped to the bottom half in 1969. The price advances of mobile home stocks were spellbinding during these positive periods.

From 1978 to 1981, the computer industry was one of the leading sectors. Traditionally, money managers then thought of the industry as consisting of IBM, Burroughs, Sperry Rand, and the like, but these were all large mainframe computer manufacturers, and they failed to perform during that cycle. Why? Because while the computer sector was hot, some industry groups within it, like mainframe computers, were not. Meanwhile, the computer sector's many other subdivisions performed unbelievably. During that period, you could have selected stocks from groups such as minicomputers (Prime Computer), microcomputers (Commodore International), graphics (Computervision), word processors (Wang Labs), peripherals (Verbatim), software (Cullinane Database), or time-sharing (Electronic Data Systems). These winners increased 5 to 10 times in price.

During 1998 and 1999, the computer sector again led with 50 to 75 computer-related stocks making *Investor's Business Daily's* new high list almost daily. However, it was Siebel Systems, Oracle, and Veritas in the enterprise software group, and Brocade and Emulex (local network stocks) that provided leadership. The computer–Internet group boomed with Cisco, Juniper, and BEA Systems; and EMC and Network Appliance in the memory group had enormous runs while the former leading personal computers group lagged in 1999. After their tremendous increases, most of these leaders then topped in 2000.

Many new subgroups have sprung up since then, and many more will spring up in the future as new technologies are dreamed up and applied. We are in the computer, communications, and space age. New inventions and technologies will spawn thousands of new and superior products and services. We're benefiting from an endless stream of ingenious offshoots from the original mainframe industry, and in the past they came so fast we had to more frequently update the various industry categories in our database just to keep up with it.

A Look at Industries of the Past and What's Coming in the Future

At one time, computer and electronic stocks may outperform. In another period, retail or defense stocks will stand out. The industry that leads throughout one bull market normally won't come back to lead in the next, though there have been exceptions. Groups that emerge late in a bull phase are sometimes early enough in their own stage of improvement to weather a bear market and then resume their advance, assuming leadership when a new bull starts.

These were the leading industry groups of each bull market from 1953 through 2000:

1953–1954	Aerospace, aluminum, building, paper, steel
1958	Bowling, electronics, publishing
1959	Vending machines
1960	Food, savings and loans, tobacco
1963	Airlines
1965	Aerospace, color television, semiconductors
1967	Computers, conglomerates, hotels
1968	Mobile homes
1970	Building, coal, oil service, restaurants, retailing
1971	Mobile homes
1973	Gold, silver
1974	Coal
1975	Catalog showrooms, oil
1976	Hospitals, pollution, nursing homes, oil
1978	Electronics, oil, small computers
1979	Oil, oil service, small computers
1980	Small computers
1982	Apparel, autos, building, discount supermarkets, military electronics, mobile homes, retail apparel, toys
1984–1987	Generic drugs, foods, confectionery and bakery, supermarkets, cable TV, computer software
1988–1990	Shoes, sugar, cable TV, computer software, jewelry stores, telecommunications, outpatient healthcare
1990–1994	Medical products, biotech, HMOs, computer peripheral/LAN, restaurants, gaming, banks, oil and gas exploration, semiconductors, telecommunications, generic drugs, cable TV
1995–1998	Computer peripheral/LAN, computer software, Internet, banks/finance, computer-PC/workstation, oil/gas drilling, retail-discount/variety
1999–2000	Internet, medical-biomed/genetics, computer-memory devices, telecommunications equipment, semiconductor manufacturing, computer-networking, fiber optic components, computer software-enterprise

As you might imagine, industries of the future create gigantic opportunities for everyone. While they occasionally come into favor, industries of the past offer less dazzling possibilities.

Here are major industries well past their peaks as of 2000:

1. Steel
2. Copper
3. Aluminum
4. Gold
5. Silver
6. Building materials
7. Oil
8. Textiles
9. Containers
10. Chemical
11. Appliances
12. Paper
13. Railroads and railroad equipment
14. Utilities
15. Tobacco
16. Airlines
17. Old-line department stores

Industries of the present and future might include:

1. Computer, computer-related services, and software
2. Internet and e-commerce
3. Laser technology
4. Electronics
5. Telecommunications
6. New concepts in retailing
7. Medical, drug, and biomedical/genetics
8. Special services

Possible future groups might include wireless, storage area networking, person-to-person networking, network security, palmtop computers, wearable computers, proteomics, and, off in the distant future, nanotechnology and DNA-based microchips.

The Importance of Tracking Many Nasdaq Stocks

Groups that emerge as leaders in a new bull market cycle can be found by observing unusual strength in one or two Nasdaq stocks and relating that strength to similar power in a listed stock of the same group.

Initial strength in only one listed stock is not sufficient to attract attention to a category, but confirmation by one or two kindred Nasdaq issues can quickly steer you to a possible industry recovery. You can see this by looking at the accompanying charts of homebuilder Centex's OTC-traded stock, from March to August of 1970, and of homebuilder Kaufman & Broad's NYSE-listed shares, from April to August of the same year:

1. Centex's relative strength in the prior year was strong and made a new high three months before the stock price did.
2. Earnings accelerated (by 50%) during the June 1970 quarter.
3. The stock was selling near an all-time high at the bottom of a bear market.
4. A strong Centex base coincided with the base in Kaufman & Broad.

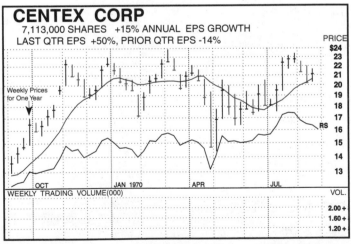

Comparing Centex Corp (above) and Kaufman & Broad Home (on the next page), note the simultaneous strength of two different stocks in the same industry.

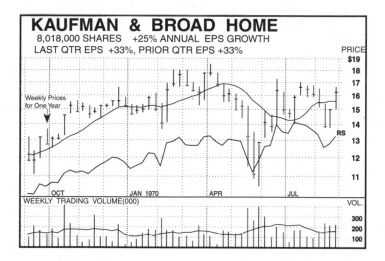

A Stock's Weakness Can Spill Over to the Group

Grouping and tracking stocks by industry group can also help get you out of weakening investments faster. If, after a successful run, one or two important stocks in a group breaks seriously, the weakness may sooner or later "wash over" into the remaining stocks in that field. For example, in February 1973, weakness in some key building stocks suggested that even stalwarts such as Kaufman & Broad and MGIC were vulnerable, despite the fact that they were holding up well. At the time, fundamental research firms were in unanimous agreement about MGIC. They were sure the mortgage insurer had earnings gains of 50% locked in for the next two years, and that the company would continue along its merry course unaffected by the building cycle. The analysts were wrong; MGIC later collapsed along with the rest of the deteriorating group.

In the same month, ITT traded between $50 and $60 while every other stock in the conglomerate group had been in a long decline. The two central points overlooked by four leading research firms that recommended ITT in 1973 were that the group was very weak and ITT's Relative Strength was trending lower even though the stock itself was not.

Oil and Oil Service Stocks Top in 1980–1981

This same "wash-over effect" within groups was seen in 1980–1981 when, after a long advance in oil and oil-service stocks, our early warning criteria caused our institutional services firm to put stocks like Standard Oil of Indiana, Schlumberger, Gulf Oil, and Mobil on the "sell" or "avoid" side.

A few months later, we recognized we had turned negative on almost the entire oil sector, and that we had seen the top in Schlumberger, the most outstanding of all the oil-service companies. One simply had to conclude that, in time, the weakness would wash over into the entire oil-service industry. Therefore, we put equities like Hughes Tool, Western Co. of North America, Rowan Companies, Varco International, and N L Industries on the sell list even though the stocks were making new price highs and showed quarterly earnings escalating, in some cases, by 100% or more. These moves baffled many experienced professionals on Wall Street and at large institutions, but we had studied and documented how groups had topped in the past. Our actions were based on historical facts and sound principles that had worked over decades, not on analyst opinions or potentially one-sided information from company officials.

The decision to advise clients to sell oil and oil-service stocks from November 1980 to June 1981 was one of our institutional firm's more valuable calls at the time. We even told a Houston seminar audience in October 1980 that the entire oil sector had topped. Seventy-five percent of those in attendance owned petroleum stocks. They probably didn't believe a word we said. We were not aware at the time, or even in the several months following, of any other New York Stock Exchange firm that had taken that same negative stand across the board on the energy and related drilling and service sectors. In fact, the exact opposite occurred. Because of decisions like this, William O'Neil + Co. became a leading research provider and adviser to many of the nation's top institutional investors.

Within a few months all these stocks began substantial declines. Professional money managers slowly realized that once the price of oil had topped and the major oil issues were under liquidation, it would only be a matter of time before drilling activity would be cut back.

In the July 1982 issue of *Institutional Investor* magazine, 10 energy analysts at eight of the largest and most respected brokerage firms took a different tack. They advised purchasing these securities because they appeared cheap and because they had their first correction from their price peak. This is just another example of how opinions, even if they come from the highest places, are frequently wrong when it comes to making and preserving money in the stock market.

In August 2000, a survey showed many analysts had high-tech stocks as strong buys, and six months later, in one of the worst markets in many years, roughly the same proportion of analysts still said tech stocks were strong buys. Analysts certainly missed with their opinions; only 1% of them said to sell tech stocks. Opinions, even by experts, are frequently wrong; markets rarely are, so learn to read what the market is telling you, and stop listening to personal opinions. Analysts who don't understand this are destined to cause some substantial losses for their clients. We measure market facts, not personal opinions.

The Bowling Boom Tops in 1961

Beginning in 1958 and continuing into 1961, Brunswick's stock made a huge move. The stock of AMF, which also made automatic pinspotters for bowling alleys, gyrated pretty much in unison with Brunswick. After Brunswick peaked in March 1961, it rallied back to $65 from $50, but for the first time, AMF did not recover along with it. This was a tip-off that the entire group had made a long-term top, that the rebound in Brunswick wasn't going to last, and that the stock—as great as it had been—should be sold.

One practical rule is to avoid buying any stock unless its strength and attractiveness is confirmed by at least one other important stock in the same group. You can get away without such confirmation in a few cases where the company does something truly unique unto itself, but these are very few in number. From the late 1980s to the late 1990s, Walt Disney fell into this category: a unique entertainment company rather than just another filmmaker in an unsteady movie group.

Two other valuable concepts turned up as we built historical models in the stock market. The first we named the "follow-on effect," and the second, the "cousin stock theory."

The "Follow-On Effect"

Sometimes, a major development happens in one industry and related industries later reap follow-on benefits. For example, in the late 1960s the airline industry underwent a renaissance with the introduction of jet airplanes, causing airline stocks to soar. The increase in air travel a few years later spilled over to the hotel industry, which was more than happy to expand to meet the rising number of travelers. Beginning in 1967, hotel stocks enjoyed a tremendous run. Loews and Hilton were especially big winners. The follow-on effect, in this case, was that increased air travel created a shortage of hotel space.

When the price of oil grew dear in the late 1970s, oil companies began drilling like mad for the suddenly pricey commodity. As a result, higher oil prices fueled a surge not only in oil stocks in 1979, but also in the stocks of oil-service companies that supplied the industry with exploration equipment and services. The roaring success of small- and medium-sized computer manufacturers during the 1978–1981 bull market created follow-on demand for computer services, software, and peripheral products in the market resurgence of late 1982. As the Internet took off in the mid 1990s, people discovered an insatiable demand for faster access and greater bandwidth. Soon networking stocks surged, with companies specializing in fiber optics enjoying massive gains in their share prices.

The "Cousin Stock Theory"

If a group is doing exceptionally well, there may be a supplier company, a "cousin stock," that's also benefiting.

As airline demand grew in the mid-1960s, Boeing was selling many new jets. Every new Boeing jet was outfitted with chemical toilets made by a company called Monogram Industries. Amid earnings growth of 200%, Monogram stock had a 1000% advance.

In 1983, Fleetwood Enterprises, a leading manufacturer of recreational vehicles, was a big winner in the stock market. Textone was a small cousin stock that supplied vinyl-clad paneling and hollow-core cabinet doors to RV and mobile home companies.

If you notice a company that's doing particularly well, research it thoroughly. In the process, you may discover a supplier company also worth investing in.

Basic Conditions Change in an Industry

Most group moves occur because of substantial changes in industry conditions. In 1953, aluminum and building stocks had a powerful bull market due to pent-up demand for housing in the aftermath of war. Wallboard was in such short supply that some builders offered new Cadillacs to gypsum-board salespeople just to buy a carload of their product.

In 1965, the onrush of a Vietnam war that was to cost $20 billion or more created solid demand for electronics used in military applications and defense during the war. Companies such as Fairchild Camera climbed more than 200% in price.

In the 1990s, discount brokerage firms continued to gain market share versus full-service firms as investing became more and more mainstream. Charles Schwab, one of the most successful discount brokerage firms, performed as well as market leader Microsoft during this time.

Watch for New Trends as They Develop

In our database research we also pay attention to areas of the country where corporations are located. In our ratings of companies as far back as 1971, we assigned extra points for those headquartered in Dallas, Texas, and other key growth or technology centers, such as California's Silicon Valley.

Shrewd investors should also be aware of demographic trends. From data such as the number of people in various age groups, it's possible to predict potential growth for certain industries. The surge of women into the workplace and the gush of baby boomers help explain why stocks like The Limited, Dress Barn, and other retailers of women's apparel soared between 1982 and 1986.

It also pays to understand the basic nature of key industries. For example, high-tech stocks are 2½ times as volatile as consumer stocks, so if you don't buy right, you can suffer larger losses. Or, if you concentrate most of your portfolio in them, they could all come down at the same time. So, be aware of your risk exposure if you get overconcentrated in the volatile high-tech sector.

Defensive Groups Flash General Market Clues

It's also important for investors to know which groups are "defensive" in nature. If, after a couple of bull market years you see buying in groups such as gold, silver, tobacco, food, grocery, and electric and telephone utilities, you may be approaching a top. Prolonged weakness in the utility average could also be signaling higher interest rates and a bear market ahead.

The gold group moved into the top half of all 197 industries on February 22, 1973. Anyone ferreting out such information got the first crystal-clear warning at that time of one of the worst market upheavals since 1929.

60% or More of Big Winners Are Part of Group Moves

Of the most successful stocks from 1953 through 1993, nearly two out of three were part of group advances. So remember, the importance of staying on top of your research and being aware of new group movements cannot be overestimated.

• CHAPTER •

The Art of Tape Reading:
Analyzing and Reacting to News

Tape reading is like seeing the Super Bowl game live from the 50-yard line rather than reading about it in the paper the next day. You see all the grand action, you feel the electricity in the air, and you experience the emotion and excitement as it happens.

What Is Tape Reading?

Tape reading is performed by investors who spend their time watching individual stock transactions as reported on the stock exchange ticker tapes and absorbing news as it flows over the news wires. With the advent of business news channels, many watch the action on television at home. Others watch via a quote terminal or the Internet, but there are still a few "boardroom sitters" who gaze at the electronic tape in their local broker's office. The accompanying New York Stock Exchange ticker tape shows a 700-share block of IBM that traded at $98.02 as well as trades in General Electric, Merrill Lynch, and Hewlett-Packard.

Most stockbrokers peek at the tape, but only a minority focus on it or really have a knack for tape reading. Most institutional traders and some professional money managers study the tape. Jack Dreyfus was such an avid tape reader that he had tapes put in every office, even his accounting department. He didn't want to miss any important trades just because he happened to leave his desk. Jesse Livermore and Gerald Loeb of E. F. Hutton always watched the tape. Of course, specialists on the floor of the New York Stock

IBM	GE	MER	HWP
700@98.02 +0.71	50K@37.45 +0.06	27K@41.20 -1.06	100K@16.45 +0.45

Sample ticker tape

Exchange have tapes throughout the Main Room, the Blue Room, and the Garage, as the different trading areas are called.

Over time, a good tape examiner acquires a feel for the market and can tell you whether stocks are behaving normally or not. However, very few tape readers actually do well, but you'd never know it for all their opinions and the bragging they do about their favorite stocks. "There goes Motors," they'll say authoritatively, as they see a stream of trading volume in General Motors' shares. But remember, there are about as many good tape readers in the stock market as there are football players good enough to play in a Super Bowl.

Tape Reading Is Emotional

Tape watching can get dangerously emotional. Sometimes a stock keeps rising to the point where everyone—including you—is convinced it's going "straight through the roof." That's when discipline is most needed because the stock is probably topping. When a stock's merits are so obvious that it looks fantastic to everyone, you can be sure almost everyone who can buy it has already done so. Remember, majority opinion is rarely right in the stock market.

Winners in the stock market need perspective, discipline, and self-control above all else. Those who continually sit in front of the ticker tape risk making emotional decisions.

Separating Leaders From Laggards via the Tape

Competent tape readers are in a better position to weed out leaders from laggards in the market. For example, after declining for several weeks, a market will finally turn and start to rebound. At this point, the very best tape readers will be able to spot the true leaders in a new bull phase. Observant tape readers watch for stocks that are the first to move up. They're also tracking the number and size of transactions to see which stocks are under the most accumulation. From price changes they're able to tell which stocks move up the easiest. Since many equities tend to move in industry groups, a seasoned tape reader will usually look for confirmation of strength in at least one other important stock in the same group. For example, if Hewlett Packard shows unusual strength, you would expect Compaq, Dell, or IBM to also show strong price and volume action.

Stocks that are the last to respond in a rally or those that trade only light volume are the laggards.

During short-term declines in a bull market, tape readers may watch for stocks that, for whatever reason, are able to resist the selling that's affecting other issues.

Tape analysts also look for sudden pick-ups in volume in previously quiet stocks. In other words, they're always on the lookout for unusual activity. The best tape readers are more concerned with volume than with just the price. Several 20,000-share trades in a single stock are much more significant than a hodgepodge of 200- and 300-share trades.

It Isn't Your Aunt Sue Buying

A 20,000-share trade in a $50 stock on a $0.30 uptick from the prior trade represents a transaction involving $1 million (20,000 × $50). The assumption is that some buyer is willing to pay up 30 cents per share to buy the stock. Because of the size of the transaction you can also be pretty certain it isn't your Aunt Sue down the street buying; more likely it's a better-informed professional buyer making the purchase.

Before you decide you've discovered an easy way to make money just by shadowing the ticker tape, let me assure you again that the obvious hardly ever works in the stock market. Experienced professionals know investors are influenced by big trades appearing on upticks, so don't get too carried away with what could be a well-advertised tape trap.

The real problem with tape analysis is that the tape reflects all trading, both good and bad. Not all of the action you see on the tape is sound and correct buying, even though professionals do it. Professionals who deal in big blocks buy a large number of mediocre or poor stocks. They also can buy good stocks but at the wrong time. Tape reading then becomes a matter of sifting the true gems from the white elephants. Market manipulation by program traders also distorts prices.

Big Block Trades Represent Institutional Trading

In today's institutionally dominated markets, large numbers of "big blocks" of stock trade every day. These blocks of 10,000 to 500,000 shares or more are crossed by block houses (institutional brokerage firms that try to find both the buy side and the sell side of a block transaction). Morgan Stanley Dean Witter, Goldman Sachs, and other highly capitalized firms handle block transactions. Block firms can take large risks and may run their block operations as a loss leader to attract greater syndicate, bond, or other commission business.

Sometimes these firms represent both sides of the block being crossed, acting as broker for both the buyer and seller. In certain of these cases it may be of value to know if a stock exchange specialist has bought part of the stock for his or her own firm's trading account. If this occurs, it is generally considered a positive sign and a show of confidence in the stock.

Block houses positioning (buying for their own trading account) a stock that trades on a big downtick from the prior trade will try to dispose of their stock as soon as possible over the next few trading days. Block trades that are unchanged or only ⅛-point (or its decimal equivalent) above or below the prior trade are confusing and misleading to the public and are sucker bait for the uninitiated. Market makers or institutional brokers sometimes use these block trades to lure other investors to their stock so that once interest is generated, they can sell. Arbitrage and deliberate "painting" of the tape by crossing blocks being sold on ⅛-point upticks all complicate the analysis of large transactions.

Learning Ticker Tape Stock Symbols

A good tape reader should learn the stock symbols of most of the leading stocks. All stocks have a ticker symbol, such as GM for General Motors, T for American Telephone & Telegraph, and XOM for ExxonMobil.

Symbols are easy to learn, but with so many new stocks each year, you have to hustle to keep up with all the new names. Many of the new listings, particularly those traded on the Nasdaq, could become exciting growth leaders in certain market cycles.

Analyze Upticks and Downticks

One helpful tool in judging overall performance is to analyze a stock's upticks and downticks. Total blocks over a period of time that occurred on upticks of ¼-point or more from the previous trade can be compared to the total volume on ¼-point or more downticks. Stocks now trade in decimals, making the evaluation more difficult to interpret, but the concept is still valid.

The Daily Graphs® charting service offers a list that tabulates the top 50 stocks in the overall market for the past week in terms of net upticks shown on the stock exchange ticker tape. A separate list of the top 50 on-balance downtick stocks is also given. These lists might be helpful in picking up accumulation or distribution (buying or selling activity), but be careful—not every stock under accumulation by an institution is a correct investment decision. Institutions, too, make many lackluster choices.

With enough study, an active, do-it-yourself investor will begin to recognize when specific large institutions are buying. This could be done by analyzing and becoming very familiar with the quarterly portfolios of several of the most active and aggressive institutions.

When a stock trades at its buy price, the individual investor can usually afford to wait for the first block or two to show on the tape. The individual investor, if skillful, has the advantage of waiting until the force behind the move is so powerful that the stock has to thrust out of its base pattern. The institutional buyer usually feels a need to start earlier, due to its size disadvantage.

Investors should be careful not to assume that a big block on the downside from the previous trade is always a dark sign. Once a block overhanging the market is out of the way, a stock customarily will rally. Specialists who take blocks on big downticks will usually try to dump their position on upticks afterwards.

Is the Stock in a Base or Is It Extended?

There's an easy way to keep your head while you keep your eye on the tape. When you see tape activity that impresses you, always refer to a chart to see if the stock is building a base or if it's extended too far past the buy or pivot point. If it's extended, leave it alone; it's too late. Chasing stocks, like crime, doesn't pay.

If the stock is in a base, then apply the CAN SLIM™ formula. Are current earnings up a meaningful amount? Is the three-year earnings record good? Have you checked all the other CAN SLIM™ criteria?

More than half the stocks that look inviting on the tape will fail the CAN SLIM™ test and prove to be deficient, mediocre investments. However, sooner or later, convincing tape action will point you to a golden opportunity that meets all your criteria for a possible star performer.

Scan Chart Books Weekly and List Buy Points

Another way to use the tape productively is to first review a comprehensive chart book every week and make a list of stocks that meet your technical and fundamental selection criteria. Then jot down the pivot point at which you would consider buying the stock. Also note the average daily volume for each stock on your prospect list so that you will easily check any noteworthy increases in volume.

Keep this shopping list with you every day for the next couple of weeks when you watch the tape. In time, one or two of the stocks on your list will begin prancing all over the tape and approach your buy point. This is the time to get ready to buy—when the stock trades at your buy point and you anticipate the day's volume will be at least 50% above average. The more demand for a stock at the buy point, the better.

Look for a Shift in Quality Around the Top

After a short-term rally or near a market top, tape readers can often discern a shift in the *quality* of the tape. Top-notch stocks are no longer leading the market up; cheap and lower-quality laggards are moving to the fore. These are warning signs that all is not right in the market, and a sharp correction might be just around the next corner.

Watch Out When Defensive Stocks Appear

After an extended rally in the market, tape readers watch for "defensive" stocks (such as foods and utilities) cropping up on the tape. This indicates that professional money is becoming apprehensive, and that you too should be cautious.

Other Subtleties of Tape Reading

There are other little symptoms and market habits that tape observers will recognize. Some stocks, for example, have delayed openings. Others will stop trading during the day. At other times, stocks may rally in rapid fashion, suggesting more short-coverings than normal. The careful eye can also spot a stock "churning" on the ticker tape. This happens when a great deal of trading volume occurs but the price barely advances.

When the pace of the market gets very slow, the tape is called "quiet" or "dull." Some traders say, "Don't sell a dull market." At certain times, activity will become so heavy that to save time, digits are deleted from the tape, with numbers left off certain prices and volumes. Previously, the sound of the mechanical tape or the old paper tape moving alerted the tape reader to a pickup or slowdown in the pace of overall market activity. Now we have modern electronic tapes that move without a whisper.

Still some markets may, to the trained tape reviewer's eye and ear, reflect a slow, steady pace of subtle accumulation. For example, on days before long holiday weekends, those on the job may quietly buy up stocks while other less-active souls are gone and miss what's happening.

Tape readers expect the pace of activity to slow down around lunchtime in New York (12 p.m. to 1 p.m. Eastern). They also know the market frequently shows its true colors in the last hour of the day, either coming on and closing strong, or suddenly weakening and failing to hold gains established early in the session.

Don't Buy on Tips and Rumors

I never buy stocks on tips, rumors, or inside information. It simply isn't sound, but, of course, tips, rumors, and inside information are what most people are looking for. However, I should remind you again that what most believe and do in the market doesn't work. Beware of falling into the typical market traps!

Certain advisory services and columns in some business newspapers are fed by Street gossip, rumors, and tips, as well as by planted personal opinions or inside information. These services and columns, in my opinion, are unprofessional and unsophisticated. There are far sounder and safer methods of gathering information.

Bernard Baruch stressed the importance of separating the facts of a situation from tips, "inside dope," and wishful thinking. One of his rules was beware of barbers, beauticians, waiters, or anyone else bearing such gifts.

The Peril of Tape Reading in a Fast-Moving Market

All stock transactions are supposed to be flashed on the ticker tape a few minutes after the trade actually occurs on the floor of the exchange. However, sometimes the volume of trading is so heavy even the high-speed tickers can't keep up with the activity, and the tape falls behind. Buying or selling at these times can be dicey because a "late tape" makes it harder to tell what the actual prices are on the floor when you enter your orders.

Watch for Tape Distortion Around Year's End

A certain amount of distortion can occur in optionable stocks around option-expiration dates. There's also a significant amount of year-end distortion in stocks during December and sometimes through January and early February.

Year-end is a tricky time for anyone to buy stock, since numerous trades are made for tax considerations. Many low-grade losers will suddenly seem strong, while former leaders lie idle or start to correct. In time, this misleading activity dissipates and the true leaders reemerge.

General market sell-offs also occasionally start after the beginning of a new year, which further adds to the difficulty. Fake-out action can occur with one big "up" day followed by a big "down" day, only to be followed by another big "up" day. There are times I'd rather take a vacation in January. The January effect, where small/mid-cap stocks get a boost during January, can be a misleading and spurious indicator. At best, it only "works" for a brief period. It's important to stick with your rules and not get sidetracked by questionable, less-reliable indicators, of which there are many.

Interpret and React to Major News

When domestic or foreign news of consequence hits the street, capable tape sleuths are sometimes less concerned with whether the news is good or bad than they are in analyzing its effect on the market. For example, if the news appears to be bad but the market yawns, you can feel more positive. The tape is telling you that the underlying market may be stronger than many believe. On the other hand, if highly positive news hits the market and stocks give ground slightly, the tape analyst might conclude the underpinnings of the market are weaker than previously believed.

Sometimes the market overreacts to or even counteracts favorable or disappointing news. On Wednesday, November 9, 1983, someone ran a full-page ad in *The Wall Street Journal* predicting rampant inflation and another 1929-type depression. The ad appeared during the middle of an intermediate correction in the market, but its warnings were so overboard that the market immediately rebounded and rallied for several days.

There's also a difference between a market that retreats in the face of news that's scary but easy to understand and explain, and one that slumps noticeably for no apparent news at all.

Experienced tape investigators have long memories. They keep records of past major news events and how the market reacted. The list would include President Eisenhower's heart attack, the Cuban missile crisis, the Kennedy assassination, an outbreak of war, the Arab oil embargo, and expectations of government actions such as wage and price controls.

Old News Versus New News

After it's repeated several times, both good and bad news become old news. Old news will often have the opposite effect on the stock market than it had when the news first broke.

This, of course, is the opposite of how propaganda and disinformation work in totalitarian countries. There, the more a lie or distortion is repeated to the masses, the more it's accepted as truth. Here, when news becomes widely known or anticipated, it's "discounted" by experienced individuals in the marketplace, blunting the effect of its release.

To market neophytes, news can be paradoxical and confusing. For example, a company can release a bad quarterly earnings report, and its stock may go up in price when the news is reported. When this occurs, it's often because the news was known or anticipated ahead of time, and a few professionals may decide to buy or cover short sales once all the bad news is finally out. "Buy on bad news" is what some wily institutions use as a guide. Others believe they should step in and provide support for their large positions at difficult times.

Analyzing the News Media

How the national news is edited and presented dramatically affects the economy and public confidence. It can also influence public opinion of our government, our president, and our stock market.

Several excellent books have been written on the subject of analyzing national news. Humphrey Neill, author of the 1931 classic *Tape Reading and Market Tactics*, also wrote *The Art of Contrary Opinion*. It carefully examines the way identical news stories are reported quite differently in the headlines of different newspapers and how that can be misleading to stock owners. Neill developed contrarian theories based on how frequently conventional wisdom or consensus opinion expressed in the national media turns out to be ill-conceived or wrong.

Media expert Bruce Herschensohn wrote *The Gods of Antenna* in 1976, which tells how some TV networks manipulate the news to influence public opinion. Another book on the subject is *The Coming Battle for the Media*, written in 1988 by William Rusher.

The most outstanding study on the subject is *The Media Elite*, written by Stanley Rothman and Robert Lichter in 1986. Rothman and Lichter interviewed 240 journalists and top staffers at three major newspapers (*The New York Times, The Wall Street Journal,* and *The Washington Post*), three news magazines (*Time, Newsweek,* and *U.S. News & World Report*), and the news departments of four TV networks (ABC, CBS, NBC, and PBS). When asked to rate their fellow workers' leanings, they said by a margin of seven to one that their coworkers were mostly on the liberal left versus the conservative right. Eighty-five percent of the top national journalists were found to be liberal and voted the Democratic ticket in recent elections. Another survey showed only 6% of national journalists voted Republican.

Emmy Award–winner Bernard Goldberg spent nearly thirty years with CBS News. His book *Bias* documents how network television has provided one-sided news with little balance or fairness.

To succeed, both as individual investors and as a nation, we need to learn to separate facts from the personal political opinions and strong biases of the majority of the national media.

In summary, tape reading is an activity possibly best left to the professionals and those individual investors who are dedicated to spending the time it takes to fully comprehend its nuances. Don't kid yourself into thinking it's an easy shortcut to big money. Follow your rules, and don't let your emotions influence your decisions.

CHAPTER 17

Should You Buy Options, Nasdaq Stocks, New Issues, Convertible Bonds, Tax Shelters, Foreign Stocks?

You may ask how I could cover all of these topics in one chapter. Most are com- plicated activities, and therefore would seem to need more space for their explanation. However, for the most part, I do not participate in these types of investments. It's been my experience that while some are worthwhile, most are often very risky, unsafe, and/or not worth your time and effort. Still, some of you will be curious about them. Before you invest, know what you're getting into. Don't jump head first into a pond before you know how deep it is.

What Are Options and Should You Invest in Them?

Options are an investment vehicle where you purchase rights (contracts) to buy ("call") or sell ("put") a stock, stock index, or commodity at a specified price by a specified future time period, known as the option expiration date. Options are very speculative and involve substantially greater risks and price volatility than common stocks. Therefore, most investors should not buy or sell options. Winning investors should first learn how to minimize the investment risks they take, not increase them. After a person has proved he or she is able to make money in common stocks and has sufficient investment understanding and actual experience, then the limited use of options might be intelligently considered.

Options are like making "all or nothing" bets. If you buy a three-month call option on General Motors, the premium you pay gives you the right to purchase 100 shares of General Motors at a certain price anytime over the

222

next three months. When you purchase calls, you expect the price to go up, so if a stock is currently trading at $95, you might buy a call at $100. If the stock rises to $130 after three months (and you have not sold your call option), you can exercise it and pocket the $30 profit less the premium you paid. Conversely, if three months go by and GM's stock doesn't perform as expected, you would not exercise the option, it would expire worthless, and you'd lose the premium. As you might expect, puts are handled in a similar manner, except you're making a bet that the price of the stock will decrease instead of increase.

Limiting Your Risk When It Comes to Options

If you do consider options, you should limit the percentage of your total portfolio committed to them. A prudent limit is 10% to 15%. You should also adopt a rule about where you intend to cut and limit all of your losses. The percentage will naturally have to be more than 8% since options are much more volatile than stocks. If an option fluctuates three times as rapidly as its underlying stock, then perhaps 20% or 25% might be a possible absolute limit. On the profit side, you might consider adopting a rule that you'll take many of your gains when they hit 50% to 75%.

Some aspects of options present challenges. Buying options where the price can be significantly influenced by supply and demand changes due to a thin or illiquid market for that particular option is problematic. Also problematic is the fact that options can be artificially and temporarily overpriced simply due to a short-lived increase in price volatility in the underlying stock or general market.

Buy Only the Best

When I buy options, which is rarely, I prefer to buy them for the most aggressive and outstanding stocks, those where the premium you have to pay for the option is higher. Once again, you want options on the best stocks, not the cheapest. The secret to making money in options doesn't have much to do with options. You have to analyze and be right on the selection and timing of the underlying stock. Therefore, you should apply your CAN SLIM™ formula and select the best possible stock at the best possible time. If you do this and are right, the option will go up along with the stock, except the option should move up much faster due to the leverage.

By buying only the best stocks, you also minimize slippage due to illiquidity. (Slippage is the difference between the price you wanted to pay and the price you actually paid at the time the order was executed. The more liquid the stock, the less slippage you should experience.) With illiquid (small capitalization) stocks, the slippage can be more severe, which ultimately could cost you money. Buying just a few contracts can cause up to 20% slippage in some cases. Buying options on lower-priced, illiquid stocks is similar to the carnival game where you're trying to knock down all the milk bottles. The game is rigged. Selling your options can be equally tricky in a thin (small capitalization) stock.

In a major bear market, you might consider buying put options on certain individual stocks or on a major stock index like the S&P, along with selling short shares of common stock. You don't have to get an uptick in the trading of the stock when you buy put options. Sometimes the uptick rule for short selling stocks listed on an exchange or the inability of your broker to borrow stock may make selling short more difficult than buying a put.

It is generally not wise to buy puts during a bull market. Why be a fish trying to swim upstream?

If you think a stock is going up and it is the right time to buy, buy it, or purchase a long-term option and place your order at the market. If it's time to sell, sell at the market. Option markets are usually thinner and not as liquid as the markets for the underlying stock itself.

Many amateur option traders constantly place price limits on their orders. Once they form the habit of placing limits, they are forever changing their price restraints as prices edge away from their limits. It is difficult to maintain sound judgment and perspective when you worry about changing your limits by ⅛, ¼, and ½ points (or their decimal equivalents). In the end, you'll get two or three executions after tremendous excess effort and frustration. When you finally pick the big winner for the year, the one that will triple in price, you'll lose out because you placed your order with a ¼-point limit below the actual market price.

You never make big money in the stock market by eighths and quarters. You could also lose your shirt when your security is in trouble and you fail to sell and get out because you put a price limit on your sell order. Your objective is to be right on the big moves, not on the minor fluctuations.

Short-Term Options Are More Risky

If you buy options, you're better off with longer time periods, say, six months or so. This will minimize the chance your option will run out of time before your stock has had a chance to perform. Now that I've told you this, what do you think most investors do? Of course, they buy shorter-term option—30 to 90 days—because these options are cheaper and move faster in both directions, up and down!

The problem with short-term options is that you could be right on your stock, but the general market may slip into an intermediate correction, and all stocks could be down at the end of the short time period. You will then lose on all your options because of the general market. This is also why you will want to spread your option buying and option expiration dates over several different months.

Keep Option Trading Simple

One thing to keep in mind is that you should always keep your investments as simple as possible. Don't let someone talk you into speculating in such things as strips, straddles, and spreads.

A *strip* is a form of conventional option that couples one call and two puts on the same security at the same exercise price with the same expiration date. The premium is less than it would be if the option were purchased separately.

A *straddle* is either long or short. A long straddle is a long call and a long put on the same underlying security at the same exercise price and with the same expiration month. A short straddle is a short call and a short put on the same security at the same exercise price and with the same expiration month.

A *spread* is a purchase and sale of options with the same expirations.

It's difficult enough to just pick a stock or an option that is going up. If you confuse the issue and start hedging (being both long and short at the same time), you could, believe it or not, wind up losing on both sides. For instance, if a stock goes up, you might be tempted to sell your "put" early to minimize the loss, and later find that the stock has turned downward and you're losing money on your "call." The reverse could also happen. It's a dangerous psychological game that you should probably avoid altogether.

Should You Write Options?

Writing options is a completely different story from buying options. I am not overly impressed with the strategy of writing options on stocks.

A person who writes a call option receives a small fee or premium in return for giving someone else (the buyer) the right to "call" away and buy the stock from the writer at a specified price, up to a certain date. In a bull market, I would rather be a buyer of calls than a writer (seller) of calls. In bad markets, just stay out or go short.

The writer of calls pockets a small fee and is, in effect, usually locked in for the time period of the call. What if the stock gets into trouble and plummets? The small fee won't cover the loss. Of course, there are maneuvers the writer can take, such as buying a put to hedge and cover oneself, but then the problem gets too complicated and the writer could get whipsawed back and forth.

What happens if the stock doubles? The writer gets the stock called away, and for a relatively small fee loses all chance for a major profit. Why take risks in stocks for only meager gains and no chance for large gains? This is not the reasoning you will hear from most people, but then again, what most people are saying and doing in the stock market isn't usually worth knowing.

Writing "naked calls" is even more foolish, in my opinion. Naked call writers receive a fee for writing a call on a stock they do not own, so they are unprotected if the stock moves against them.

It is possible that large investors who have trouble making decent returns on their portfolio may find some minor added value in writing short-term options in stocks that they own and feel are overpriced. However, I am always somewhat skeptical of new methods of making money that seem so easy. There are few free lunches in the stock market.

Great Opportunities in Nasdaq Stocks

Nasdaq stocks are not traded on a listed stock exchange but are traded through over-the-counter dealers. The over-the-counter dealer market has in recent years been enhanced by a wide range of ECNs (electronic communication networks) like Instinet, SelectNet, Redibook, Archipelago, which bring buyers and sellers together within each network, and through which orders can be routed and executed. The Nasdaq is a specialized field, usually of newer, less-established companies. But now even established NYSE firms have large Nasdaq operations. In addition, reforms during the 1990s have removed any lingering stigma that once dogged the Nasdaq.

There are usually hundreds of intriguing new growth stocks on the Nasdaq. It's also the home of some of the biggest companies in the United States. You should definitely consider buying the better quality Nasdaq stocks that have institutional sponsorship and fit the CAN SLIM™ rules.

Sometimes over-the-counter securities may prove to be less liquid in very poor markets. In truly terrible markets, some over-the-counter dealers may just stop making markets or be very slow to answer their telephone when you want out. New order-handling rules, the Internet, and competing ECNs have made that less of a problem.

For maximum flexibility and safety, it is vital to maintain marketability in all of your investments, regardless of whether they're traded on the NYSE or Nasdaq. An institutional quality common stock with larger average daily volume is your best defense against an unruly market.

Should You Buy Initial Public Offerings (IPOs)?

An initial public offering is a company's first offering of stock to the public. I usually don't recommend investors purchase IPOs. There are several reasons for this.

Out of the numerous IPOs that occur each year, there are a few outstanding ones. Those that are outstanding are going to be in such hot demand by institutions (who get first crack at them) that if you are able to buy them, you will only receive a tiny allotment. Logic dictates that if you, as the individual investor, can acquire all the shares you want, they are probably not worth having.

The Internet and some discount brokerages have made IPOs more accessible to individual investors, although some brokers place limits on your ability to sell soon after a company comes public. This is a dangerous position to be in since you may not be able to get out when you want. You might recall that in the IPO craze of 1999 and early 2000, there were some new stocks that rocketed on their first day or two of trading only to collapse and not recover.

Many IPOs are deliberately underpriced and therefore shoot up on the first day of trading, but more than a few could be overpriced and drop. Because IPOs have no trading history, you can't be sure whether they're overpriced. In most cases, this speculative area should be left to experienced institutional investors who have access to the necessary in-depth research and who are able to spread their new issue risks among many different equities.

That's not to say that you can't purchase a new issue in its infancy. The safest time to buy an IPO is on the breakout from its first correction and base-building area. Once a new issue has been trading in the market for two or three months or more, you have valuable price and volume data on which to judge the situation. There are always standout companies with superior new products and excellent current earnings to be considered from among the broad list of new issues of the previous three months to three years. (*Investor's Business Daily's* "The New America" page explores most of them. Past company research articles can be purchased for a small fee on investors.com.)

Experienced investors who understand correct selection and timing techniques should definitely consider buying new issues that have formed proper price bases. They can be a great source for new ideas if dealt with in this fashion. Most big winners in recent years were IPOs at some point in the stock's prior eight years. Even so, new issues can be more volatile and occasionally suffer massive corrections during difficult bear markets. This usually happens after a period of wild craze in the IPO market where any and every offering seems to be a "hot issue." For example, the new-issue booms that developed in the early 1960s and in the beginning of 1983, as well as those in late 1999 and early 2000, were almost always followed by a bear market period.

Congress, at this writing in 2002, should again lower the capital gains tax to create a strong incentive for thousands of entrepreneurs to start up fast-growing, new companies. Our research proved that 80% of the stocks that had outstanding performance in the 1980s and 1990s were ones that had been brought public in the prior few years. America now needs a renewed flow of new companies to spark new inventions and new industries . . . and with that, a stronger economy, more jobs, and more taxpayers. It has always paid off for Washington to lower capital gains taxes. This will be needed to reignite the IPO market and the American economy after the enormous collapse in high techs in 2000 and 2001.

What Are Convertible Bonds and Should You Invest in Them?

A convertible bond allows you to exchange (convert) your bond for another investment category, typically common stock, at a predetermined price. Convertible bonds provide a little higher income to the owner than the common stock typically does, along with the potential for some of the possible profits commonly associated with stock ownership.

The theory goes that a convertible bond will rise almost as fast as the common stock rises but that the convertible bond will decline less during downturns. As so happens with most theories, the reality may be different. There is also a liquidity question to consider, since many convertible bond markets may dry up in extremely difficult periods.

Sometimes investors are attracted to this medium because they can borrow heavily and leverage their commitment (obtain more buying power). This simply increases your risk. Excessive leverage can be dangerous. It is for these reasons that I do not recommend that most investors buy convertible bonds.

Should You Invest in Tax-Free Securities and Tax Shelters?

The typical investor should not use these investment vehicles (IRAs, 401(k) plans, and KEOGHs excepted), the most common of which are municipal bonds. Overconcern about taxes can confuse and cloud normally sound investment judgment. Common sense should also tell you if you invest in tax shelters, there is a much greater chance the IRS may decide to audit your tax return.

People seeking too many tax benefits frequently end up investing in questionable or risky ventures. The investment decision should always be considered first and tax considerations made a distant second. This is particularly true in the new millennium, an environment with a lower top tax bracket. One of the tax advantages during the 1980s and again in the 1990s was the reduction in the capital gains rate.

This is America, where anyone who really works at it can be successful at investing. Learn how to make a net profit, and when you do, be happy about it rather than complaining about having to pay tax because you made a profit. Would you rather hold on until you could have a loss so you have no tax to pay? Recognize at the start that Uncle Sam will always be your partner, and he will receive his normal share of your wages and investment gains.

I have never bought a tax-free security or a tax shelter. This has left me free to concentrate on finding the best investments possible. When these investments work out, I pay my taxes just like everybody else. Always remember that the U.S. system of freedom and opportunity is the greatest in the world. Learn to use and appreciate it.

Should You Invest in Income Stocks?

Income stocks are stocks that produce high and regular dividend yields, providing taxable income to the owner. These stocks are typically found in more conservative industries, such as utilities and banks. Most people should not buy common stocks for their dividends or income.

People think income stocks are conservative and that you can just sit and hold them because you are getting your dividends. Talk to any investor who lost big on Continental Illinois Bank in 1984 when the stock plunged from $25 to $2, or on the electrical utilities caught up in nuclear power plant problems. Investors got hurt when electric utilities nose-dived in 1994, and the same was true when certain California utilities collapsed in 2001. In theory, income stocks should be safer, but don't be lulled into believing they can't decline sharply. In 1999–2000, AT&T dropped from over $60 to below $20.

If you do buy income stocks, don't strain to buy the highest dividend yield available. That will likely entail greater risk and lower quality. Trying to get an extra 2% or 3% yield can expose your capital to larger losses. A company can also cut dividends if its earnings per share are not adequately covering those dividends, leaving you without the income you expected to receive.

If you need income, my advice is to concentrate on the very best stocks and simply withdraw 6% or 7% of your investment each year for living expenses. You could sell off a few shares and withdraw 1½% per quarter.

Higher rates of withdrawal are not generally advisable, since in time they could lead to the depletion of your principal.

What Are Warrants and Are They Safe Investments?

Warrants are an investment vehicle that allows you to purchase a specific amount of stock at a specific price, sometimes for a certain period of time, but it's common for them not to have time limits. Many warrants are cheap in price and therefore seem appealing.

However, most investors should shy away from low-priced warrants. It is another complex, specialized field that sounds fine in concept but which few investors truly understand. The real question comes down to whether the common stock is correct to buy. Most investors will be better off to forget the field of warrants.

Should You Invest in Merger Candidates?

Merger candidates can often behave erratically, so I don't recommend investing in them. Some merger candidates run up substantially in price on rumors of a possible sale only to suddenly drop sharply in price when a potential deal falls through or other unforeseen circumstances occur. In other words, it can be a risky, volatile business and in most instances should be left to those experienced professionals who specialize in this field. It is usually better to buy sound companies, based on your CAN SLIM™ evaluation, than to try to guess whether a company will be sold or merged with another.

Should You Buy Foreign Stocks?

A few foreign stocks have good potential if bought at the right time and the right place, but I don't advise people to waste much time investing in them. The potential profit in a foreign stock should be two or three times as large as that in a standout U.S. company to justify the additional risk. For example, foreign securities investors must understand and closely follow the general market of the particular country involved. Sudden changes in the country's interest rates, currency, or governmental policy could, in one sweeping action, make your investment considerably less attractive.

It is really not necessary for individuals to search out foreign stocks when there are over 10,000 securities to select from in the United States. In 1982, some of our large banks learned the hard way the substantial added risk they assumed when making large loans and investments in foreign countries. Foreign stocks should be left to professionals who specialize in this field and can spread their risk among several different stocks. There are a few good mutual funds that excel in this specialty, so if you absolutely must invest in foreign stocks, buy a small amount of a mutual fund run by such professionals.

Avoid Penny Stocks and Low-Priced Securities

The Canadian and Denver markets list many stocks you can buy for only a few cents a share. I strongly advise that you avoid gambling in such cheap merchandise because everything sells for what it's worth. You get what you pay for.

These seemingly cheap securities are unduly speculative and extremely low in quality. The risk with them is much higher than with better-quality, higher-priced investments. The opportunity for questionable or unscrupulous promotional practices is also greater with penny stocks. I do not like to buy any common stock that sells below $15 per share, and neither should you. Our studies of super winners shows that most broke out of chart bases between $30 and $50 a share.

What Are Futures and Should You Invest in Them?

Futures refer to buying or selling a specific amount of a commodity, financial issue, or stock index at a specific price on a specific future date. Most futures fall under the categories of grains, precious metals, industrial metals, foods, meats, oils, woods, and fibers (known collectively as commodities), financial issues, and stock indices. The financial group includes government T-bills and bonds, plus foreign currencies. One of the more active stock indices traded is the S&P 100, better known by its ticker symbol OEX.

Large commercial concerns, such as Hershey, use the commodity market for "hedging." For example, Hershey might lock in a current price by temporarily purchasing cocoa beans in May for December delivery, while arranging for a deal in the cash market.

It is probably best for the individual investor not to participate in the futures markets. Commodity futures are extremely volatile and much more speculative than most common stocks. It is not an arena for the inexperienced or small investor unless you want to gamble or lose money quickly.

However, once an investor has four or five years of experience and has unquestionably proven his or her ability to make money in common stocks, the "strong of heart" might consider investing in futures.

With futures, it is even more important to be able to read and interpret charts. The chart price patterns in commodity prices are similar to those in individual stocks. Being aware of futures charts can also help stock investors evaluate changes in basic economic conditions in the country.

There are a relatively small number of futures in which you can trade. Therefore, astute speculators can concentrate their analysis. The rules and terminology of futures trading are different and the risk is far greater, so investors should definitely limit the proportion of investment funds that might be committed to futures. There are worrisome events involved in futures trading, such as "limit down" days where a trader is not even allowed to sell and cut a loss. Risk management (i.e., position size and cutting losses quickly) is never more important than when trading futures. You should also never risk more than 5% of your capital in any one futures position. There is an outside chance of getting stuck in the position that has a series of limit up or limit down days. Futures can be treacherous and devastating; you could definitely lose it all.

Should You Buy Gold, Silver, or Diamonds?

As you can surmise, I do not normally recommend investing in metals or precious stones.

Many of these investments have questionable histories; they were once promoted in a super aggressive fashion with little protection afforded the small investor. There was no Securities & Exchange Commission to protect against exaggerated, even fraudulent, claims made by some dealers in precious metals. Many books were written boldly predicting gold would bolt to several thousand dollars and our country would go down the drain. Diamonds were hawked to the public with almost fraudulent sales pitches, claiming diamonds were guaranteed to go up every year in price because they had always gone up. People were erroneously told that the diamond market price is totally controlled and set by DeBeers.

These types of investments can be highly speculative, and after periods of frenzy and hype, many investors are left with investments they bought at inflated price levels. In addition, the dealer's profit markup in these investments is sometimes excessive. Furthermore, these investments do not pay interest or dividends.

Gold, silver, and diamonds all made very major long-term tops in 1980 and have not recovered. At some point these commodities will rally back to a degree. However, due to the wild speculative furor that occurred, there is no way to know how much time must pass to completely clean out past excesses.

Generally, there will be periodic, short, quick run-ups in gold caused by fears or panics regarding potential problems in certain foreign countries.

This type of commodity trading can be a pretty emotional and unstable game, so I suggest care and caution.

It is possible at some point that small investments in such items will become timely and reasonable. However, even in this case, investors still may have to contend with large price markups and a lack of ready marketability. Marketability becomes a vital issue when you decide to sell and have trouble finding a willing buyer at your price.

Today, many of these investments are just not as relevant or safe as they appear to be. Silver may find fewer uses as photography companies convert to discs and films that no longer use this precious metal. As a result, silver might become less attractive as an investment vehicle in the future. Supply and demand is also a factor. As prices for diamonds collapsed in 1980, many investors were surprised to learn that the law of supply and demand could seriously impact their investments. New sources of supply for diamonds entered the world market and caused prices to fall. Some investors have lost a great deal of money investing in such commodities.

Should You Invest in Real Estate?

Yes, at the right time and in the right place.

I am completely convinced that everyone should work toward owning a home, building a savings account, and investing in common stocks or a growth-stock mutual fund. Home ownership has been a goal for most Americans. Their ability to obtain long-term borrowed money with only a small down payment has created the leverage necessary for Americans to make large real estate investments possible.

Real estate is a popular investment vehicle because it is fairly easy to understand and can be highly profitable. Over two-thirds of American families currently own their own homes. Time and leverage usually pay off. However, this is not always the case. People can and do lose money in real estate under the following unfavorable conditions:

1. They make a poor initial selection by buying in an area that is slowly deteriorating or is not growing, or the area in which they've owned property for some time deteriorates.

2. They buy at inflated prices after several boom years and just before severe economic setbacks in the economy or in the particular geographic area where they own real estate. This might occur if there are major industry layoffs or closes of an aircraft or steel plant that is an important mainstay to a local community.

3. They get themselves personally overextended with real estate payments that are too high, or their source of income is reduced by the loss of a job or an increase in rental vacancies should they own rental property.

4. They are hit by fires, floods, tornadoes, earthquakes, or other acts of nature.

Money and skill are usually best developed by concentrating on the correct buying and selling of higher-quality growth stocks rather than scattering your efforts among the myriad of higher risk or less rewarding investment alternatives. Like all investments, do the necessary research before you make your decision. Remember, there's no such thing as a risk-free investment. Don't let anyone tell you there is.

How You Could Make a Million Dollars Owning Mutual Funds

What Are Mutual Funds?

A mutual fund is a diversified portfolio of stocks managed by a professional investment company, usually for a small management fee. Investors purchase shares in the fund itself and make or lose money based on the combined profits and losses of the stocks within the fund.

What you're buying when you purchase a mutual fund is professional management to make decisions for you in the stock market. You should handle a mutual fund differently from the way you handle individual stocks. A stock may decline and never come back in price. That's why you *always* need a loss-cutting policy. In contrast, a well-selected, diversified domestic growth-stock fund run by an established management organization will, in time, always recover from the steep corrections that naturally occur during bear markets. The reason they come back is that mutual funds are broadly diversified and generally participate in each recovery cycle in the U.S. economy.

How to Become a Millionaire the Easy Way

Mutual funds are outstanding investment vehicles if you learn how to use them correctly. However, many investors don't understand how to manage them to their advantage.

The first thing to understand is that the big money in mutual funds is made by owning them through several business cycles (market ups and downs). This means 10, 15, or 20 years or longer. To sit tight for that long requires patience and confidence. It's like real estate. If you buy a house and then get nervous, selling out after only three or four years, you may not make anything. It takes time for your property to appreciate.

Here's how I believe you, as a shrewd fund investor, should plan and invest. Pick a diversified domestic growth fund that performed in the top quartile of all mutual funds over the last three or five years. It will probably have averaged an annual rate of return of about 20%. The fund should also have outperformed many other domestic growth stock funds in the latest 12 months. You'll want to consult a reliable source for this information. Many investment-related magazines survey fund performances every quarter. Your stockbroker or library should have special fund performance rating services, such as Wiesenberger Thomson Financial or Lipper Inc., so you can get an unbiased review of the fund you're interested in purchasing. *Investor's Business Daily* also rates mutual funds based on their 36-month performance records (on a scale from A+ to E) as well as other performance percentages based on different time periods. Focus your research on mutual funds with an A+ or A performance rating in IBD. The fund you pick does not have to be in the top three or four in performance each year to give you an excellent profit over 10 to 15 years.

You should also reinvest your dividends and capital gains distributions (profits derived from a mutual fund's sales of stocks and bonds) to benefit from compounding over the years.

The Magic of Compounding

The way to make a fortune in mutual funds is through compounding. Compounding happens when your earnings themselves (the performance gains plus any dividends and reinvested capital) generate more earnings, allowing you to put ever-greater sums to work. The more time that goes by, the more powerful compounding becomes.

In order to get the most benefit from compounding, you'll need a carefully selected growth-stock fund, *and* you'll need to stick with it over time. For example, if you purchase $10,000 of a diversified domestic growth-stock fund that averages about 15% a year over a period of 35 years, here is an approximation of what might occur, compliments of the magic of compounding:

First five years	$10,000	becomes	$20,000
Next five years	$20,000	becomes	$40,000
Next five years	$40,000	becomes	$80,000
Next five years	$80,000	becomes	$160,000

Next five years	$160,000	becomes	$320,000
Next five years	$320,000	becomes	$640,000
Next five years	$640,000	becomes	**$1.28 million!**

Suppose you also added $2,000 each year and let it compound as well. Your total would then come to more than $3 million! Now, how much more do you think you'd have if you also bought a little extra during every bear market while the fund was temporarily down 30% or more from its peak?

Nothing's guaranteed in this world, and yes, there are always taxes. However, the example above is representative of what has happened with the better growth funds over the last 50 years, and what could happen to you if you plan and invest in mutual funds correctly.

When Is the Best Time to Buy a Fund?

Anytime is the best time. You'll never know when the perfect time is, and waiting will usually result in paying a higher price. You should focus on getting started and building capital that will compound over the years.

How Many Funds Should You Own?

As time passes, you may discover you'd like to develop an additional long-term program. If so, do it. In 10 or 15 years, you might have hefty amounts in two or even three funds, but don't overdo it. There's no reason to diversify broadly in mutual funds. Individuals with multimillion dollar portfolios could spread out somewhat further, allowing them to place sums into a more diverse group of funds. If this is to be done correctly, some attempt should be made to own funds with different management styles. For example, money may be divvied up among a value-type growth fund, an aggressive growth fund, a mid- to large-cap growth fund, small-cap fund, etc. Many fund organizations, including Fidelity, Franklin Templeton, MFS Funds, Nicholas-Applegate, Strong Funds, AIM, Scudder, American Century, Oppenheimer, Dreyfus, Vanguard Group, IDS Mutual, and others, offer families of funds with varied objectives. In most cases, you have the right to switch to any other fund in the family at a nominal transfer fee. These families could offer you the added flexibility of making prudent changes many years later.

Are Monthly Investment Plans for You?

Programs that automatically withhold money from your paycheck are usually sound if you choose to deposit that money into a carefully selected, diversified domestic growth-stock fund. However, it's best to also make a larger initial purchase that will get you on the road to serious compounding all that much quicker.

Don't Let the Market Diminish Your Long-Term Resolve

Bear markets can last from six months to, in some rare cases, two years or more. If you're going to be a successful long-term investor in mutual funds, you'll need courage and perspective to live through many discouraging bear markets. Have the vision to build yourself a great long-term growth program, and stick to it. Each time the economy goes into a recession, and the newspapers and TV are saying how terrible things are, consider *adding* to your fund when it's 30% or more off its peak. You might go so far as to borrow a little money to buy more if you feel a bear market has ended. If you're patient, the price should be up nicely in two or three years.

Growth funds that invest in more aggressive stocks should go up more than the general market in bull phases, but they will also decline more in bear markets. Don't be alarmed. Instead, try to look ahead several years. Daylight follows darkness.

You might think that buying mutual funds during periods like the Great Depression would be a bad idea because it would take 30 years to break even. However, on an inflation-adjusted basis, had investors bought at the top of 1929, they would have broken even in just 14 years, based on the performance of the S&P 500 and the DJIA. Had these investors bought at the top of the market in 1973, they would have broken even in just 11 years. If, in addition, they had dollar-cost averaged throughout these bad periods (meaning they had purchased additional shares as the price went down, lowering their overall cost per share), investors would have broken even in half the time. Even during the worst two market periods in history, growth funds did bounce back and did so in less time than you'd expect. In other words, if you took the absolutely worst period of the twentieth century, the Great Depression, and you bought at the top of the market, then dollar-cost averaged down, at worst, it would have taken seven years to break even. This is compelling evidence that dollar-cost averaging into mutual funds and holding them for the long haul is smart investing.

Some may find this confusing since we tell people never to dollar-cost average down in stocks. The difference is that a stock can go to zero, while a domestic, widely diversified, professionally managed mutual fund will find its way back when the market gets better, often tracking near the performance of benchmarks like the S&P 500 and Dow Jones Industrial Average.

The super big gains from mutual funds come from compounding over a span of many years. Funds should be an investment for as long as you live. They say diamonds are forever. Well, so are your funds. So buy right and sit tight!

Should You Buy Open- or Closed-End Funds?

"Open-end" funds continually issue new shares when people want to buy them, and they are the most common. Shares are normally redeemable at net asset value whenever present holders wish to sell.

A closed-end fund issues a fixed number of shares. Generally, shares are not redeemable at the option of a shareholder. Redemption takes place through secondary market transactions. Most closed-end fund shares are listed for trading on exchanges. Better long-term opportunities are found in open-end funds. Closed-end funds are subject to the whims and discounts below book value of the auction marketplace.

Should You Buy Load or No-Load Funds?

The fund you choose can be a "load" fund, where a sales commission is charged, or a "no-load" fund. If you buy a fund with a sales charge, discounts are offered based on the amount you invest. Some funds have back-end loads (sales commission charged when withdrawals are made, designed to discourage withdrawals) that you may also want to take into consideration when evaluating a fund for purchase. Whatever the case, the commission on a fund is much less than the markup you pay to buy insurance, a new car, a suit of clothes or your groceries. You may also be able to sign a letter of intent to purchase a specified amount of the fund, which may allow a lower sales charge to apply to any future purchases made over the following 13 months.

Few people have been successful trading aggressive no-load growth funds on a timing basis using moving average lines and utilizing services that specialize in fund switching. Most investors shouldn't try to trade no-load funds because mistakes can be easily made in the timing of buy and sell points. Again, get aboard a mutual fund for the long term.

Should You Buy Income Funds?

If you need income, you will find it more advantageous *not* to buy an income fund. Instead, you could select the best fund available and set up a withdrawal plan equal to 1½% per quarter, or 6% or 7% per year. Part of the withdrawal would come from dividend income received and part from your capital. If selected correctly, the fund should generate enough growth over the years to more than offset 6% to 7% annual withdrawals from your total investment.

Should You Buy Sector or Index Funds?

Steer away from funds that concentrate in only one industry or area. The problem with them is that sectors go in and out of favor all the time. Therefore, if you buy a sector fund, you will probably suffer severe losses when that sector is out of favor or a bear market hits, unless you decide to sell it if and when you have a worthwhile gain. Most investors don't sell and could end up losing money, which is why I recommend not purchasing sector funds. If you're going to make a million in mutual funds, your fund's investments should be diversified for the long term. Sector funds are generally not a long-term investment.

It's OK if you want to pick an index fund, where the fund's portfolio matches that of a given index, like the S&P 500. Index funds have outperformed many actively managed funds over the long run.

Should You Buy Bond or Balanced Funds?

I also don't think most people should invest in bond or balanced funds. Stock funds tend to outperform bond funds, and in combining the two, you're ultimately just watering down your results.

Should You Buy Global or International Funds?

These funds might provide some diversification, but limit the percentage of your total fund investment in this higher-risk sector to 5% or 10%. International funds can, after a period of good performance, suffer years of laggard results, and investing in foreign governments creates added risk. Historically, Europe and Japan have underperformed the U.S. market.

The Size Problem of Large Funds

Asset size is a problem with many funds. If a fund has billions of dollars in assets, it will be more difficult to buy and sell large positions in a stock. Thus, it will be less flexible in retreating from the market or in acquiring meaningful positions in smaller, better-performing stocks. For this reason,

I'd avoid most of the largest mutual funds. If you have one of the larger funds that's done well over the years, and it still does reasonably well even as it has grown large, you should probably sit tight. Remember, the big money is always made over the long haul.

Management Fees and Turnover Rates

Some investors spend a lot of time evaluating a fund's management fees and portfolio turnover rates, but in most cases, such nitpicking isn't necessary.

In my experience, some of the best-performing growth funds have higher stock turnover rates. (A portfolio turnover rate is the ratio of the dollar value of buys and sells during a year compared to the dollar value of the fund's total assets.) Average turnover topped 350% in the Fidelity Magellan Fund during its three biggest performance years. CGM Capital Development Fund, managed by Ken Heebner, was the top-performing fund from 1989 to 1994. In two of those years, 1990 and 1991, it had turnover rates of 272% and 226%, respectively.

You can't be successful and on top of the market while not making any trades. Good fund managers will sell a stock when they think it's overvalued, are worried about the overall market or a specific group, or find another, more attractive stock to purchase. That's what you hire a professional to do. Also, institutional commission rates that funds pay are extremely low—only a few cents per share of stocks bought or sold. So don't be overly concerned about turnover rates. It's the fund's overall performance that is key.

The Five Most Common Mistakes Mutual Fund Investors Make

1. Failing to sit tight for at least 10 to 15 years.
2. Worrying about a fund's management fee, turnover rate, or the dividends it pays.
3. Being affected by news in the market when you're supposed to be investing for the long term.
4. Selling out during bad markets.
5. Being impatient and losing confidence too soon.

Other Common Mistakes

Typical investors in mutual funds tend to buy the best-performing fund after it's had a big year. What they don't realize is that history virtually dictates that the next year or two will probably show much slower results. If the economy goes into a recession, the results could be poorer still. Such conditions are usually enough to scare out those with less conviction and those who want to get rich quick.

Some investors switch (usually at the wrong time) to another fund that someone convinces them is much safer or has a "hotter" recent performance record. Switching may be OK if you have a really bad fund or the wrong type of fund, but too much switching quickly destroys what must be a long-term commitment to the benefits of compounding.

America's long-term future has always been a shrewd investment. The U.S. stock market has been growing since 1790 and the country will continue to grow in the future in spite of wars, panics, and recessions. Investing in mutual funds—the right way—is one way to benefit from America's growth and to secure your and your family's long-term financial future.

Improving Management of Pension and Institutional Portfolios

Having managed individual accounts, pension funds, and mutual funds, as well as supervised research analysts and dealt with many top portfolio managers, I have a few observations about the field of professional money management.

Individual investors need to know as much as they can about institutional money managers. After all, they represent the "I" in our CAN SLIM™ formula and account for roughly 80% of the important price moves. They also exert far greater influence on prices than specialists, market makers, daytraders, or advisory services do.

I've learned from my grand share of mistakes in the past, and that's how all of us learn and become wiser about investing. Perhaps my hands-on experience with all sides of The Street through many economic cycles will provide some key insights.

Institutional Investors: An Overview

The mutual fund you own or the pension fund you participate in is quarterbacked by an institutional money manager. You have a vested interest in knowing whether those managers are doing a good job, but it's also of value to understand how it is they do their job.

Today's markets are dominated by such pros, and almost all institutional buying is done with 100% cash rather than by using borrowed money (margin). As a result, you might have a sounder foundation for most securities than if speculative margin accounts ruled our stock markets. For example, in 1929, the public was heavily involved in the market, speculating with 10%

cash and 90% margin. This is one of the reasons why so many people got hurt when the market collapsed. However, margin debt as a percentage of the market capitalization of NYSE stocks also reached an extreme level at the end of March 2000.

Professional investors usually do not panic as easily after prolonged declines as the public might. In fact, institutional buying support often comes in when prices are down. The severe problems the stock market encountered from 1969 to 1975 had nothing to do with institutional or public investors. They were the result of economic mistakes and bad policy decisions made by politicians in Washington, D.C. The stock market is like a giant mirror that reflects basic conditions, political management (or mismanagement), and the psychology of the country.

Stiff competition among money managers and close scrutiny of their performance records has probably made today's best professional investment managers a little more proficient than they were 30 years ago.

The First Datagraph Books Evolve Into WONDA®

One of the first products we developed for institutional investors was the O'Neil Database® Datagraph books, which contain extremely detailed charts on thousands of publicly traded companies. They were the first of their kind and represented an innovation in the institutional investment research world. We were able to produce these books on a timely weekly interval, updating them at the market close every Friday. These comprehensive books were delivered to institutional money managers over the weekend in time for Monday's market open. This quick turnaround (for its time) was achieved not only because of the equity database we compiled and maintained on a daily basis, but also because of our high-speed microfilm plotting equipment. When we started out in 1964, this costly computer machinery was so new no one knew how to get a graph out of it. Once this barrier was cleared, it was possible to turn out complex, updated graphs through an automated process, at the rate of one per second.

Today, the technology has advanced so far that we can generate the most complex stock datagraphs with hardly a second thought, and the O'Neil Database books have become a mainstay at many of the leading mutual fund organizations around the globe. Initially, each datagraph displayed price and volume information along with a few technical and fundamental data items. Today, each datagraph displays 98 fundamental and 27 technical items, and these are available for over 10,000 stocks in 197 proprietary industry groups. This means an analyst or portfolio manager can compare any company to any other, either in the same industry or in the entire database.

We still offer the O'Neil Database books with their 600 pages of Datagraphs to our institutional clients as part of our overall institutional investment advisory business. With the advent of the Internet and highly sophisticated computer technology, these old-technology, hard-copy books are being replaced by our newest and most innovative flagship service, WONDA®. WONDA stands for William O'Neil Direct Access and provides all institutional clients with a direct interface to the O'Neil Database. The O'Neil Database contains over 3000 technical and fundamental data items on over 10,000 U.S. stocks, and WONDA allows users to screen and monitor the database using any combination of these data items.

We originally developed WONDA as an in-house system used to manage our own money. In the 1990s after years of real-time use, refinement and upgrading, the service was rolled-out as the newest William O'Neil + Co. service available strictly to the institutional investment community. Because WONDA was conceived and created by our in-house portfolio managers, research analysts, and computer programmers, the service was designed with the institutional money manager in mind. Institutional money managers frequently must make rapid decisions while under fire during the market day, and WONDA offers a wide range of features that allows for instantaneous access to and monitoring of crucial stock data and related information as the market is moving. Some of our institutional clients who use WONDA say they can "practically print money" with the system. These clients run the gamut from very conservative value-type managers to fast-trading hedge fund managers. Clearly, no computer system can print money, but that type of comment from some of the biggest and best institutional clients points out the functionality and effectiveness of WONDA.

Interpreting Dome Petroleum's Datagraph

One of the secrets that you, as a winning individual investor, should never forget is that you want to buy a stock before its potential is obvious to others. When numerous research reports show up, it might actually be time to consider selling. If it's value is obvious to almost everyone, it's probably too late.

The accompanying Datagraph of Dome Petroleum on the has been marked up to highlight a few of the ways to interpret and use this display of fundamental and technical information. We recommended Dome to institutions in November 1977 at $48. Fund managers didn't like the idea or the company's nonconservative accounting, so we bought the stock ourselves. Dome became one of our biggest winners at that time. This and the following case studies are real-life examples of how it's actually done.

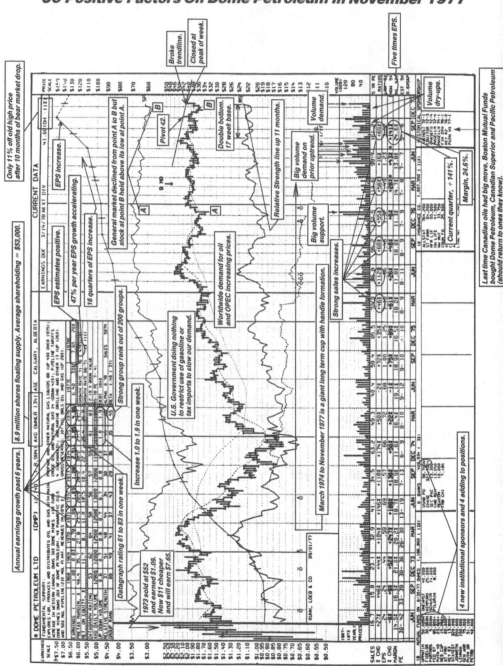

The Pic'n'Save Story

In July 1977 we recommended another stock that no institution would touch: Pic'n'Save. Most felt the company was entirely too small because it traded only 500 shares a day, so we began purchasing it several months later. We had the successful historical computer models of Kmart in 1962, when it traded only 1000 shares a day, and of Jack Eckerd Drug in April 1967, when it traded 500 shares a day, so we knew that, based on historical precedent, Pic'n'Save could become a real winner.

Precedent was on our side. Both retailers became big winners after they were discovered, and average daily trading volume increased steadily as a result. The same thing occurred with Pic'n'Save. This little, unknown company headquartered in Carson, California, turned in a steady and remarkable performance for seven or eight years. In fact, Pic'n'Save's pretax margins, return on equity, annual earnings growth rate, and debt-to-equity ratio were at that time superior to the other, more widely accepted institutional growth favorites—such as Wal-Mart Stores—that we had also recommended.

I've always believed in finding an outstanding stock and buying it every point on the way up. That's almost what happened with Pic'n'Save. We bought it every point or two on the way up for several years. I liked the company because it provided a way for families of meager means to buy most of the necessities of life at exceptionally low prices. All told, we bought Pic'n'Save on 285 different days and held it for 7½ years. When it was finally sold, the stock was trading several hundred thousand shares a day and our early purchases showed more than a 10-fold gain.

Radio Shack's Charles Tandy

We first uncovered Tandy Corp. in 1967, but we were only able to convince two institutions to buy the stock. Among the reasons given for not buying were that it didn't pay a dividend and that Charles Tandy was just a promoter. (Qualcomm was another stock considered to be too promotional from 1996 to 1998. We picked it up straight off of the weekly chart at the very end of 1998. It became the leading winner of 1999, advancing 20-fold).

When I met Tandy in his office in downtown Fort Worth, Texas, my reaction was just the opposite. He was a brilliant financial man who also happened to be an outstanding salesman. He had innovative incentives, departmental financial statements, and highly detailed, daily computer reports on sales of every item in every store by merchandise type, price, and category. His automated inventory and financial controls were almost unbelievable for that time.

After the stock tripled, Wall Street analysts started to acknowledge its existence. There were even a few research reports noting Tandy as an undervalued situation. Isn't it strange how far some stocks have to go up before they begin to look cheap to everyone?

The Size Problem in Portfolio Management

Many institutions think their main problem is size. Because they manage billions in assets, there never seems to be enough big-capitalization stocks they can buy or sell easily.

Let's face it: size is definitely an obstacle. It's easier to manage $10 million than $100 million; it's easier to manage $100 million than $1 billion; and $1 billion is a piece of cake compared to running $10 billion, $20 billion, or $30 billion. The size handicap simply means it's harder to buy or get rid of a huge stock holding in a small- or medium-sized company.

However, I believe it's a mistake for institutions to restrict investments solely to large-cap companies. In the first place, there aren't always enough outstanding ones to invest in at any given time. Why buy a slow-performing stock just because you can easily acquire a lot of it? Why buy a big-cap stock with earnings only growing 10% to 12% a year? If institutions limit themselves to large-cap investments, they could miss out on the truly powerful growth in the stock market.

During the Reagan years from 1981 through 1987, more than 3000 dynamic, up-and-coming companies incorporated or had initial public offerings of stock. This was a first and was due mainly to several lowerings of the capital gains tax during the early 1980s. Many of these small- to medium-sized entrepreneurial concerns became enormous future market leaders and were responsible for driving the unprecedented technology boom and big expansion of new jobs in the 1980s and 1990s. Although most of these names were small unknown companies at the time, you'll recognize them now as some of the biggest names and greatest winning companies of that period. This is just a partial list of the thousands of ingenious innovators that reignited growth in America until the March 2000 market top.

Adobe Systems	Clear Channel Communications
Altera	Compaq Computer
America Online	Comverse Technology
American Power Conversion	Costco
Amgen	Dell Computer
Charles Schwab	Digital Switch
Cisco Systems	EMC

Emulex
Franklin Resources
Home Depot
International Game Technology
Linear Technology
Maxim Integrated Products
Micron Technology
Microsoft
Novell
Novellus Systems

Oracle
PeopleSoft
PMC-Sierra
Qualcomm
Sun Microsystems
Unitedhealth Group
US Healthcare
Veritas Computer
Vitesse Semiconductor
Xilinx

As mentioned earlier, our government should seriously consider lowering the capital gains tax again and possibly shortening the time period to six months to help fuel a new cycle of entrepreneurial start-up companies. Today's markets are more liquid than markets of the past, with volume of many medium-sized stocks averaging 500,000 to 5,000,000 shares a day. In addition, significant crossing of blocks occurs between institutions, which also aids liquidity. The institutional manager who handles billions of dollars would best be advised to broaden his or her prospects to the 4000 or more innovative companies available. This is better than restricting activities to the same few hundred large, well-known, or legal-list-type companies. At one point, the research department of one of the nation's largest banks followed only 600 companies.

A sizable institution would likely be better off owning 500 companies of all sizes than 100 large, mature, slow-moving companies. However, mutual funds that concentrate in small-cap, big performers have to be more careful. If they have only a few hundred million to manage, it can be exceptionally rewarding. If these same funds, through their own success, grow to several billion dollars, they can't continue to concentrate solely in fast-moving, more speculative smaller names. The reason is that these stocks in one phase perform well and then later top; some never come back or lag in performance for years. Several Janus and Putnam funds ran into this problem during the late 1990s and early 2000 period. Success can breed overconfidence.

Pension funds can address size problems of their own by spreading their money among several different managers with different investment styles.

Size Is Not the Key Problem

However, size isn't the number one problem for institutional investors. Frequently, it's their investment philosophies and methods that keep them from fully capitalizing on the potential of the market.

Many institutions buy stocks based on their analysts' opinions about the supposed value of a company. Others mainly buy stories. Still others follow economists' top-down predictions of the broad sectors that ought to do well. We believe working from the bottom up (concentrating on locating stocks with winning characteristics) produces better results.

For many years past, some institutions used the same standard names and rarely changed their approved lists. If a list had a hundred widely accepted names, four or five might be added each year. Many decisions had to be approved by investment committees. However, market decisions made by committees are typically poor. To make matters worse, some committees had members who weren't experienced money managers. This is questionable investment policy.

Even today, investment flexibility is sometimes hamstrung by antiquated rules. Some more conservative institutions, for example, can't buy stocks that don't pay dividends. This seems right out of the Dark Ages because many outstanding growth stocks deliberately don't pay dividends; they reinvest their profits into the company to continue funding their above-average growth. Other restrictions mandate that half or more of the portfolio be invested in bonds. Most bond portfolios have produced weak results over the long term. Also, in the past, some bond portfolios have used misleading accounting that did not value their portfolio to current market prices.

In these few situations, reporting of portfolio results is too infrequent and the true overall performance is unclear. Too much emphasis is on yield and not enough on the increase or decrease in market value of the assets in the portfolio.

The main problem is that most of these antiquated, institutionally accepted investment decision processes have a deeply rooted legal basis. They have become, in a word, "institutionalized." Many institutions are forced to adhere to legal concepts such as the "prudent man rule," "due diligence," and "fiduciary responsibility" when making investment decisions. In most cases, a trust department could be liable for poor or derelict investment decisions, but the standard for determining whether an investment decision is poor or derelict has nothing to do with the performance of the investment itself! If an institution can show that a stock it decided to invest in was selected on the basis of a "prudent man" analysis (meaning the institution acted as a prudent man or woman would be expected to act) that took into account valuation based on a static view of a company's fundamental situation, or that it was part of an overall "asset allocation" model or some other similar reason arrived at by due diligence, then the institution can show it exercised its fiduciary responsibility properly and thus side-step any liability.

Years ago, institutions had relatively few fund managers to choose from, but today there are many outstanding professional money-management teams using a variety of systems. However, many of them can't buy a stock that's not on their preapproved list unless it's accompanied by a long, glowing report from one of their analysts. Since the institutions already own a substantial number of companies which they insist their analysts continue to follow and update, it might take an analyst more time to get all the interesting new names onto an approved list and reports prepared on these companies. Superior performance comes from fresh ideas, not the same old overused, stale names or last cycle's favorites. For example, the super tech leaders of 1998 and 1999 will probably be replaced by many new consumer and defense sector leaders in the twenty-first century.

Bottom Buyers' Bliss

Many institutions buy stocks on the way down, but bottom fishing isn't always the best way to achieve superior performance. It can place decision makers in the position of buying stocks that are slowly deteriorating or decelerating their growth.

Other money management organizations use valuation models that restrict investments to stocks in the lower end of historical P/E ranges. This approach works for a few unusually capable, conservative professionals, but over time, it rarely produces truly superior results. Several major Midwest banks that use this approach have continually lagged in performance. Entirely too many analysts have a P/E hang up. They want to sell a P/E that's up and looks high and buy one that comes off. Fifty years of models of the most successful stocks show that low or "reasonable" P/Es are not a cause of huge increases in price. Those faithful to low P/Es would probably have missed almost every major stock market winner of the last half century.

I am familiar with hundreds of institutions and virtually every investment philosophy imaginable. Most of those that concentrate on the undervalued theory of stock selection invariably lag today's better managers. Sometimes these undervalued situations get more undervalued or lag the market for a long time.

Comparing Growth Versus Value Results

Over the previous 12 business cycles, it's been my experience that the very best money managers produced average annual compounded total returns of 25% to, in a few cases, 30%. This small group consisted of either growth-stock managers or managers whose most successful investments were in growth stocks.

The best undervalued type managers in the same period averaged only 15% to 20%. A few had gains over 20%, but they were in the minority. Most individual investors haven't prepared themselves well enough to average 25% or more per year, regardless of the method used.

Value funds will do better in down or poor market periods because their stocks typically don't go up a large amount during the prior bull market period, and so they typically will correct less. Therefore, most people trying to prove the value case will pick a market top as the beginning point of a 10-or-more-year period to compare with growth investing. This leads to an unfair comparison in which value investing may "prove" more successful than growth-stock investing. The reality is that if you look at the situation fairly, growth-stock investing usually outperforms value investing over most periods.

Value Line Dumps the Undervalued System

From the 1930s up to the early 1960s, the Value Line service rated stocks it followed as undervalued or overvalued. The company's results were mediocre until they dumped the system in the 1960s and began rating stocks based on earnings increases and relative market action. Since the switch, Value Line's performance has improved materially.

Overweighting and Underweighting to the S&P

Many institutions invest primarily in stocks in the S&P 500 and try to overweight or underweight positions in certain sectors. This practice assures they'll never do much better or worse than the S&P 500 Index. However, an outstanding small- or mid-sized growth-stock manager should potentially be able to average about 1¼ to 1½ times the S&P 500 Index over a period of several years. The S&P 500 is a tough index for a mutual fund to materially beat because the S&P is really a managed portfolio that continues to add newer, better companies and discard laggards.

Weaknesses of the Industry Analysts System

Another widely used, expensive, and ineffective practice is to hire a large number of analysts and then divvy up coverage by industry. Much of this is done for the investment banking side in order to develop and maintain client relationships. Thus, at a minimum, analysts have split loyalties.

The typical securities research department has an auto analyst, an electronics analyst, an oil analyst, a retail analyst, a drug analyst, and on and on. However, this setup is not efficient and tends to perpetuate mediocre performance. What does an analyst assigned to two or three out-of-favor groups do? Recommend the least bad of all the poor stocks he or she follows?

On the other hand, the analyst who happens to follow the year's best-performing group may only put forth two or three winners, missing many others. When the oil stocks boomed in 1979 and 1980, all of them doubled or tripled. The best shot up five times or more.

The theory behind dividing up research is that a person can be an expert on a particular industry. In fact, Wall Street firms go so far as to hire a chemist from a chemical company to be their chemical analyst and a Detroit auto specialist to be their automotive analyst. These individuals may know the nuts and bolts of their industries, but in many cases, they have little understanding of the general market and what makes leading stocks go up and down. Maybe this explains why virtually every analyst appearing on CNBC after September 2000 continually recommended buying high-tech stocks as they were on their way to 80% to 90% declines. People lost a lot of money if they followed this free advice on TV.

Firms also like to advertise they have more analysts, the largest department, or more top-ranked "all star" analysts. I'd rather have 5 good analysts who are generalists than 50, 60, or 70 who are confined to limited specialties. What are your chances of finding 50 or more analysts who are all outstanding at making money in the market or coming up with money-making ideas?

The shortcomings of Wall Street analysts were never made plainer to institutional and individual investors than during the 2000 bear market. While the market continued to sell off in what would become the worst bear market since 1929 as measured by the percentage decline in the Nasdaq Index, and many former high-flying tech and Internet stocks were being decimated, Wall Street analysts continued to issue "buy" or "strong buy" recommendations on these stocks. In fact, in October 2000 one major Wall Street firm was running full-page ads calling the market environment at that time "One of the Ten Best Times to Own Stocks" in history. As we now know, the market continued to plummet well into 2001, making that period in fact one of the worst times to own stocks in history! It was not until many of the tech and Internet high-flyers were down 90% or more from their peaks that these analysts finally changed their tune. Many days late and many dollars short!

A December 31, 2000, *New York Times* article on the subject of analysts' recommendations quoted Zacks Investment Research, "Of the 8,000 recommendations made by analysts covering the companies in the Standard & Poor's 500 Stock Index, only 29 now are sells." In the same article, Arthur

Levitt, Chairman of the SEC, stated, "The competition for investing banking business is so keen that analysts' sell recommendations on stocks of banking clients are very rare." A mutual fund manager quoted by the *Times* stated, "What passes for research on Wall Street today is shocking to me. Instead of providing investors with the kind of analysis that would have kept them from marching over the cliff, analysts prodded them forward by inventing new valuation criteria for stocks that had no basis in reality and no standards of good practice." *Vanity Fair* also ran an interesting article in August 2001 on the analytical community. Clearly, at no time in the history of the markets has the phrase *caveat emptor* had more meaning for investors, both institutional and individual alike.

The year-2000 implementation of SEC Rule FD, governing the fair disclosure of material company information to institutional as well as individual investors, has restricted the ability of major brokerage research analysts to receive inside information from a company before it is released to the rest of the street. This has further reduced any advantage to be gained by listening to most Wall Street analysts. We prefer to deal only with facts and historical models rather than opinions about supposed values. Many research analysts in 2000 and 2001 had not been in the business for 10 years or longer and therefore never experienced the 1987, 1974–1975, and 1962 terrible bear markets.

On still another subject, many large money-management groups probably deal with entirely too many research firms. For one thing, there aren't that many strong research inputs, and dealing with 30 or 40 dilutes the value and impact of the few good ones. Confusion, doubt, and fear created by conflicting advice at critical junctures can prove to be expensive.

Financial World's Startling Survey of Top Analysts

A *Financial World* magazine article dated back in November 1, 1980, also found that analysts selected by *Institutional Investor* magazine as the best on Wall Street were overrated and overpaid, and they materially underperformed the S&P averages.

As a group, on two out of three stock picks the "superstar" analysts failed to match either the market as a whole or their own industry averages. They also seldom provided sell recommendations, limiting most of their advice to buys or holds.

The *Financial World* study confirmed research we performed in the early 1970s. We found that only the minority of Wall Street recommendations were successful. We also concluded that during a period in which many sell opinions were in order, only 1 in 10 reports made sell suggestions.

One of the problems is that a lot of the research on Wall Street is done on the wrong companies. Every industry analyst has to turn out a certain amount of product, but only a few industry groups lead a typical market cycle. There's insufficient front-end screening or control to determine the superior companies on which research reports should actually be written.

Database Power and Efficiency

On any given day, most institutional money managers receive a stack of research reports a foot high. Trudging through them in search of a good stock is usually a waste of time. If they're lucky, they may spot 1 out of 20 that's really right to buy.

In contrast, those with access to WONDA can rapidly screen through 10,000 companies in our database. If the defense industry pops up as one of the leading industries, they can call up 84 different corporations whose primary business is in that area. The typical institution might look at Boeing, Raytheon, United Technologies, and two or three other big, well-known names. With more than 3000 comparable technical and fundamental variables on each of the 84 companies stretching back a number of years, as well as the ability to display these variables quickly on identical graphic displays, it's possible in 20 minutes for an institutional money manager to determine the 5 or 10 companies in the entire group that possess outstanding characteristics worthy of more detailed research.

In other words, there are ways for an institution's analysts to spend their time more productively. Yet, few research departments are organized to take advantage of such advanced and disciplined procedures.

How well has this approach worked? In 1977, we introduced an institutional service called New Stock Market Ideas and Past Leaders to Avoid (NSMI). It is published every week, and its documented, recent 10-year performance record is shown on the accompanying graph.

Buy selections over 23 years outperformed *avoids* more than 135 to 1, and *buy* picks outran the S&P 500 stocks more than 30-fold. The compounding over the 23 years' time helps make an unbelievable long-term record like this possible. For the 13 years ended 2000, overall stocks listed in NSMI as stocks to avoid made zero performance. Institutions could have improved performance just by staying out of all of the stocks on our avoid list. As a service to our institutional clients, we provide them with computerized quarterly performance reports for every *buy* and *avoid* recommendation made in the New Stock Market Ideas® service.

Having a massive amount of factual data on every firm and proven historical models for 50 years, we're able to discover a stock beginning to

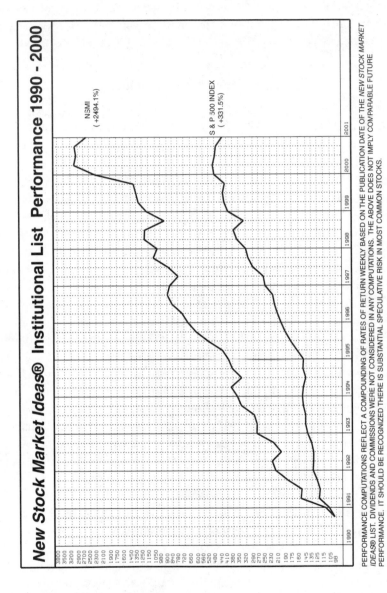

New Stock Market Ideas® Institutional List Performance 1990 - 2000

NSMI
(+2494.1%)

S & P 500 INDEX
(+331.5%)

PERFORMANCE COMPUTATIONS REFLECT A COMPOUNDING OF RATES OF RETURN WEEKLY BASED ON THE PUBLICATION DATE OF THE *NEW STOCK MARKET IDEAS®* LIST. DIVIDENDS AND COMMISSIONS WERE NOT CONSIDERED IN ANY COMPUTATIONS. THE ABOVE DOES NOT IMPLY COMPARABLE FUTURE PERFORMANCE. IT SHOULD BE RECOGNIZED THERE IS SUBSTANTIAL SPECULATIVE RISK IN MOST COMMON STOCKS.

Performance record of NSMI over ten years

improve or get in trouble much earlier—without visiting the company. It may be naïve to believe companies are going to always tell you when they are beginning to have problems. By using our own data and research, we also discourage any reliance on tips, rumors, and personal opinions. We just don't need, want, or believe such information. We also do not have investment banking clients or market-making activities, and we do not manage money for others, so those areas of potential bias are nonexistent.

The 1982 and 1978 Full-Page Bullish Ads

We usually don't try to call every short-term or intermediate correction. For institutional investors, this would be a little foolish and shortsighted. Our primary focus is recognizing and acting upon the early stages of each new bull and bear market. This work includes searching for the market sectors and groups that should be bought and those that should be avoided.

In early 1982, we placed a full-page ad in *The Wall Street Journal* stating that the back of inflation had been broken and the important stocks had already made their lows. That May, we mailed out two wall charts to our institutional clients: one of defense-electronic stocks and the other of 20 consumer growth stocks we thought might be attractive for the bull market ahead. We also made a point of going to New York and Chicago to meet with several large institutions. In these meetings, we stated our bullish posture and provided a list of names that should be purchased.

The stance we took was diametrically opposed to the position of most institutional research firms at that time, as well as the negative news flooding daily out of the national media. Most investment firms were downright bearish. They anticipated another big down-leg in the market. They also projected that interest rates and inflation were going to soar back into new high ground as a result of massive government borrowing that would crowd the private sector out of the marketplace.

The fear and confusion created by these questionable judgments frightened large investors so much that they hesitated. As a result, they did not fully capitalize on the fact that the two leading groups for the coming bull market had already been identified. It appeared professional managers had been bombarded with so much negative "expert" Wall Street input that they found it hard to believe our positive findings. As for us, we invested fully on margin in the summer of 1982 and enjoyed our best performance ever up to that time. From 1978 to 1991, our account increased 20-fold. From the beginning of 1998 through 2000, our firm account, run out of our separate holding company, increased 1500%. Results such as this remind us it may be

DON'T LET THE GLOOM BUGS FOOL YOU... INFLATION'S BACK IS BROKEN AND IT'S TIME TO INVEST FOR THE RECOVERY AHEAD

Now's the time for both corporations and individuals to grab on to President Reagan's powerful incentive programs and invest.
William O'Neil & Co. believes the stock market averages may be near their lows now. We also think the *best* individual stocks have seen their lows and will one by one find their way back to new high ground over the next 6 months.

It is very normal to have gloom, doubt and pessimism during the low point of a recession and the bottom of a bear market. However, we do not agree with Henry Kaufman's recent negative conclusion that inflation will move back toward old record levels when the economy recovers. We believe the backbone of excessive inflation has definitely been broken and will wind down more in the year ahead. There are a number of reasons for our optimistic outlook on inflation.

Long Term Trend Of Oil, Real Estate And Commodity Prices Has Broken
To begin with, oil prices, as well as oil company stocks, topped a year ago. OPEC should consider lowering prices; otherwise they may have to continue reducing production and income. The large oil price jumps of recent years caused widespread changes to other fuels, increased energy efficiency, lower overall demand and a loss of world oil markets. High prices also stimulated exploration and new production. The old law of supply and demand still works.

Gold, silver, diamonds and other inflation-hedge commodity prices have made major long term tops and are down substantially from their highs. And we do not agree with a well-known economist nor a prominent member of the House of Representatives who advocate the U.S. must return to the gold standard. This out-moded concept did not prevent government's financial mismanagement since 1965, and it can not now substitute for competence.

Real estate prices, after tremendous increases, have been coming down. In Southern California where building trends frequently lead other areas of the country, condominiums and homes became so overpriced that both prices and interest rates need to decline further before sales can pick up. The reason is simple. People can not make or qualify for monthly payments of $2,000 or more.

The auto giants' bad management decisions and high interest rates have caused them to permanently lose share of market. Their best hope is for both big labor and big management to reduce all costs and auto prices with no strings attached and try to regain part of their lost market. If they do not act together, the auto industry will likely be a declining U.S. industry in the future.

Airline fares have been too high and are being lowered to attract more customers.

The Consumer and Producer Price Indexes have fallen and the trend of money supply has been down for almost a year and a half. This should lead to lower inflation ahead.

Reasons Why Interest Rates Should Be Lowered
The Federal Reserve Board discount rate is now substantially higher than the inflation rate, and so are long term Bond yields.

A few years ago the discount rate was raised several times by abnormal amounts to protect the American dollar from attack. This problem no longer exists. Confidence in the U.S., its leadership and the dollar have materially improved.

Interest rates at the low point in each past recession have progressively been at higher levels. If this trend continues, we could have higher low points and higher high points for interest rates in each new business cycle. The Federal Reserve Board should consider lowering the rate over the next 6 months to a point slightly below the 10% low of the previous cycle, thus breaking the escalating trend.

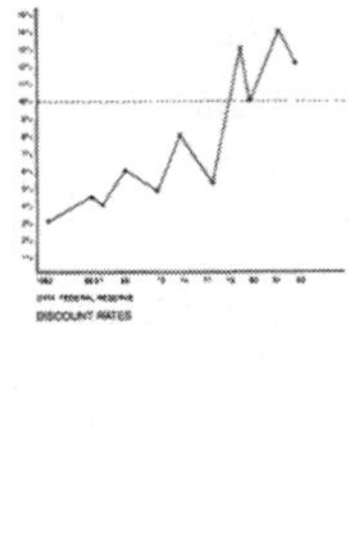

The Federal Reserve Board should probably not try to fight inflation all by itself. Tight money did not solve the inflationary problem in the recession in 1974, nor in 1977-78. While money supply is the primary determinant of the rate of inflation, it is not the sole cause as some people believe. Last year's decline in inflation was caused primarily by a leveling in oil prices and farm prices. Money supply policy, in no way, created good weather, good crops and an over-supply of oil.

Our government may also want to consider having money supply figures available monthly, rather than weekly since weekly guessing, over-reaction and public over-emphasis make sound interpretation of the major trend unlikely. The Fed may want to consider the possibility of better control of new sources of money supply.

For example, Money Market funds have no reserve requirements. What might occur if a run were to happen on Money Market funds? The high rates Money Market funds offer drain funds from other more productive areas and forces other agencies to raise their rates in order to try and compete.

Congress also has an important responsibility to cut spending and government inefficiency. Congress can also deregulate natural gas and include a windfall tax to help lessen the 100 billion dollar deficit.

Because of new tax incentives for saving there should be an increased pool of savings available as business begins to borrow in the recovering economy.

The auto industry and its supplier industries will not recover until interest rates decline further. Ten percent unemployment economically should be unacceptable and could be dangerous to the country as well as politically damaging.

High interest rates are hurting the world economy.

Why You Should Buy Common Stocks Now
Stocks are the only remaining area in the economy that appears greatly undervalued. Gold, real estate, diamonds, commodities have all had excessive increases and as a result seem over-priced with less potential for profit. The number of shareholders in America, after declining for many years, should increase significantly. The cause of this increase will be the substantially lower capital gains tax (20% vs. nearly 50% in recent years) and the new investor's retirement accounts with their flexibility and tax saving features.

Stocks on average are currently selling at 6 and 7 times annual earnings. Such low price earnings ratios have not occurred since the 6 P E at the bottom of the Dow Jones in 1974, the 7 P E in 1949 and the 5 P E in 1932. And as you know prices and P E's improved materially from these historical lows. We believe the decline in price earnings ratios that began in 1962 has ended and the future will show progressive upward reevaluation for stocks.

If channel lines are drawn along the tops and bottoms of the Dow Jones Industrial average since the early 1930's the Dow is once again sitting on its major long term bottom trendline.

The lower tax for all consumers, combined with lower inflation, will ease the pressure on consumer's discretionary income for the first time in many years. This should result in a resurgence in the better consumer growth stocks.

The William O'Neil & Co. Senior Growth Stock Index is performing stronger than general market indexes; and the Dow Jones Industrials failed to confirm the recent new lows in the transportation index.

Not only have we seen several brokerage house economists being very bearish, but a preponderance of public advisory services have been preaching total gloom and doom. This usually happens around market bottoms.

Odd lot short selling accelerated in January—another psychological sign of bottom market action. Those who expect a climax bottom with heavy selling will likely be disappointed since this phenomenon occurred mainly in past years when markets had greater public involvement. Institutions, which dominate our markets today, do not panic as readily along bear market lows. They tend to pull back from selling or actually buy on the way down.

What Areas Of The Market Seem Favorable Now?
We are in the midst of a revolutionary computer and communication age. The better, innovative leaders in this area should continue to do well.

As mentioned earlier, we believe there will be a resurgence in selected consumer growth stocks. As time passes, various defense electronic stocks should benefit from our planned defense build-up. Companies producing automated teller equipment should benefit from increased branch banking and automation. Selected drug and medical companies that show superior earnings per share increases should be favored. Speciality retailers plus entertainment companies with new products in areas such as video games seem to be succeeding. As the economy slowly recovers, other areas will emerge with improved and accelerating earnings.

Why Corporate America Should Be Investing Now
Big corporate America, in the past, has invested somewhat backwards and been slow to take innovative new risks. Traditionally, big business only expands at the end of a business cycle. It seems to us that the top of a cycle is the poorest time to invest in new plant capacity and automation, because interest rates and competition are at a peak. The shrewdest and cheapest time to invest is at the low point in a business cycle where prices will be the best and your bargaining power the greatest. Andrew Carnegie, an earlier industrial leader, used to say, "the first man gets the oyster, the second the shell."

The American people and in particular American businessmen and women, in our opinion, may have one of the best Presidents since Abraham Lincoln. They should get off the dime and take advantage of the tremendous tax incentives now available. President Reagan's incentive programs are broad and very workable. The sole cause of the current recession has been the Federal Reserve's tight money policy. The press, the country and many politicians may be making the mistake of continually underestimating Ronald Reagan's ability and leadership.

Big companies need to change in order to survive. All growth is built on change. They need new products and some of them need new management. Giants like Mobil, U.S. Steel and DuPont, trying to acquire other large companies for the most part is counterproductive only making a giant larger, less creative and less efficient. Few conglomerates know how to run more than one or two businesses correctly and the high prices paid for such acquisitions are questionable to say nothing of the poor utilization of billions of dollars of this nation's badly needed capital.

The Administration's recently announced council to study productivity is primarily staffed with big business representatives. The makeup of this group should be amended to include several leaders of small to medium-sized, innovative growth companies. These are the companies that have shown the greatest productivity in our country. Big business has been the least productive, least creative and least imaginative. Having a council loaded with big business leaders is a little like a council of losing football coaches meeting to tell everyone how to be No. 1.

How Many Truly Successful Pessimists Do You Know?
In summary, we see a psychological comparison to 1947-49. This was the time our troops returned home after World War II. The common thinking then was that bad times were ahead because there wouldn't be enough jobs to absorb those returning from war. The common fears turned out to be wrong as pent-up demand launched a new economic surge. Likewise, today we believe the common fears may turn out to be wrong. The economy will be stimulated with the strongest incentives in decades and the needs of mankind. We are also reminded of old Sewell Avery forever hoarding his money and completely missing his market. Springtime is only around the corner and it makes us think. How many truly successful pessimists do you know? So, don't let the gloom bugs fool you.

If you are an institutional or a corporate investor you may be interested to know that our latest January issue of *New Stock Market Ideas & Past Leaders To Avoid* lists 170 stocks as buy recommendations and only 38 stocks that should be avoided. Our advice to all Institutional consulting clients throughout the month of January was to buy specific growth stocks into the correction.

If you are an individual investor you may wish to examine our latest new service titled, *Long Term Values*. We introduced this investment service, which covers 4,000 securities, at the bottom of the market in October. This, along with our Daily Graphs Services have over 22,000 annual subscribers, and can be seen in full page ads in *Barron's* every week.

William O'Neil + Co.
INCORPORATED

Member NYSE, ASE and other major regional exchanges.
11915 LaGrange Avenue, Los Angeles, California 90025
(213)820-7011

Reprint from The Wall Street Journal February 5 and 8, 1982

February 1982 bull market ad

an advantage not to be headquartered in rumor-filled and emotion-packed Wall Street.

You, as a savvy individual investor, have a gigantic advantage in not having to listen to 50 different, strongly held opinions. You can see from this example that majority opinions seldom work in the market and that stocks seem to require doubt and disbelief—the proverbial "wall of worry"—to make meaningful progress. The market generally moves to disappoint the majority.

Our first full-page ad in *The Wall Street Journal* was placed in March 1978. It predicted a new bull market in small- to medium-sized growth stocks. We had written the ad weeks ahead of time and waited to run it until we felt the time was right. The right time came when the market was making new lows, which caught investors by surprise. Our only reason for placing the ad was to document in print exactly what our position was at that juncture, so there could be no question with institutional investors later on.

It is at these extremely difficult market turning points that an institutional research firm can be of most value. At such times, many people are either petrified with fear or carried away with excessive fundamental information.

Our institutional research firm has more than 600 leading institutional accounts in the United States and around the world that receive our periodic confidential market memos when we feel a major market change could be in process. We were one of the few firms to tell its accounts to sell tech stocks and raise cash in March, April, and September 2000.

The following is a confidential market memo written before the second edition of this book was published. It projects a moderately bearish 1994, with most growth stocks topping. Sometimes these memos are right and sometimes they're not. This one gave institutions 10 weeks of rally to sell into before the market topped in late January. Almost all institutions who got the memo weren't so sure. They argued with the conclusions or just found it impossible to reduce commitments and hold cash when the market was strong and going up. As a result, in April 1994, most institutions had less cash than they had in November 1993. (A similar divergence of opinion happened when we recommended home builders Ryland in April 2001 at 46 and NVR in November 2001 at 180. Most analysts ignored the continuous decline in interest rates and said to sell the builders.)

TO: Institutional Clients

FR: William O'Neil

RE: November 19, 1993 Market Memo

For the past four weeks, we have continued to add a large number of this year's growth leaders to the sell/avoid side in our *New Stock Market Ideas and Big Cap* service. We believe a bear market has started in these stocks. Examples included companies like Best Buy, Promus, Int'l Game Technology, Cabletron, Countrywide Credit, Dial Page, Glenayre, Newbridge, Nextel, Qualcomm, Tellabs, etc. These stocks are different from the Philip Morris, Novell, Nike, and Waste Management names added to the avoid category earlier this year. The recent changes cover a broad area in the high tech and gambling sectors, the two leading groups of the year. If you combine this with noticeable weakness in banking, insurance, and utilities stocks, the breadth of the distribution that has taken place is significant.

Here are a few other pertinent facts: the general market (S&P and DJIA) on Tuesday, Wednesday, and Thursday, November 2–4, came under abnormal liquidation on heavy volume. Likewise, the daily breadth suffered its sharpest two-day drop in two years and was unable to rally back. The IBD Mutual Fund Index also had its sharpest two-day break, as did the Nasdaq average. We believe that the Nasdaq and AMEX average had a speculative price climax on heavy volume four weeks earlier and has since been in a topping process. On Wednesday, November 17, the relative price strength line on the Nasdaq Composite shown in *Investor's Business Daily* broke below its support low of four weeks ago on 360 million shares.

Laggard stocks have been up in recent weeks and the bond market has been down. Last month was an all-time record for new issues, and both Zacks and Value Line introduced major new investment services for the public. Both the DJIA and the S&P 500 have shown wedging patterns with no ability to follow through. Interest has revived in gold as a place to hide, even though the fundamentals are not powerful. Finally, the market on a yield and P/E basis has been in overvalued territory for some time now. On a worldwide perspective, Europe and Japan still do not have strong economies.

We do not believe this is just another short-term correction and do not believe a stock like Intel is a value simply because it sells for nine times earnings. We expect an earnings slowdown over the next several quarters for Intel. Furthermore, we see a number of market leaders that are topping and expect the next three months and much of 1994 to be a somewhat more difficult year.

Many of President Clinton's proposals appear to us to be unsound, particularly in the healthcare area. Our estimate is that 10 years from now, more than $1 trillion in new taxes will be needed to fund his enormous new program. Price controls along with government management could lead to other difficulties. There also seems to be a credibility problem with the President. The Administration says they've decided against price controls, everyone will get to choose his or her own doctor, the system will be better, and we'll save more money. Most of his statements are misrepresentations of the facts contained in his plan submitted to Congress.

Our suggestion is to reduce your portfolio volatility and reduce portfolio concentration in aggressive stocks and groups. We do not, however, expect any bear market correction that might occur to be of a substantial nature (when compared to historical bear markets). Perhaps 15% might be a reasonable guesstimate because America is in an entrepreneurial phase with hundreds of emerging new companies and new technologies that will cushion any adjustment. We are also in a low interest rate, low inflation environment with the economy showing a degree of pickup.

Institutional Investors Are Human

If you don't think fear and emotion can ride high among professional investors after a prolonged decline, think again. I remember meeting with the top three or four money managers of one important bank at the bottom of the market in 1974. They were as shell-shocked, demoralized, and confused as anyone could possibly be. (They deserved to be. The ordinary stock in the market at that time was down 75%.) About the same time, I recall visiting with another top manager. He too was thoroughly worn out and, judging from the peculiar color of his face, suffering from market sickness. Yet another top fund manager in Boston looked as if he'd been run over by a train! Of course, all of this is preferable to 1929, when some people jumped out of office buildings in response to the devastating market collapse.

I also recall a high-tech seminar given in 1983 in San Francisco attended by 2000 highly educated analysts and portfolio managers. Everyone was there, and everyone was ebullient and self-confident, and that marked the exact top for high-tech stocks.

I also remember a presentation we gave to a bank in another large city. All its analysts were brought in around an impressive table in the boardroom, but not one analyst or portfolio manager asked any questions during or after the presentation. It was the strangest situation I've ever been in. Needless to say, this institution consistently performed in the lower quartiles when compared to its more alert and venturesome competitors. It's important to communicate and be open to new ideas.

Years ago, one medium-sized bank for which we did consulting work insisted we give them recommendations only from the stocks they carried on their limited approved list. After consulting with them each month for three months and telling them that there was nothing on their approved list that met our qualifications, we had to honorably part company. A few months later we learned that key officials in that trust department were relieved of their jobs due to their laggard performance.

We provided recommendations to another Midwest institution, but they were of doubtful value because the institution had a cast-in-concrete belief that any potential investment must be screened to see if it passed an undervalued model. The best investments rarely show up on any undervalued model, and there's probably no way this institution will produce first-rate results until it throws out this model. This isn't easy for large organizations to do. It's like asking a Baptist to become a Catholic or vice versa.

Some large money-management organizations with average records tend to fire the head of the investment department and then look for a replacement who invests pretty much the same way. Naturally, this doesn't solve the problem of deficient investment methods and philosophy. Security Pacific Bank in Los Angeles was an exception to this rule. In July 1981, it made a change in its top investment management. It brought in an individual with a completely different approach, a superior investment philosophy, and an outstanding performance record. The results were dramatic and accomplished almost overnight. In 1982, Security Pacific's Fund G was ranked number 1 in the country.

Penny Wise and Performance Foolish

Some corporations put too much emphasis on saving management fees, particularly when they have giant funds to be managed. It's usually an actuary who convinces them of the money their pension fund can save by shaving the fee by 0.125 of 1%.

If corporations have billions of dollars to be managed, it makes sense to increase fees and incentives so they can hire the best money managers in the business. The better managers will earn the extra 0.25 or 0.50 of 1%, 10 or 20 times over. The last thing you ever want is cheap advice in the stock market. If you were going to have open heart surgery, would you look for the doctor who'll charge the absolute least?

How to Select and Measure Money Managers Properly

Here are a few tips for corporations and organizations that want to farm out their funds to several money managers.

In general, portfolio managers should be given a complete cycle before their performance is reviewed for the purpose of changing managers. Give them from the peak of one bull market period to the peak of another cycle or the trough of one cycle to the trough of another. This will usually cover a three- or four-year period and will allow all managers to go through both an up market and a down market. At the end of this period, the bottom 20% or so of the managers in total overall performance should be replaced. Thereafter, every year or two the bottom 5% or 10% of managers over the most recent three- or four-year period should be dropped. This avoids hasty decisions based on disappointing performance over a few short quarters or a year. Given time, this process will lead to an outstanding group of proven money managers. Because this is a sound, longer-term, self-correcting mechanism, it should stay that way. Then it won't be necessary to pay as many consultants to recommend changes in personnel.

In the selection of managers, consideration could be given to their latest three- to five-year performance statistics as well as to a more recent period. Diversification should be considered among the types, styles, and locations of managers. The search should be widespread and not necessarily limited to one consultant's narrow, captive universe or stable of managers.

The corporate or pension fund client with money to be managed also has to be careful not to interfere at critical junctures—deciding, for example, when a greater proportion of the portfolios should be either in stocks or bonds or that undervalued stocks should be emphasized.

Clients can also interfere by directing where commissions should go or insisting that executions be given to whoever does it cheapest. The latter, while a well-meaning attempt to save money, commonly results in forcing upon a money manager someone that provides poorer executions or no research input of real value. This handicap costs the portfolio money as it pays ⅛, ¼, or ½-point or more (or their decimal equivalents) on trades being executed by more inexperienced people. Another practice that should possibly be curtailed is dictating that portions of the commissions from execution of fund orders be directed to a third party who will then rebate them to the corporation. This siphons off incentive dollars that should be used to pay for the best research, execution, and market ideas available. A fund will never be able to buy the "best market brains" at a cheap price.

Is an Index Fund the Way to Go?

Finally, a word about the indexing of equity portfolios. There's an assumption that a pension fund's objective is to match some general market index. This theoretically could be a risky conclusion.

If we were to go through another 1929 market collapse, and the general market indices were to decline 90% in value, no intelligent trustee could possibly believe his or her fund's objective should be to lose 90% of its value. No one will be happy just because the fund achieved its target of matching the index's disastrous performance.

I saw a small version of this happen in 1974, when I was called in to evaluate a fund that had lost exactly 50% of its assets because it was managed by an organization that specialized in and promoted index funds. People were very upset but too embarrassed to publicly state their conclusion.

Why should anyone expect the majority of money managers to do any better at their jobs than the majority of musicians, ball players, doctors, teachers, artists, or carpenters do at theirs? The fact of the matter is that the typical person in a given field might be slightly subpar. The answer in money management is the same as in other occupations: to get above-average results, you have to go out of your way to find the minority of managers who can fairly consistently beat the market indices.

Some will say this is impossible, but that's not true. To say that all information is already known, that stocks can't be selected in a way that outperforms market averages, is nonsense.

Value Line's rating system since 1965 is ample evidence that stocks can be selected in a way that materially outperforms the market. Our own top Datagraph-rated stocks have dramatically outperformed the market.

During a sabbatical at the University of Chicago, Professor Marc Reinganum of the University of Iowa, and now at Southern Methodist University, conducted an independent research study titled "Selecting Superior Securities." For his research, he picked nine variables comparable to those discussed in this book and achieved a 1984–1985 result 36.7% greater than the S&P 500.

He's not alone. We've received hundreds of testimonials from investors who also have materially outperformed the market indices.

Those who say the stock market is a random walk are misinformed. There are a number of systems and services that can and do outperform the market. Unfortunately, there are also too many poorly based opinions, too many faulty interpretations, and too many destructive emotions that come into play. Sometimes judgments are just bad or shallow. Sometimes there are too many complex variables. Some events change too fast to keep up with, and finally, there are just too many fundamental and technical research reports recommending mediocre stocks on the way down. That's why sell recommendations are few and far between when each bear market begins.

In the future, the indexing of a small part of Social Security investments will probably be wise if rules can be created to keep the government away from influencing any of the investment decisions. After all, the pathetic existing Social Security investments do not even keep up with inflation.

You can see that even the pros need to evaluate and alter preconceived methods if they aren't working. We all make mistakes, but the answer is to learn what's working once you see what's not. History will give you solid examples that should guide you in your investing. Only by careful study and research—and by not accepting conventional wisdom—have we uncovered these valuable findings. Use them and profit. You can do it.

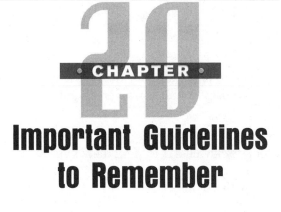

Important Guidelines to Remember

1. Don't buy cheap stocks. Buy Nasdaq stocks mainly selling between $15 and $300 a share and NYSE stocks from $20 to $300 a share. Avoid the junk pile.

2. Buy growth stocks that show each of the last three years' annual earnings per share up at least 25% and the next year's consensus earnings estimate up 25% or more. Most growth stocks should also have annual cash flow of 20% or more above EPS.

3. Make sure the last two or three quarters' earnings per share are up a huge amount. Look for a minimum of 25% to 30%. In bull markets, look for EPS up 40% to 500%. (The higher, the better.)

4. See that each of the last three quarters' sales are accelerating in their percentage increases or the last quarter's sales are up at least 25%.

5. Buy stocks with a return on equity of 17% or more. The best companies will show a return on equity of 25% to 50%.

6. Make sure the recent quarterly after-tax profit margins are improving and near the stock's peak after-tax margins.

7. Most stocks should be in the top five or six broad industry sectors in IBD's daily "New Price Highs" list or in the top 20% of "IBD's 197 Industry Group Rankings."

8. Don't buy a stock because of its dividend or P/E ratio. Buy it because it's the number one company in its particular field in terms of earnings and sales growth, ROE, profit margins, and product superiority.

9. Buy stocks with a Relative Price Strength Rating of 85 or higher in *Investor's Business Daily's SmartSelect®* Ratings.

10. Any size capitalization will do, but the majority of your stocks should trade an average daily volume of several hundred thousand shares or more.

11. Learn to read charts and recognize proper bases and exact buy points. Use daily and weekly charts to materially improve your stock selection and timing. Buy stocks as they initially break out of sound and proper bases with volume for the day 50% or more above normal trading volume.

12. Carefully average up, not down, and cut every single loss when it is 7% or 8% below your purchase price with absolutely no exceptions.

13. Write out your sell rules that show when you will sell and nail down a profit in your stock.

14. Make sure your stock has at least one or two better-performing mutual funds who have bought it in the last reporting period. You want your stocks to have increasing institutional sponsorship over the last several quarters.

15. The company should have an excellent new product or service that is selling well. It should also have a big market for its product and the opportunity for repeat sales.

16. The general market should be in an uptrend and either favoring small- or big-cap companies. (If you don't know how to interpret the general market, read IBD's "The Big Picture" column every day.)

17. Don't mess around with options, stocks trading in foreign markets, bonds, preferred stocks, or commodities. It doesn't pay to be a "Jack of all trades" or to overdiversify or over-asset allocate. Either avoid options outright or restrict them to 5% or 10% of your portfolio.

18. The stock should have ownership by top management.

19. Look for a "new America" entrepreneurial company (a new issue within the last seven or eight years) rather than laggard, "old America" companies.

20. Forget your pride and ego; the market doesn't know or care what you think. No matter how smart you think you are, the market is always smarter. A high IQ and a master's degree are not guarantees of market success. Your ego could cost you a lot of money. Don't argue with the market, and never try to prove you're right and the market is wrong.

21. Read "Investor's Corner" and "The Big Picture" in IBD daily. Learn how to recognize general market tops and bottoms. Read up on any company you own or plan to buy; learn its story.

22. Watch for companies that have recently announced they are buying back 5% to 10% or more of their common stock. Find out if there is new management in the company and where it came from.

23. Don't try to buy a stock at the bottom or on the way down in price, and don't average down. (If you buy at $40, don't buy more if it goes down to $35 or $30.)

Key Reasons People Miss Buying Big Winning Stocks

1. Disbelief, fear, and lack of knowledge. Most big winners are newer companies (IPOs in the last seven or eight years). Everyone knows Sears and General Motors, but most people are simply unaware or unfamiliar with the hundreds of new names coming into the market every year. The new America names are the growth engine of America, creating innovative new products and services plus most of the new technology. (A chart service is one easy way to at least be aware of the basics of price, volume, sales, and earnings trends of all these younger companies.)

2. P/E bias. Contrary to conventional wisdom, the best stocks rarely sell at low P/Es. Just like the best ballplayers make the highest salaries, the better companies sell at better (higher) P/Es. Using P/Es as a selection criteria will prevent you from buying many of the best stocks.

3. Not understanding that the real leaders start their big moves by selling near or at new price highs, not near new lows or off a good amount from their highs. Investors like to buy stocks that look cheap because the stocks are lower than they were a few months ago, so they buy stocks on the way down. They think they are getting bargains. They should be buying stocks on the way up, just making new price highs as they are breaking out of a base or price consolidation area.

4. Selling too soon, either because they get shaken out or they are too quick to take a profit, and psychologically having a hard time buying back the stock. They also sell too late, letting a small loss turn into a devastating one by not cutting all their losses at 8%.

One Final Thought

You could definitely become a millionaire once you learn to save and invest properly. My parting advice: Have courage, be positive, and don't ever give up. Great opportunities occur every year in America. Get prepared, study, learn, and go for them. What you'll find is that little acorns can grow into giant oaks, and that with persistence and hard work anything is possible. You can do it, and your own determination to succeed is the most important element.

We at *Investor's Business Daily*, investors.com, and Daily Graphs Online® are here to help you every step of the way, and we look forward to hearing your success stories. Please email or write us, letting us know how you're doing with the CAN SLIM™ system. And of course, we're here to answer any questions you might have along the way.

Success Stories

Labor Day, 2001

Dear Mr. William O'Neil and *Investor's Business Daily,*

As a huge enthusiast of *Investor's Business Daily* and all of your written material, I can't write enough explaining how much your works have changed my life.

I first came across *How to Make Money in Stocks* in the fall of 1997 through reading reviews of it on Amazon.com. I was living and teaching in Guatemala at the time, and was looking to get involved in investing and the stock market. Consequently, I ordered *How to Make Money in Stocks* and a few other books, but it was your book, based on historical research, that intrigued me the most. I reasoned that you had seen both great times and rough times in your over 40 years of trading, while most other books had research based only from the 1990s. In addition to that, you used both technical and fundamental analysis rather than concentrating on just one method. The other books I read advocated either one analysis or the other. I was further convinced that your system of trading was for me when you wrote how David Ryan and Lee Freestone had won U.S. Investing Championships using the CAN SLIM method.

What complements *How to Make Money in Stocks* perfectly is *Investor's Business Daily.* I had clipped out the coupon in the back of your book for a free two-week subscription to IBD, and when I received the paper for the first time, the whole system made sense to me. Finding the CAN SLIM stocks was so much easier to do using IBD, and the paper had so many other great articles including "Leaders & Success," "The New America," "Stocks in the News," and my favorite, "Investor's Corner," that further enhanced my in-

269

sights into trading. I immediately subscribed to it, even though $180 was a lot for me at the time. Then, even though the paper would arrive in Guatemala three days late each day, I could still use its valuable information for research.

I read everything I could in the paper and decided to use it in my profession of teaching. That year, as I was teaching English as a Second Language in Guatemala, I also taught one class of 5th-grade gifted and talented students. I introduced them to IBD, and they ate it up. These students, and my other students later, especially loved the stock tables because each stock is graded like they are graded using 1–99 and A through E or F. Students were always coming up to me and saying things like, "Look at this one! It's got a 99, 99, and AAA." I have even taught my students to look for cup with handles, and they have enjoyed the challenge of that, too.

I moved back to Denver in the summer of 1998 and continued using IBD both personally and professionally. I had the same success here with many of the same student reactions as I did in Guatemala. Then, last year, during the 2000–2001 school year, I taught a 6th through 8th grade after-school business club. Using IBD, I helped my students participate in the *Denver Post* annual stock market competition. One team, a group of two Ethiopian boys and one boy from the Philippines, all of whom had only been in America for a year, won second prize in the state! In fact, the only problem I've had using IBD in my classroom is when these students fought over who got IBD's "Your Weekend Review" section on Fridays.

As a result of this success utilizing IBD in my classroom, I have a lot of other ideas for using IBD in education. If you ever think about creating a curriculum outreach program, I'd love to share them with you. There is so much in IBD that would be great for schools!

As far as my own investing, I still read IBD daily and subscribe to Daily Graphs Online. I am more confident now and strongly feel that when this bear slowly turns itself into a bull, I will be able to find and buy, at the pivot point, the next Qualcomm, JDSU, or Qlogic. (The pivot point took me about three years to completely appreciate!) At first, I was the typical beginner with no discipline. I would cheat on the CAN SLIM rules, simply buying anywhere and anytime regardless of what the chart showed. I also bought Internet stocks simply because they were Internet stocks. And I tried many other methods looking for instant profit and success. All in all, during my first two years of investing I "nickeled and dimed" my account to very low points, dragging my ego down with it.

Finally, I disciplined myself and made a CAN SLIM checklist. I swore that I wouldn't violate any of the system's rules. As a result, my successes have increased. And even though the market during the last year and a half has been rough, I did make a few nice trades such as with Techne, Skechers, International Gaming, and Direct Focus. I have read and reread Chapter 10 ["When to Sell and Take Your Profit"] in *How to Make Money in Stocks* about 20 times so that I can remain focused for the next rally. I'll be shooting for the stars like you did from 1962 to 1963.

In conclusion, I would also like to express my appreciation for your love and respect of America. I have taught and traveled in many countries, and it is easy to say that America isn't perfect, but I feel, as you do, that if you work hard in America, great things will come. My father came to America as a poor, young immigrant in 1950 and has built up a great mason business, all through hard work. He always told me that if you work hard and remain positive you can achieve anything you want. I feel that you and IBD express this same sentiment every day. And believe it or not, I bought my father a subscription to IBD for his birthday, and now he loves it, quotes from it, and reads it every day!

Most importantly, however, I want to thank you for the great work you do and the great information you print daily. It is greatly appreciated!

Sincerely,

David Claussen

J. Barkasy: For the last four years, I've had over 200% gains, and it's also helped me get a job with a major exchange. My returns of the last two years are equivalent to three years of my salary! In just four and a half years, I went from $2,000 to $600,000 (pre-tax) in my portfolio by going to Bill's seminars and workshops a few times and reading *How to Make Money in Stocks.*

P. Vartanian, investor: IBD and Mr. O'Neil's books have changed my life. I have no background in finance, no MBA, and very little time. However, I have beaten the market the last two years! IBD has given me the chance to work from my home . . . I quit my job last August and now consider investing my career. Everyday, I begin with "Investor's Corner" and then "The Big Picture." Needless to say, I'm a believer. . . . IBD works, and without it and Mr. O'Neil's books, I would be a lot poorer and not nearly so happy.

Mike Goode, investor: Investor's Business Daily has made a big difference in the types of stocks I'm picking now. It brings a lot of investment information to investors that's not available anywhere else. There is a lot of opportunity; there are new companies being formed no one has heard of yet, and the first place you're going to find out about them is *Investor's Business Daily.*

Ladd King, investor: "The New America" page is an opportunity to learn about new companies, and I save them (so) I can quickly refer back. *Investor's Business Daily* is one of the best ways to take 10 to 15 or 20 minutes in the morning to find out what's going on in the market. I haven't opened *The Wall Street Journal* for the entire week, whereas I've read all five IBDs. When I first started reading IBD, I was able to become very comfortable with the newspaper in just days. I can look at the charts very quickly to help me select my stocks.

Yihong Cai, software engineer: I love and respect Mr. O'Neil because he is not only highly successful himself in investments, but also is willing to help hundreds of thousands of ordinary people. He is truly original and smart. Without Mr. O'Neil, I would have continued to lose in the stock market. Thank you very much, Mr. O'Neil.

Chris Cox, obstetrician/gynecologist: I was playing golf with a friend of mine and he was a retired airline pilot. And I asked him, "You're only 55 years old. How did you retire?" He said, "Chris, the best thing you could ever do is go out and get Investor's [Business] Daily." He told me to buy the book [*How to Make Money in Stocks*] and read it twice, then study the paper. And he said, "It is the absolute best way to manage your portfolio."

So *Investor's Business Daily* has changed my philosophy of buying stocks. In the past I would maybe purchase some stock if a physician told me it was a good stock. But today I put it through *Investor's Business Daily* criteria . . . *Investor's Business Daily* is the first opinion . . . I pick stocks on the fundamentals that are found in *Investor's Business Daily*.

By using *Investor's Business Daily* techniques, I was actually able to increase my portfolio by 75%! The paper is the only reason I was able to turn my portfolio around because I had no other means of investing other than recommendations by friends. The paper taught me discipline and how to evaluate companies. I've really become a student of the market by using *Investor's Business Daily*.

Rai Chowdhary: "I have been using IBD since 1995 and have several clippings dating back to that time. I have been saving many articles and each Friday's paper. Quite possibly, my collection may be the largest you may find among your readers.

I am a new investor, yet I have made money on every stock I bought using IBD information and following Bill O'Neil's advice on investing as provided in *24 Essential Lessons for Investment Success* and *How to Make Money in Stocks*. This may not be the Horatio Alger story, but it sure works for me! Thanks!

Ed Sanders, investor: Our son financed a trip around the world through his investing. A lot of the knowledge he gained was learned from IBD. I would describe it as a tool in your ongoing education on what investing can do for you. New investors need to understand that education is what will take you forward . . . not a hot stock tip . . . IBD gives them that education.

Michael Galligan, investor: I would like to take this opportunity to thank you all for making it possible for me to invest in not only the various markets but in the future of my family. I have found your information to be interesting, easily understood, and, when used correctly, profitable. The results have been the same for those of my friends and family who have chosen to read and subscribe to IBD. Your complete approach to investing is excellent, from mind-set to execution. Whenever I have been able to successfully apply information/insight you provide (industry, EPS/RS, chart pattern, etc.), I have traded successfully. The greater my understanding of your information, the more successful the trade. I have now been taught the tools to recognize when a trade may not go as planned, and, most importantly, WHEN to sell. That lesson alone has been invaluable.

Johanne Schroeder, investor: A heartfelt thank you for your books and the newspaper. I can finally make informed decisions, and I am beginning to understand a little how the market works, the basic "how to's of investing." I can't begin—and don't need—to tell you what a difference that makes! Don't laugh—but I consider you one of the major benefactors I have had the good fortune to be touched by in my life. My gratitude is profound. All the best.

Randy Albertson, CPA: I have been impressed with the wealth of knowledge you dispense daily (in IBD). I have recently been recommending your publication to selected clients, which is something I do not do lightly.

David Kutz: I want to thank you for the fantastic market analysis in "The Big Picture" section of the "General Markets & Sectors" page. This section is extremely helpful in understanding general market behavior and is the best part of the recent changes that you've made. Keep up the great work.

I'd also like to express my interest in the "Investor's Corner" column. It is one of the first sections of the paper I read, and I appreciate the educational value of it. Thanks for an exceptional newspaper.

Rick Baca: Congratulations for a job well done! In my opinion, you already led the pack of competitors. I doubt your former competitors are even in your rear-view mirror. You have a life-long subscriber.

Michael D. McLennan: I subscribe to IBD. My daughter in the 5th grade reads ("Leaders & Success") a bio from IBD every day as I drive her to school. What an education she is getting. Thank you, thank you!

Nicholas Pishvanov, Lt. Col. USAF (Ret): You have surpassed yourselves! Congratulations on your upgraded edition and your editorials. Your financial pages were superior to all competition. Now they are light years ahead.

Marilyn Ellis: "I saw Bill O'Neil on CNBC in the late 80s and tracked his market calls, and he was accurate! An eye opener! In learning Mr. O'Neil's CAN SLIM method, my husband and I have been able to retire early and build the house of our dreams, and look forward to years of travel in Europe . . . a life we never dreamed we could achieve before we had IBD in our lives. We have now happily become accustomed to annual 100% returns in our portfolio in up markets and appreciate being safely on the sidelines in the bear markets. Thank you!

Midge E.: I feel you are taking me by the hand and saying, "Here, look . . . this is how you can make money!" No other publication is in your league. Thank you.

Tim Cotie, MD: I am truly impressed by "Leaders & Success." It is inspiring! My only disappointment is that your paper is only published five days a week, for Sunday and Monday I suffer with withdrawal.

I find the stories of successful people and demonstrations of personal courage and persistence very helpful and a light to my path. Never allow yourselves to even consider stopping the series.

Jared R. Larson, Sr., investment education consultant for a financial services firm: I do national "How to Invest" seminars for our 401(k) participants. Your paper is without peer in the industry and the ONLY one I read. Many investors ask me if I read the WSJ, and I tell them that it is OK if you want to read what happened in the market yesterday. I tell them that if they really want to learn how to succeed and become better investors, then IBD is the ONLY way to go.

Peter Siracusa: "Leaders & Success" is read by my 15-year-old and his friends daily. Keep up the good work.

Bennet Simonton: Your paper is a great improvement over *The Wall Street Journal*, which I have read for years. WSJ just doesn't have what an investor needs. Your articles about companies are very useful.

Joey Wilson: Thank you so much for your service as the change in my life is beyond what I ever imagined. I have enough cash to last me the rest of my life at age 52. When the working world dumped me due to my affliction, I found "yawl." Thanks are not enough, but it's all I have to offer and to tell folks the word you pass on. Thanks for my life back.

Don Carbonari: "Thanks to *Investor's Business Daily*, I have been able to take the emotion out of my investment decisions. Although I have been an investor for 15 years and was a stockbroker from 1988 to 1991, I never previously utilized your newspaper. And, unfortunately, never had the phenomenal success I have had the past three years.

Due to the results I have achieved, I am now managing money on a fee basis for other people. In my personal account I have almost tripled my money in two short years, as I am up 177% from Sept. 1994 through Sept. 1996. During these same time periods, the S&P 500 was up less than 60%. Your newspaper was instrumental in helping me identify the right growth-oriented companies, even though the general market did poorly. Your paper has helped me tremendously in owning winners.

Charles Slany, Jr., certified financial planner: Just a note to let you know what a great job you are doing. Your investment advice is legend, but many people who appreciate your effort may not find the time to tell you. Thank you and keep up the good work.

M. Lorenzen, portfolio manager: Your paper and other products are the linchpin to my investment analysis and recommendations to clients.

David Brown: There is no better financial daily newspaper out there. It helps to sharpen decision-making capabilities based on the extensive number of facts it provides.

John J. Barston, Jr.: FACT: Trading without *Investor's Business Daily's* proprietary RS, EPS, and volume data is like flying without an instrument panel.

Fred Benedetto, arbitrator: I've been reading IBD since its inception. I started with $5,000 and three years later, it escalated to $50,000. Why? Because of IBD. If you want to be on top of the stock market, the only tool is *Investor's Business Daily* . . . Need I say more?

Eloise Rivers, administrative coordinator: I'm a long-time subscriber to *Investor's Business Daily.* IBD helps me level the financial playing field. It's jam-packed with useful information and provides a financial education you cannot get in any school. You learn at your own pace and . . . you learn quickly what works and what doesn't. "Investor's Corner" is very helpful in this area.

Thanks to early investing (in the right stocks), I can live where I choose and travel to remote corners of the globe when I want. I place IBD in the same category as my top ranking wealth creation stocks. It's a very important part of my financial assets.

Marie Fritz, school teacher: I use IBD's "Ten Secrets to Success" in a language assessment program developed for students. I believe that "Ten Secrets" presents a great opportunity to engage students with authentic texts that are both fun and informative. I plan to use this tool in my programs for nearly six thousand middle school students in a southwest urban school district to assess each student's level of mastery of the language arts.

Masayo Taylor, retired realtor/broker: During year 2000, I made a net reportable gain of $201,205 from stock trading. And this was my first year investing. I began on November 16, 1999, after attending IBD's seminar in California. IBD taught me to stay away from trading during the bear market.

J. Hart, individual investor: Using your information, I was able to retire way ahead of my expectations. Profits were 172% in 1999 and 40% in 2000.

J. Kakvand, an early retiree: I had only been reading IBD for four years when I quit my engineering job in April 1999 and have been concentrating on trading, strictly based on the CAN SLIM method. I owe my success to Mr. O'Neil and his CAN SLIM method.

John M.: "Kudos, thanks, praise God for you! You have helped take me from a net worth of $697 to over $1 million dollars—honest—since I began reading your paper in 1995. Your paper seems to get better and better, too. I buy two copies from the newsstand every day—one to read and underline and the other to reread and to reiterate. The only complaint I have about your publication is that it is too hard to throw away."

Dr. L. Richmond, a pastor: I started studying the market in March 1999. After six months with a broker and no results, I went to the library, found *Investor's Business Daily,* and decided to learn to invest on my own. I started last September with $50K. When I sold everything in March after reading your latest book, I had $174K. Made most of my money on cup-with-handle formations and reading your book, *How to Make Money in Stocks.* I am a minister and want to use the money to start churches here in Illinois. My goal is to start 13 churches in the next few years. Thanks so very much for sharing your strategy with others.

Ed Sanders, investor: I read Mr. O'Neil's book, *How to Make Money in Stocks,* twice, and my account went into new high ground! His book has helped me to piece together all the information in IBD and Daily Graphs. I would say that Mr. O'Neil, IBD, and Daily Graphs are solely responsible for my portfolio performance. IBD gives me more of the information I need to make decisions on what companies to invest in. And it gives the individual investor, who doesn't have time to do the research that high-powered Wall Street firms do, a shortcut to the same end!

F. Rutherford and F. Jones: CAN SLIM and *Investor's Business Daily* provide an investor with all the information needed to consistently make great decisions in a user-friendly way. For more than 10 consecutive years, we've realized a compounded 57% annual return, and CAN SLIM and IBD played a pre-eminent role in that success. O'Neil's wisdom really works.

V. Strautmanis: Four years ago, as a father of five, I entered the brokerage business as a $1000-a-month cold-caller. Last year, I earned a multiple six-figure income for the first time in my life! This year, I've started my own fund and owe it 100% to Bill O'Neil. Thank you.

H. Rogers: I subscribed to IBD and have not been sorry one bit. Had it not been for IBD, I would never have known of the company that to date has been my winningest stock purchase. My initial investment has now grown 1100%! Am I rich yet? No, but that one investment and the fact that your paper teaches as well as it reports has brought me success. I want to thank Bill O'Neil for creating the best daily investment news printed anywhere.

ABOUT THE AUTHOR

William J. O'Neil is one of Wall Street's most seasoned and successful veterans. At age 30, he bought his own seat on the Big Board with profits made in the stock market and founded William O'Neil + Co., Inc., a leading institutional investment research organization based in Los Angeles. The firm's current clients are over 600 of the top institutional investment firms in the world. Mr. O'Neil is also the founder of *Investor's Business Daily*, the fastest-growing national competitor of The Wall Street Journal.

INVESTORS.COM

THE ONLINE COMPANION TO
INVESTOR'S BUSINESS DAILY

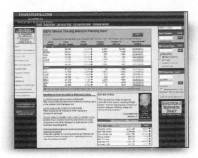

INVESTORS.COM

- A robust, interactive Web site designed to complement the proprietary features of Investor's Business Daily.

- Receive timely access to select Investor's Business Daily articles including "Internet & Technology", "The New America", "Investor's Corner", "Leaders & Success" and more.

- Delve into both educational and research tools expanding upon key ideas found in *How to Make Money in Stocks*.

IBD POWER TOOLS, AVAILABLE TO IBD SUBSCRIBERS ONLY

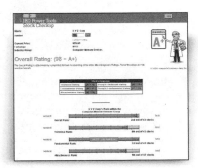

- **IBD STOCK CHECKUP**^{SM}**.** Assess the health of your stocks with this powerful evaluation tool, based on our most sophisticated model of winning characteristics.

- **IBD CHARTS.** Full screen, color charts to help you identify patterns and trends — view the daily and weekly charts you want when you want them.

- **SCREEN OF THE DAY.** Get new stock ideas every day through a list of noteworthy companies based on criteria selected by investors.com editors.

- **MY STOCK LISTS.** Keep tabs on your current portfolio and potential investments. Each list includes Earnings Per Share and Relative Price Strength Ratings, intraday Volume Percent Change, research links, and more!

Date:	08/28/2000
High:	133.19
Low:	129.75
Last:	130.56 1.44
Vol:	8,533,400

ADDITIONAL FEATURES

- **ASK BILL O'NEIL**

- **IBD LEARNING CENTER**

- **WHERE THE BIG MONEY'S FLOWING NOW**

www.investors.com